The Labour of Loss

The Labour of Loss explores how mothers, fathers, widows, relatives and friends dealt with their experiences of grief and loss during and after the First and Second World Wars. Based on an examination of private loss through letters and diaries, it makes a significant contribution to understanding how people came to terms with the deaths of friends and family. The book considers the ways in which the bereaved dealt with grief psychologically, and analyses the social and cultural context within which they mourned their dead. Damousi shows that grief remained with people as they attempted to rebuild an internal and external world without those to whom they had been so fundamentally attached. Unlike other studies in this area, *The Labour of Loss* considers how mourning affected men and women in different ways, and analyses the gendered dimensions of grief.

JOY DAMOUSI is a senior lecturer in the Department of History at the University of Melbourne. She is the author of *Women Come Rally: Socialism, Communism and Gender in Australia 1890–1955* (1994); co-editor of *Gender and War: Australians at War in the Twentieth Century* (Cambridge University Press, 1995), and author of *Depraved and Disorderly: Female Convicts, Sexuality and Gender in Colonial Australia* (Cambridge University Press, 1997).

For A.T.

Studies in the Social and Cultural History of Modern Warfare

General Editor
Jay Winter *Pembroke College, Cambridge*

Advisory Editors
Paul Kennedy *Yale University*
Antoine Prost *Université de Paris-Sorbonne*
Emmanuel Sivan *The Hebrew University of Jerusalem*

In recent years the field of modern history has been enriched by the exploration of two parallel histories. These are the social and cultural history of armed conflict, and the impact of military events on social and cultural history.

Studies in the Social and Cultural History of Modern Warfare intends to present the fruits of this growing area of research, reflecting both the colonization of military history by cultural historians, and the reciprocal interest of military historians in social and cultural history, to the benefit of both. The series will reflect the latest scholarship in European and non-European events from the 1850s to the present day.

Titles in the series

1 *Sites of memory, sites of mourning*
   The Great War in European cultural history
   Jay Winter
   ISBN 0 521 49682 9 (hardback) ISBN 0 521 63988 3 (Canto)

2 *Capital cities at war: Paris, London, Berlin 1914–1919*
   Jay Winter and Jean-Louis Robert
   ISBN 0 521 57171 5

3 *State, society and mobilization in Europe during the First World War*
   Edited by John Horne
   ISBN 0 521 56112 4

4 *A time of silence*
   Civil war and the culture of repression in Franco's Spain, 1936–1945
   Michael Richards
   ISBN 0 521 59401 4

5 *War and remembrance in the twentieth century*
   Edited by Jay Winter and Emmanuel Sivan
   ISBN 0 521 64035 0

6 *European culture in the Great War*
   The arts, entertainment and propaganda, 1914–1918
   Edited by Aviel Roshwald and Richard Stites
   ISBN 0 521 57015 8

7 *The labour of loss*
   Mourning, memory and wartime bereavement in Australia
   Joy Damousi
   ISBN 0 521 66004 1 (hardback) ISBN 0 521 66974 X (paperback)

The Labour of Loss

*Mourning, Memory and
Wartime Bereavement in Australia*

Joy Damousi
University of Melbourne

PUBLISHED BY THE PRESS SYNDICATE OF THE UNIVERSITY OF CAMBRIDGE
The Pitt Building, Trumpington Street, Cambridge, United Kingdom

CAMBRIDGE UNIVERSITY PRESS
The Edinburgh Building, Cambridge CB2 2RU, UK   http://www.cup.cam.ac.uk
40 West 20th Street, New York, NY 10011–4211, USA   http://www.cup.org
10 Stamford Road, Oakleigh, Melbourne 3166, Australia

© Joy Damousi 1999

This book is in copyright. Subject to statutory exception
and to the provisions of relevant collective licensing agreements,
no reproduction of any part may take place without
the written permission of Cambridge University Press.

First published 1999

Printed in Singapore by Craft Print Pte Ltd

Typeset in Plantin 10/12 pt

A catalogue record for this book is available from the British Library

National Library of Australia Cataloguing in Publication data
Damousi, Joy, 1961–
The labour of loss: mourning, memory and wartime
bereavement in Australia.
Bibliography.
Includes index.
ISBN 0 521 66004 1.
ISBN 0 521 66974 X (pbk).
1. Grief – Psychological aspects. 2. World War, 1914–1918 –
Psychological aspects. 3. World War, 1939–1945 –
Psychological aspects. 4. World War, 1914–1918 – Social
aspects – Australia. 5. World War, 1939–1945 – Social
aspects – Australia. I. Title. (Series: Studies in the
social and cultural history of modern warfare 7).
155.9370994

ISBN 0 521 66004 1 hardback
ISBN 0 521 66974 X paperback

Contents

Abbreviations	*page* viii
Acknowledgements	ix
Introduction	1

Part I The First World War

1 Theatres of Grief, Theatres of Loss	9
2 The Sacrificial Mother	26
3 A Father's Loss	46
4 The War Widow and the Cost of Memory	65
5 Returned Limbless Soldiers: Identity through Loss	85

Part II The Second World War

6 Absence as Loss on the Homefront and the Battlefront	105
7 Grieving Mothers	126
8 A War Widow's Mourning	144
Conclusion	161
Notes	164
Bibliography	195
Index	206

Abbreviations

AA	Australian Archives
AIF	Australian Imperial Force
AFW	Anzac Fellowship of Women
AWM	Australian War Memorial
CIB	Commonwealth Investigation Branch
ML	Mitchell Library, Sydney
NLA	National Library of Australia
RAAF	Royal Australian Air Force
RSA	Returned Soldiers' Association
RSL	Returned and Services League (*later* Returned Services League)
RSSILA	Returned Soldiers' and Sailors' Imperial League of Australia
SLQ	State Library of Queensland
SLSA	State Library of South Australia
SLV	State Library of Victoria

Currency

During the period discussed in this book, Australian currency was pounds, shillings and pence.

There were 12 pennies (d) in one shilling (s), and 20 shillings in one pound (£). A guinea was 21 shillings. Amounts such as 2s and 2s 6d were sometimes written as 2/- and 2/6.

Acknowledgements

Many people offered me wonderful help and support during the course of this project. Foremost among these was Stuart Macintyre who read and reread countless drafts, offered valuable suggestions, made appropriate criticisms and never wavered in his support of this book. His contribution to my writing and to my research has been immeasurable.

Others also offered their time and thoughts generously. Jay Winter kindly commented on earlier drafts and his suggestions have been invaluable in sharpening and refining this work. Emma Grahame exercised expert editorial flair and provided intellectual input which has markedly improved the text. Katie Holmes, Robert Reynolds and Charles Zika offered important insights and arguments which have significantly enhanced my perspectives.

At Cambridge University Press, Phillipa McGuinness has been, as always, an unflagging source of strength, support and encouragement. Her faith and commitment to this project sustained me through many trials. I have very much appreciated the work of Janet Mackenzie, a meticulous, thorough and perceptive editor whose deft hand added so much more to the manuscript, and Paul Watt who provided much valued assistance and reassurance.

I am indebted to Carmel McInerney for the rich archive she so meticulously documented for me from the Australian War Memorial and to Garry Disher for his generosity in passing on several important references. Katherine Ellinghaus provided much more than anyone could ever ask of a research assistant; she answered each query with warmth, efficiency and good humour. Robyn Harper saved me from several computing catastrophes with a calm reassurance, while no request was ever too difficult for Erica Mehrtens, Marcia Gilchrist, Martine Walsh or Lynne Wrout.

The section on war widows could not have been written without the assistance of the War Widows Guild of Australia. I wish to acknowledge, in particular, the help given to me by Mrs Margaret Feeney, the state secretary of the NSW branch, and to Mrs Eileen Watt, the president of the Victorian branch, both of whom generously allowed me access to their records and provided a congenial place to work.

My research was also aided by funding from the Australian Research Council, and from the helpful assistance of the staff at the State Library of Victoria, the State Library of NSW, the Australian War Memorial and the Australian Archives in Melbourne and Canberra.

I was fortunate to be the recipient of warm hospitality from Suzanne Rickard and Marion K. Stell in Canberra and John Dillane and Peter Langmede in Sydney. Other friends and colleagues have also at various times provided encouragement through their conversation, conviviality and generosity. I wish to thank Verity Burgmann, Julie Brown, Barbara Caine, Georgine Clarsen, Paul Collins, Ann Curthoys, Jenny Dawson, Sarah Ferber, Esther Faye, Patricia Grimshaw, Phillip Harvey, Lucy Healey, Diane Kirkby, Rose Lucas, Marilyn Lake, Susan Magarey, Jill Matthews, Peter McPhee, Carmel Reilly, Lyndall Ryan, Sue Sheridan, Judith Smart, Charles Sowerwine, Shurlee Swain, Christina Twomey and Julie Wells.

Finally, this book is for Ann Turner who advised me while writing it that I should try to make my words sing. Through her guidance she has shown me how this may be possible, and much else besides.

Introduction

'No event has ever destroyed so much', wrote Sigmund Freud a year after the outbreak of the First World War, 'that has confused so many of the clearest intelligences, or so thoroughly debased what is highest.'[1] This war, he observed,

> tramples in blind fury on all that comes in its way as though there were to be no future and no peace among men after it is over. It cuts all the common bonds between the contending peoples and threatens to leave a legacy of embitterment that will make any renewal of those bonds impossible for a long time to come.[2]

It is the bonds that war so effectively severs – bonds that are our most intimate and fundamental – that are the subject of this book. I attempt to explore how mothers, fathers, widows and soldiers dealt with the grief that resulted from the deaths during and immediately after the two world wars. My starting-point is a psychological and emotional one. I examine the process of mourning and the expression of grief, drawing on the understanding that bereavement is 'the objective situation of loss', grief is the psychological and emotional response to loss, and mourning is 'expressive of grief'.[3] Within this context, my study is concerned not only with the psychological strategies that these groups adopted to cope with death, but also examines the cultural and social context of these experiences and thus considers the ways in which grief and loss, like notions of sacrifice, have a history.[4]

This examination reveals the ways in which the relatives of those who perished attempted to claim a legitimacy for their loss. A paradox emerges in their stories: men and women were complicit in sustaining the memory of war and its celebration, but in their demands for remuneration they tried to shape an expression of grief which the myths of war sought to deny. In this regard, mourning of wartime loss involved a process of sustaining both a continuity with, and a detachment from, the lost soldier.[5]

Mourning was channelled into various activities, such as political agitation, social networks, and shaping new identities, which gave the bereaved a public and political voice. In terms of wartime grief, then, it is shown that mourning can be an active, dynamic and creative process, rather than one which negates activism.[6] Those who were lost in war were mourned in many ways, at the same time as mourners pined for a time and place without loss. But mourners also strongly resisted the loss of memory of *their* particular sacrifice in giving their sons and husbands.

This work builds on the insights of other studies which consider the responses of those left to deal with grief.[7] Here the emphasis is on the psychological experiences of relatives rather than on the ordeal of frontline soldiers, although the two are inter-related. The pathbreaking scholarship of Jay Winter, David Cannadine, Pat Jalland, Eric Leed and George Mosse provides contexts within which to consider these experiences, as does the work of Eric Santner.[8] Santner, one of the few historians who examines the psychological aspects of this experience, has observed that historians are reluctant to consider the psychology of grief partly because they 'strive for intellectual and not psychic mastery of events'.[9]

Discussions of wartime grief have concentrated on an examination of public expressions of mourning, through art, religion, cinema and literature.[10] Symbols such as military cemeteries, war monuments, museums and commemorative ceremonies for the dead have been analysed to explore how death, brutality and the pain of war have been denied and rewritten as glorious sacrifice.[11] Through these accounts, historians have considered how wartime grief has been managed publicly, rather than emotionally expressed. This research is marked by an emphasis on national rather than individual and familial grief, on material symbols and artefacts at the expense of the psychological expressions of loss.[12] The impact of war has also been assessed in terms of the history of welfare and repatriation and of shifting roles of gender.[13]

Few studies have considered how the experience of mourning affected men and women in different ways. Historians have universalised rather than particularised the mourning experience, and its gendered dimensions remain largely unexamined.[14] Nor have they related issues of welfare and gender to the psychological expressions of grief. The anger and resentment associated with the repatriation demands of mothers have not been linked, for instance, to their projection of unresolved grief and a sense of neglect by the state.[15]

In order to examine these processes, I draw on those who argue for the need to connect the psychic, the cultural and the historical,[16] and examine how these have intersected to shape aspects of culture.[17] Freud's fine distinction between mourning and melancholia points to possible understandings of the differentiation and complex 'layering of mourning'.[18] For Freud, mourning is the process whereby the loss is negotiated and worked through; in melancholia, the loss cannot properly end.[19]

But as others have pointed out since, the process of grieving has many layers.[20] A complicating factor which disrupts the easy binary between melancholia and mourning is that the 'self' is transformed over time, for subjectivity is not an ahistoric, unchanging entity.[21] There are examples of this multi-layering and shifting identity throughout this study. War widows, for instance, were often reluctant to assume a different identity or to imagine 'the invention of new symbolic worlds and selves'.[22] But in other respects, many of them were rebuilding a new identity as *war widows*.

Particularly useful for this study have been those works which consider mourning within its specific cultural and social context, and in its various expressions.[23] The insights of Melanie Klein and Judith Butler shed light on the productive potential of mourning and, especially in the case of Butler, illuminate how grief has been used by groups to mobilise politically.[24] One key argument is that wartime bereavement among relatives was often expressed through a displacement and projection of grief, which channelled their anger and resentment into political militancy as a way of resisting the loss of the memory of their sacrifices.[25]

These themes relate to another aim of the book, which is to link mourning to the shifting parameters of memory.[26] Although the world wars produced conditions that shaped the grieving process and made it particular to time and to place, what bonded men and women across the generational divide was their relationship to the past – a past which, to use Julia Kristeva's words, 'does not pass by'. For some men and women remained 'riveted to the past', 'faithful to those bygone days' and, in some cases, 'nailed down to them'.[27] This intersection between the past and the present through memory is the key to understanding the complex relationship between wartime loss and the expression of grief as it was played out during what turned out for some to be the trauma of peacetime.

Memory does not grasp an event, accurately or inaccurately, but subjects events to a process of rewriting.[28] In this way, memory links history to the practice of psychoanalysis, which can be considered 'the construction of a history, and history, in its turn, an act of remembering'.[29] The departure point here is the premise that both the historical and the psychoanalytic explore ways in which the present is shaped by the past through memory.[30] Drawing on these arguments, memory and grief are linked in this work in ways new to investigations of memory in Australian studies.[31] Most recently, Stephen Garton and Alistair Thomson have dwelt on the cost of repatriation and the myths surrounding war experience and identity. Their studies continue the emphasis on the narratives of returned soldiers, but the *process* of loss and grief and its relationship to identity is unexplored.[32] The work of Raelene

Frances and Bruce Scates, Michael McKernan and K. S. Inglis has unearthed a fascinating archive of grief, but the psychological layering of wartime loss in Australia remains untheorised.[33] Raymond Evans' study of violence between women during the First World War tantalisingly alludes to this psychology but does not discuss it further.[34] The lingering *cost* of memory was also different for relatives as it carried with it a financial and social burden. Widows, for example, not only endured financial deprivation but also came under surveillance for their moral behaviour.

The process of forgetting is as important as that of remembering, and forgetting forms a subtle, but discernible, theme in my study. Cultural amnesia, especially in relation to Aboriginal people and to the role of women, is linked to grief and mourning in twentieth-century Australia. Powerful notions of sacrifice were shaped by white male understandings of citizenship and nationhood.

Another key theme, related to remembering and forgetting, is the relationship between memory, mourning and identity. I have attempted to move away from examining the shaping of national identities, which has universalised and homogenised individual experiences,[35] to consider the formation of individual identities. As parents began to find a new sense of themselves without sons, and widows without husbands, they developed individual rituals and practices which assisted them to relinquish their former roles.[36] Mourning is a highly individual process, but the networks that mourners formed facilitated a community which was sustained through these psychological transitions. While there was a collective spirit of remembrance, as Winter and others have shown,[37] mothers, fathers, widows and disabled soldiers were, paradoxically, also at pains to demand that their particular sacrifices be acknowledged. To lose the recognition of their specific contribution from public commemoration would mean they would endure another loss: that of relinquishing *their* special place in the memory of war, at a time when others were trying to forget, repress or rewrite war.[38] These experiences differed for men and for women, as different cultural expectations governed the behaviour of mothers, fathers and widows after the war.[39]

This study also makes a contribution to the history of grief in Australia, which remains a small field in cultural and social history. A few studies have considered the practice and ritual of death,[40] and Peter Read examines this issue in his study, *Returning to Nothing: The Meaning of Lost Places*, but a full-scale history of grief awaits its historian.[41]

Loss in war is a profound emotional and psychological experience, most powerfully conveyed in the detail of its telling. In these stories of grief I have tried to capture the evocative force which drives the personal narratives, and also to read the silences and gaps which suggest psychological expression. The stories are told through sites of grief other than public memorials and monuments, which have been privileged by historians as representing *the* iconography of loss.[42] Even when private mourning has been considered, it has been done so in relation to public commemoration and collective histories, rather than in its own terms.[43] These narratives are shaped in the privacy of letters and diaries; in public petitions and rallies; in applications for financial assistance; and in the newsletters and magazines which were published by various organisations. In each of these archives, a new identity and persona was forged – that of a childless father, a fatherless family, a sole mother, a husbandless wife – which symbolised a process of renewal, a necessary part of moving towards a life without the deceased.

In what follows, Part I is concerned with the First World War. Chapter 1 explores the ways in which the experience of grief was shaped by an intersection between the battlefront and the homefront. It examines the interaction between soldiers and parents of the deceased, and considers the ways in which soldiers' experiences of grief shifted their identity, influencing the ways they told the stories of their comrades' deaths, and shaped the ways in which they conveyed the details of death. This chapter also shows that through the news of death which circulated in letters and newspapers, women were drawn together into a community of mourners.[44] This produced a particular form of grief, that of anticipating loss.[45] Both for soldiers and for women at home expecting bereavement, we can see the ways in which identity becomes shaped by their experience of grief.

Chapter 2 considers how memories of the 'sacrificial mother' changed over time. The campaigns undertaken by mothers for remuneration reveal a projection of unresolved grief and a feeling of abandonment. This was particularly pronounced when the identity of the 'sacrificial mother' was subsumed into the generic category of 'women's sacrifice', effectively erasing mothers' particular sacrifice.

Chapter 3 turns to fathers and considers how some fathers dealt with the loss of their sons as a challenge to their own masculine identity. In attempting to keep alive the memory of their deceased sons, they were also trying to resist the loss of their status and their own sacrifices.

Widows are the subject of Chapter 4, which discusses the cost of sustaining the memory of loss in both financial and cultural terms. The ambiguous sexual status of widows created anxiety for the repatriation authorities; but there was also deep resentment *between* widows as some remarried, while others politicised their grief through protest. The moral codes that widows were expected to uphold, because of their connection with the memory of the fallen, made them targets of surveillance.

Chapter 5 discusses the ways in which limbless soldiers created a new postwar identity by privileging their physical loss. They expressed political militancy by channelling their grief and embitterment into an affirmation of their physical disabilities.

Part II deals with various aspects of grief and the Second World War. Chapter 6 explores the ways in which grief and loss on the battlefront and the homefront shaped each other; as in the First World War, anticipating loss could be as debilitating as loss itself. Chapter 7 shows how familial memories and mythologies were formed through grieving mothers' stories, while Chapter 8 considers how the identity of the war widow – framed through anger and resentment – was an empowering and sustaining one for war widows immediately after the war.

In this complex tapestry of emotions, the common threads are the ways in which individuals created new identities and a different sense of self through their experience of grief. Through their memories, we can see how 'events become experiences', in that they assume a particular meaning over time.[46] Grief is expressed in diverse ways, and it can be a productive process that can forge political mobilisation.

In 1945, the writer Gertrude Stein, who witnessed both world wars, reflected prophetically, 'And when there is no war, well just now I cannot remember just how it is where there is no war.'[47] This book examines the stories of those for whom loss in war remained the experience through which they understood themselves, and through which they shaped their lives. After the wars ended, their lives had been irrevocably changed through continuing grief, for the burden of memory would remain with them as they attempted to rebuild an internal and external world without those to whom they had been so fundamentally attached.

Part I

The First World War

1 Theatres of Grief, Theatres of Loss

> No mail now brings his cheery lines to read;
> No message breaks the silence of that grave.[1]

In writings on war, the enactment of grief is often overshadowed by the drama of battle. As in the wider conflict where loss is born, grief leaves no one unaffected by its devastation: like combat, there is no space to retreat and to take refuge from the havoc grief unleashes among those who give and those who receive the news of death.

Soldiers were messengers and chroniclers, as well as watchers and sufferers of grief. Unlike the theatre of war, where they played out their performances like actors trained in melodrama, they were given no script for this role.[2] Their confrontation with death meant they could not act out their military selves with the control and certainty expected of them by others who witnessed battle. One soldier, E. W. D. Laing, wrote to the mother of his deceased friend, expressing his awkwardness, reluctant responsibility and individual mourning:

I was a friend of your son, Mort, & his death was a blow to me. I was away from the Bn at the time he was killed & have just got your address. Your son was one of the most loveable straight forward chaps I have ever met. This I know is the opinion of all the officers & men in the Bn ... [the] world is considerably poorer through his death ... I wish I could express all I feel, but believe me all my sympathy is with you ... Please forgive me if I have put things crudely but [I am not] very good at expressing myself.[3]

Writing to the families of the dead allowed soldiers to share their anguish as a way of coming to terms with their harrowing loss and sense of guilt as survivors. The effort to mourn and then revive a persona bonded soldiers with the families of the fallen, and they became complicit in exalting the dead and resisting the finality of loss.[4] In this task they had been given no instruction, however, for the etiquette of letter-writing had not equipped them to transmit the news of carnage to strangers.

As elsewhere, the First World War brought a new shock to the experience of death.[5] In early colonial Australia, rituals of death and mourning were, as one historian has described it, characterised by directness and emotion 'largely unfettered by concerns of ritualised propriety'. The funeral processions of both rich and poor passed through the streets, and it was during the 1820s that the commercial funeral began to appear.[6]

The Victorian ritual of death introduced not only a more elaborate system of public and private ritual according to social class, but also a more formal and polite expression of grief.[7] This was a generation that was accustomed to strict regulation of people's actions in mourning, both in public and in private. Mourners wore black; women were expected to abide by this social custom longer than men. The required etiquette could be costly, demanding of women that they were adorned with appropriate jewellery and silk dresses.[8] The period of time for mourning depended on one's relationship to the deceased. The spectacle of a slow public procession from the service to the grave site and, for the wealthy, of an elaborate and ornately decorated hearse with horses decked in feathers, was an essential part of the cultural expression of grieving. Many of these conventions were shaped by religious and Christian beliefs which enforced a public respectability and propriety in the grieving process.[9] The war ushered in less ornate mourning rituals, leading to an increasing acceptance of cremation as a burial practice where the public spectacle of death was far simpler.[10]

After the war broke on 5 August 1914, death in combat demanded that soldiers express themselves in a new way. Without the remnants of a body, or the ritual of a funeral, their descriptions were more than just words. Psychologically, these details were crucial: they carried the weight of reality and truth, providing a presence which filled the empty void of unknown events.[11] The details of death which soldiers conveyed offered an emotional comfort to families, but at the same time their words would also scar those families forever.

Surrounded by an unimaginable number of men who had died prematurely, soldiers fumbled to find a voice to convey the meaning of such extraordinary circumstances. In this process, they shed their innocence and had to realign their sense of self and their perspective on reality. The identity of survivors, as others have noted, is deeply affected by death.[12] Self-understanding is dependent on others: the loss of someone who has been part of shaping one's identity can be a shattering experience, precipitating a crisis, because the bereaved must create a new identity without the deceased.[13] Letter-writing was one way soldiers began to shape another self in their correspondence. Through letters, they attempted to order, contain and control the chaos which surrounded them.[14]

To deal with the death of their fellow-combatants, soldiers were required to accept another identity, one which expressed the frailties of the warrior. For while the rhetoric of war insisted that men repress their emotions, war paradoxically created the very conditions which feminised them as they searched, panic-stricken and ill-prepared, for a response to its pain and sorrow.[15] They nurtured the parents of those who had been killed, a task seemingly superfluous in war where public proclamations overtly disparaged the feminine. It was not that they had forgotten their lines, only that they unexpectedly discovered that the words they had rehearsed so well could not communicate the unspeakable. While the havoc of war created a spectacle of grief which left its protagonists speechless, it also produced incessant conversation about war.

Writers and soldiers alike have emphasised the inadequacy of language to convey the experience of trench warfare. The inability to describe the trenches became, as Paul Fussell has observed, one of 'the motifs of all who wrote about the war'.[16] Letters by soldiers are said to have been clichéd, uniform and flat, but my reading of soldiers' correspondence to family members of deceased soldiers shows that this was not always the case. In meticulously documenting the details of death, soldiers took care to describe the particular circumstances of a special loss, rather than use tired clichés which denied the family the distinctiveness of their son's death.[17]

Battlefronts

Soldiers felt acutely the loss of a comrade in combat, and much has been written about the bonds forged between soldiers in battle.[18] These intimate bonds sustained and protected them, and they sought to replicate them through writing letters to their friends' parents. Lieutenant John Archibald wrote of the collective grief experienced by his brigade following the death of Morton Allan:

I do not exaggerate when I say the whole of the Third Brigade will feel his loss for he had friends in every battalion in the Brigade & all will miss his cheery, gallant personality & his cheery smile, that he never lost, no matter how bitter were the prevailing hardships or how hot the fight. He was one of those great spirits who could never die but who became one of 'your Deathless Army', whose grace and example whilst amongst us render their influences for good eternal.[19]

An entire battalion would share the grief. Sergeant Livingstone wrote to Mrs Chapman saying that her soldier son was 'respected by all', and that his loss was a very severe blow to everyone of us as he was looked upon by everyone in the Battalion as one of the very best Soldiers that ever left Australia ... I never heard anyone speak a single disrespectful word of him ... some of the lads brought his remains back ... our Pioneers erected a very nice cross of Wood ...[20]

It was not always the occasion of death that inspired soldiers to write to parents. J. K. Forsyth wrote to Mrs Ellen Derham, regarding her son Alfred, that 'we have been very closely associated for almost a year now, and I have grown to love him as if he were my own boy ... I know how a mother likes to be able to tell you these fine things to his credit.'[21] He also very 'often talks to me of you all, and I know from what he says how very fondly he regards all his dear ones at home'.[22] When Derham was hospitalised, another soldier wrote paternally to his mother with the reassurance that 'I shall look after your boy & do my best to send him back all the better for the experience ... when all this sad business is over.'[23]

But it was not usually under these circumstances that soldiers communicated with the parents of men with whom they bonded. They more frequently found themselves describing the pain of severing ties, rather than the delight of consolidating a friendship. The family of George Naylor, who died in 1917, received a letter from the man who had witnessed his death. His sacrifice was elevated to glory and the loss bonded both family and soldier. 'I thought you would like to have a few lines from one of George's friends', wrote Private Wallace to Naylor's father in April 1917.

I am trying to express the sympathy we his mates feel towards you and your family in losing him. We lost a cheery good pal and staunch comrade and understand your deepest feelings. Struck down by a shell – George died as he lived – a man – a soldier striking for Honour and Freedom and I am glad to know I was counted amongst his friends.[24]

Allan Hislop died a year earlier, in 1916, after contracting abscesses on both his lungs. After he went missing, his friend Alex wrote to Hislop's parents, believing it was his duty to let them know as much as possible. He conveyed, in considerable detail, the course of events which led to his disappearance. 'I was with Allan during the afternoon & he was in the best of spirits & was looking forward [to] the charge.' Unable to capture the trenches, 'we were mostly back behind our own lines at day break ... I looked for Allan but could not find him & he has not since turned up.' He promised Hislop's parents that he would send his watch, which was being repaired at the jewellers, and news of any other developments.[25]

Many found this instantaneous intimacy and emotional expression difficult. 'I am afraid I am a very bad hand at expressing myself,' wrote Captain R. F. French to the mother of Private Donald Anderson, who was killed in 1916, 'but I would like you to know how awfully sorry we all are for you ... we thought a great deal of your son who was as brave as a man as one could wish and we all feel his loss immensely'.[26] An awkward intimacy was also expressed by C. S. D. Adamson on the occasion of the death of his friend, Sidney Brooks. 'Perhaps Sid spoke of me to you', he wrote in 1918; he 'often told me of his wife and little child. He had never seen the latter and was very anxious to. Poor little fellow. Later on I hope he will know what a brave fellow his dad was and how much he was loved by his comrades. It seems a cruel fate.'[27]

It was particularly difficult for these soldiers to find an appropriate language because their role shifted from combatant to nurturer.[28] The father of Edgar Briggen received several letters relating to his son's death at the age of twenty-two in February 1918. Will Brydie wrote how his letter was 'really a poor attempt of expressing my sympathy to you and Ted's dear sister and loved ones at "Home", however, should I be spared to reach "Home" again I will then be able to give in detail, verbally that which I cannot find words to write'. Brydie wrote that 'my only regret is that I cannot find words to write to let you know of his fine qualities. I really feel so grieved about it myself that I find writing this rather difficult.'[29]

The difficulty of expression came to soldiers because of the frailties and vulnerabilities they exposed in themselves. In October 1916, William Goodman wrote to Mrs Hislop: 'I hardly know how to perform this painful and sad duty. Your son Allan gradually sank and on the morning of the 18th at 8.25 am he passed away ... he was very peaceful when the end came ... this may come as a surprise after having such cheery letters from Allan.' He assured her he 'will go to his funeral myself and so pay my last respects also represent you there'. He also promised to send his belongings after the war.[30] 'Allan had a decent funeral,' he later wrote, 'and a wreath I sent for you personally & myself I attended the cemetery.' He confessed he had been 'a prisoner now since Oct 1914 & am looking forward to a speedy return home ... Hoping some day [to] meet you and also to hear from you.'[31] Their shared anguish bonded them. From the

> 1st day Allan came to Göttingen I felt drawn towards him & I went with him when it was necessary to amputate his hand. Later Allan improved and actually walked with me but unfortunately he seemed to get thin & he fell away and so to satisfy myself & also to represent you & family I assisted at the post-mortem exam ...[32]

The subsequent correspondence with the family was close and intimate, the parents requesting a photograph of Goodman, asking after his health and well-being. A year later, he was corresponding with them describing his influenza, 'general depression' and hoping to see 'them some day'.[33] At times, fellow-combatants became surrogate sons, drawn into families who sought to replace their absent son with one who was present at the loss.

The desire to capture the minute details of death was crucial even to those who had never met the soldier. Captain Norman W. Sunder, who knew the family, wrote to Morton Allan's father soon after Morton's death. He described how he stumbled across him, and reassured the family that he had died with minimal pain and in triumph:

> He was killed on the morning of September 20th by a shell fragment which penetrated the back of his head, death would be instantaneous. I was passing over the battlefield on the morning of the 21st & came across his body in a shell crater. I had never met your son but on examining his papers I discovered who he was & immediately had him buried & made a cross with all his particulars printed on it. I am enclosing a little map showing the exact spot, as near as I could possibly locate it, where he is buried ... Your son was not disfigured & had a smile on his face & as we buried him I thought of you and your grief but it must be a comfort to know that he gave his life for his country ... I am so glad that I was able to see that your son was buried properly. It was not possible to have a Chaplain but my thoughts were sufficient & he rests in a soldier's grave.[34]

Soldiers who did know the dead men often wrote apologetically, burdened by the weight of grief and sense of guilt but also, as Thomas Laqueur has pointed out, an acute sense that they had not abandoned their comrades.[35] One Red Cross worker wrote to the father of Percy Chapman, killed in action in March 1917:

> You will no doubt be surprised to hear from me ... I feel I ought to tell you what I can. I never met him [but] often saw him with his co. when on parade ... Captain wandered onto the German line ... I am told he must have been killed instantly and not suffered ... If I have harrowed you with too much detail I am sorry; but I think you will understand my motive ... I felt you would rather know the facts. Captain Chapman was a brave man ... & I hope the knowledge that he was so may help to soften the weight of your trouble ...[36]

Sometimes family members wrote wanting to know further information and the final news often came as a relief. F. McInerney wrote to 'Earnie', a soldier who had sent him details of his brother's death, claiming, 'I cannot thank you too kindly for having written the details of my poor Brother's death. I was longing & thinking for weeks past ... his sufferings are at an end and he died a noble death one that we are proud of.' There was a moment of familiarity they shared: 'Harry must have been a bit too hasty jumping up on the Parapet but he was one of that sort – as game as they make them'.[37] McInerney requested further knowledge about his brother's behaviour: 'I oft times wonder did he ever get a German during the time he was there if you could find out if he accounted for any of the Huns I would only be too pleased to know. Also any further details that you may dig up.'[38] The lack of details frustrated other soldiers who apologised for their inability to shed light on death. 'I am afraid I can give you no details of the end', wrote one soldier; 'I was wounded on another part of the Battlefield at the time he fell & only heard of it when in hospital.'[39]

It was in the public appeals to manhood, patriotism and the Empire that this grief and pain was given purpose. As Fussell and others have noted, soldiers understood and made sense of battle through the chivalrous and heroic tales of poets such as Tennyson.[40] In an atmosphere of 'euphemism and rigorous, impenetrable language', heroic language obscured grief.[41] J. E. Norman Osborne wrote to his friend's father using the language of glory, claiming that his son was buried in 'a Military Cemetery near Ploegsteert in Belgium ... A wooden Cross has been erected to mark the spot ... I trust and pray that God will give you comfort and strength to bear it. You have at least the satisfaction of knowing that your son died doing his Duty nobly and that he gave his life in the highest cause.'[42] Captain R. M. Anderson wrote of one soldier that he was 'much respected and well liked by officers and Men of this unit. He was a good soldier and a very fine MAN.'[43]

Soldiers eulogised the military persona of the deceased, a role that they themselves were shedding. This militaristic role-playing suggested a disavowal, for the language of glory shielded an unresolved loss. But while it did not name grief, it was a response against which recipients could at least identify their pain. Notions of duty replaced emotions of grief. The mixture of loss and patriotism came to the fore in soldiers' letters. Roy Youldale wrote to the mother of Lieutenant William Stanley Martin of her irreparable loss, 'but at the same time I cannot but congratulate you on being able to give to the state so splendid a soldier'. He assured her that the service was an impressive one, and that he would attempt to obtain a photograph of the cross. 'I cannot but feel', he concluded, 'that your great pride in his gallant memory will help to ease the blow you have suffered. For what more could a man do than that he lay down his life for his friends.'[44] R. A. McDonald received a letter outlining the circumstances of the death of Allan Albert in 1916. He 'met his death', noted another soldier, 'whilst at duty with machine gunners in front line of trenches at Pozières on morning of 7th August 1916'. The enemy, he continued, 'were attacking strongly ... and it was whilst engagement with other machine gunners repelling this attack that Pte Albert met his death. He with others being killed by enemy shells his body was buried on the battle field ... it will be comforting to them [his parents] to know that their son died doing his duty'.[45] Politicians in particular celebrated the idea of the comfort of heroism. The mayor of Brisbane wrote to Annie Hislop, expressing his sympathy and the hope that it would be of some consolation that her son died as a gallant soldier 'in support of a righteous cause, and in the true interests of humanity'.[46] An impassioned letter was sent to Emily Duncan, following the death of her son Alfred, from the premier, A. H. Peake: 'No man can render a greater service to his country than to give his life for it, and the heroic deeds of those who have fallen in the cause for liberty, justice and civilisation will be ever remembered.'[47]

When Claude Leahy was killed in Palestine in October 1917, the secretary of the shire which included Nhill, Victoria, wrote to Leahy's widow claiming that 'the noble patriotic spirit which prompted him to volunteer and give his life for his King and Country is the highest and noblest sacrifice [a man] can make and the deeds of the Australians of which he was one will make a world's everlasting history. Believe me.'[48]

Perhaps men of the church were better equipped than most to perform the role of accommodating death, familiar as they were with providing rituals of and meanings to it. But even they often acted out an unacknowledged grief, by drawing on the familiar rhetoric of sacrifice. Religious comfort was very important for some soldiers. 'I trust that God will be with you & yours in these sad hours,' wrote Lieutenant John Archibald, '& that He will give you the comfort of his Holy Spirit to sustain you all through this great sorrow that He in His Infinite wisdom has called on you to bear for His sake.'[49] But the chaplains who were sent to the front were not accustomed to the indifference they met from many of their charges. Some chaplains were idealistic and joined the chaplaincy 'dreaming of glorious opportunities for spiritual work with men'.[50] All of them were required to conduct church parades on Sundays and to bury the dead, but the role they played – either as counsellors or companions – was left up to individual chaplains. Many must have felt the contradiction between their role as Christian men devoted to peace and their complicity through their official involvement in the war.[51] The turnover of chaplains was extremely high – some 414 chaplains were commissioned between 1914 and 1919 – with many serving for a year or less.[52]

Families sought details of the burial, as knowledge of such a ritual could serve to help in the healing process.[53] Australia did not bring the dead home and there was no public ceremony.[54] Without a body, the resolution and reality of death were harder to accept.[55] Mrs Leahy received a letter from Chaplain A. E. Lapthorne in January 1917 describing her son's burial:

I buried him with his companions on the slope of a hill close to Beersheba. He gave his life for a noble and a grand cause and now lies at rest in Holy ground in this country ... I feel for you in your great loss and grief and pray earnestly that God Himself will be your comfort and stay.[56]

Some described the heroic loss as an act of God and soldiers as His followers. On the death of Private Allan Albert in 1916 at Pozières, Alex MacDonald wrote to this effect in no uncertain terms: 'Look upon all this as from God and remember that your son was a hero, and that his memory will never die.'[57] Chaplain F. W. Rolland wrote to Mrs Albert from 'a dug out near where your boy fell' to tell of how her son was esteemed by his mates and his officers and that:

The autumn leaves are very glorious here – God makes beautiful what is going to die – The pathos of this War is that our young men forgo their summer and fall in their spring. But me feels in them too a glory and a beauty of soul born of God – they have the spirit of Jesus Christ. He claims them proudly as His followers – he loves them with the love of those who have passed thro' terrible experiences together – a love that cannot be broken but only cemented by death. God help you dear lady with His peace. You know today something of what He did when He let His own son go and suffer and gloriously give Himself away for the world's advantage.[58]

Army chaplains had little preparation for how to deal with the scale of death they encountered in the trenches. The theology they knew did not serve them well in the ghastly situation in which they found themselves. As one historian has observed, 'much of the theology before, during and after the war lacked the qualities and ambivalence, paradox, irony, tragedy, grief, sophistication, which are necessary to cope with the complexity of experience'.[59] Chaplains wrote to parents on behalf of the battalion of which their sons were a part. But all too often they relied on reassurances of heroic glory to understand the purpose of death:

I should like to tell you especially how greatly I as Chaplain, valued your splendid boy's life & influence & what a real power for good it was in the Bn. Life on active service can be very hard in many ways – temptations that at home mean nothing, out here become very real sources of trouble – but I always knew I could depend on Mort to go straight all the time ... For a while now you only have his memory, but it should be a very proud one for you.[60]

Chaplains often adopted a feminine role of comforting the bereaved. C. Bullock, a Catholic chaplain, wrote to Mrs Armstrong whose son, Colville, had died after the war had ended:

I am writing to you as I promised but this time with the utmost difficulty ... It is so hard to have to send this sad news esp'lly after the anxious time you have had.

The poor boy was so patient & brave through it all. Obedient in everything he never gave a bit of trouble. Naturally therefore the nurses & the orderlies were much upset when he died ... I promise you I will mention him in every Mass that I may have the privilege of saying. May he rest in peace & also may God give you all the grace to bear this sad bereavement with resignation.[61]

Bullock also wrote to Armstrong's sister, with an awkward and embarrassed attempt to convey details. He reassured her that her brother had

received all the condolences of his Holy religion ... cemetery exceedingly well kept ... nicest I was ever in ... But if you wish to give any instructions will you send them to me & I will forward them to some civilian friends of mine who live quite close to the cemetery. I sincerely hope your dear Mother is quite well again ... writing as if I knew you all ... pardon me ... only way showing my sympathy ... photo enclosed of place where your dear Brother buried & of the Chaplain who performed the Last Rites. Once more I promise you all & especially your Brother an ever remembrance in my Masses.[62]

Another chaplain wrote to the mother of Percy Chapman, that her son 'left a great record [and] ... a great blank ... The fine monument erected by the battalion expressed what his men thought of him ... they brought a fine cross for many, many miles & have placed it on his grave ... I have applied for an official photograph of the Grave.'[63]

Other chaplains became more cynical, changed by the experience of war and disillusioned by what it revealed about human nature. William Moore, the Army Chaplain in the Australian Imperial Force (AIF), observed that

[War] is an animal process. Not human, not reasonable ... Worse still, men tend to become callous in the face of death in horrible forms and the corollary of that condition is that they grow to hold human life cheaply. That too comes back to the national character – and we do experience crime in its most violent forms following in the wake of war. What else can be expected.[64]

Homefronts

Meanwhile, on the homefront, war had extinguished any certainty, and replaced it with absence as a way of life. Emotional life was determined by the stark columns of casualty and death lists in the daily press, and the arrival of telegrams announcing death had a shattering impact. Clergymen witnessed the effect of the war on families as they delivered the casualty telegrams to the door. It was a 'grievous lot to pay a solemn call', recalled one clergyman,[65] and the sight of a priest in the street was enough to send households into a wave of panic and fear.⁶⁶ This task became an awkward and difficult one for the clergy to perform. They carried the message of death to strangers, imparting news which would not only devastate these families but also create distress for themselves.⁶⁷ In Britain, the practice was somewhat less personalised, as telegraph boys riding on red bicycles delivered the death notice.⁶⁸ The majority of the bereaved in Germany similarly received a 'terse official telegram'.⁶⁹

There were dislocations of another sort, too: war affected the ways men and women came to identify themselves. Women understood themselves as sisters, mothers and wives of soldiers, while men could not escape the military culture which defined their manhood. Fatherhood was spoken about in ways which assumed an unusual national importance, for fathering a nation of heroes was seen as worthy of respect and public commentary.

In receiving their news through personal letters and the daily press, families with a serving soldier were drawn together into a collective experience of anticipating mourning.⁷⁰ Letters became precious, even sacred; valued and treasured, circulated and distributed, read and reread aloud. Like immigrant letters, they became public property – the arrival of a letter allayed fear of death for friends and families. Relationships were sustained and forged through correspondence.⁷¹ People counted letters, noticing any change in frequency. Ruth Derham wrote to her brother, Alfred, in December 1914, noting that 'I got your letter yesterday – made the family jealous as no letter has arrived for them – they seem to let them through gradually.'⁷² Frances Anderson, Alfred's fiancée, rationalised the decline in letters optimistically in terms of her high expectations: 'I suppose it is because we have been so lucky up till now that we feel it even more.'⁷³

In Australia, as elsewhere in the world, the volume of correspondence dispatched overseas escalated during the war. With this pressure on postal services and the delays imposed by wartime restrictions, it took considerably longer for letters and parcels to reach overseas destinations. In 1913, the average time taken for the mail carrier, the *Orient Pacific*, to travel between London and Adelaide was 28½ days. The return journey averaged 29¾ days. During 1916–17, this increased to almost 45 days and almost 50 days, respectively.⁷⁴ Letters were a cheap form of communication. The cost of sending a parcel to Britain was one shilling up to one pound weight and sixpence for every additional pound.⁷⁵ This was within reach of most – the average weekly earnings were 55s 7d for men and 27s 5d for women in 1914, climbing to 66s 5d for men and 30s 5d for women by the end of the war.⁷⁶ The British postal service was similarly strained. In October 1914, the army postal service handled

650 000 letters and 58 000 parcels a week. Within five months, this had increased to 3 million letters and 230 000 parcels. By 1916, mail for the troops had reached a weekly average of 11 million letters and 875 000 parcels.[77]

While this swell of correspondence may suggest sustained contact across the seas, censors carved out words and silenced voices. The uniform postcard which was sent out allowed soldiers to delete the relevant lines and sanitised their experience in the process.[78] Frances Anderson wrote to her fiancé in frustration:

Mother got a p.c. [postcard] from Uncle Henry from the front last mail, one of the printed things with set sentences, you know, I expect ... they cross out whatever they don't want. They are evidently not allowed to write & I am wondering if we'll be allowed news from you – it doesn't look as if we would. Wish I knew if you'll get any letters.[79]

Letters were the main source of personal information available but could also bring confusion:

Mail is in and nothing from you for anyone and I am wondering where you are. That cable from you was apparently from Alexandria & so we expected to hear ... this mail, but now we are wondering if it had really been dispatched from Lemnos. And if after the 2nd Brigade's rest it would go back to the Dardanelles, or [participate] in the landing at Salonika? Everyone is in the dark about everything, conjectures are rife, but few of them are optimistic. Things about the Dardanelles are coming out now & it is openly acknowledged a failure. And the details of the failures are appalling. What we do hear – there must be ten times as much that we don't hear & never will.[80]

When letters continued to come after death, they inflicted cruel reminders. Marianne Wiggins has powerfully dramatised this process of denial and fear, presence and absence, in her novel *John Dollar*. Writing of Charlotte Lewes, whose husband Henry had been killed in the war, Wiggins observed:

For two months after he was killed ... his letters written from the trench continued to arrive. A dead man can't send letters, Charlotte knew. She also knew that they'd been written months before, but she pretended ... But then the letters stopped. A month went by without a word from him ... Sometimes she smoothed the paper of the letters that he'd written like shrouds over her face as she lay still. Sometimes she tried to hear his voice. She missed his face.[81]

It is easy to see how a steady correspondence of this macabre sort would arouse false hope and a desire to cheat rather than to accept the inevitable pain of death. A constant contact with others helped in this path of acceptance.

Through letters of condolence we can see see how there emerged a network of women immersed in an atmosphere of preparing for the possibility of further loss.[82] Following the death of her son, Lance-Corporal Sidney Brooks, Mrs Brooks received letters of condolences from those anxious about their sons. 'My own son', one correspondent began, 'is also in France with the Artillery, therefore I can feel for you in your sad bereavement: for at the present juncture, we never know what any day may bring forth ... Mere words fail us at the supreme crisis, but you know how we all feel, and I pray that time may heal your sorrow.'[83]

It was through reading the daily newspapers that her friends were drawn into a collective support group. Before the widespread use of radio and television, newspapers were the key form of communication. Prior to the outbreak of war, newspaper prices reached their lowest point ever, and even afterwards they remained cheap. The *Daily Telegraph*, the *Sydney Morning Herald*, and the *Argus* cost only one penny each in 1914. The *Sydney Morning Herald* was only twopence in 1920.[84] The newspaper became the primary form of communication during the war and never before or since have newspapers so dominated public communication.[85] Under the scrutiny of the censors, newspaper war reports could not be entirely reliable. In October 1914 the War Precautions Act came into effect, giving governments wide powers. Under these laws it was illegal to publish any material likely to discourage recruiting or undermine the Allied effort. But the casualty lists and death notices could not deny the reality of war, and they stood as bold pronouncements against its sanitised reportage.

The 'lists' drew women together, forming a common identity. In May 1915, Alfred Derham was wounded in battle. His mother, Ellen Derham, received several letters wishing her son well, and a rapid recovery. M. Barrett observed in her letter how confronting the casualty and death lists were: 'I have not been able to look at those lists', she confessed, 'and only heard of your misfortune today.'[86] 'How harrowing it is to read daily of the heavy list of casualties', wrote Isabelle Walker; 'it makes our hearts ache for the many parents whose homes are desolated by the cruel war.'[87] Another friend had noticed in the *Argus* that 'Alfred had been wounded', and appreciated the 'anxious time you must all be going through',[88] and another reported that she 'looked at the papers at what might be awaiting me'.[89] Mary Gibson wrote that it

gave me quite a shock when I read over the list in paper this morning, to see that poor dear Alfred has been wounded and I know how sore your heart will be at present ... the war comes very near homeward ... it is terrible to think of good lives sacrificed we need all pray God that he will be on our side ...[90]

'Our first thought', wrote another friend, 'is for the lists which are greedily scanned. The last week has been one of horror.'[91] Fannie Billing was saddened by the news that Derham's son's name was 'amongst the wounded' and was thankful it was not worse. As a public spectacle of the wounded and the dead, the casualty lists spared no one who cast their eyes over them. Even those who did not experience the immediacy of death in their family could not ignore the names listed in the daily newspaper, mounting like the bodies in the trenches they represented. In 1915, one correspondent confessed, 'I think the boys are brave who join now. After reading the papers'.[92] The papers could also bring relief and triumph, for it was the place of volatile emotions. 'In this morning's paper', wrote Myrtle Forrester, 'I see Alf has been honoured by the King with a military cross – How glorious! . . . I have looked for some mention of his name each day in the papers, and it was good to see it this morning in a column of distinction . . . the casualty list is so dreadfully long, isn't it?'[93]

Women spoke to each other through the fate of their men and forged a collective identity through absence.[94] Ruth Falkingham wrote to Ellen Derham, 'We have had many letters from Harry he writes cheerfully and his last letter he had dinner in Cairo with Miss Spoule.'[95] D. G. Cullen wrote in hope that the next news would be better: 'My brother's son John is there, and of course we are anxious. I trust you will all bear up in this time of grief and trial – it is His will.'[96] Annie Samuel stressed that 'We, too, are passing through an anxious period as we have had no word from our boy for sometime.'[97] M. Barrett remarked that 'I feared Keith was in the Dardanelles too but last mail brought me news that he had been kept back at the last minute with 39 others who are to train as second lieutenants.'[98] Ethel Clarke wrote, 'My brother Cecil cabled last Monday, he was still in Egypt – though expected to be leaving soon, but was not sure if he was to go to the Dardanelles or France – Oh isn't it all awful.'[99] Kitty Fraus confessed she had 'lost a cousin of mine last week', while Elsie Barker was glad that at least Alfred was removed from the front, for one 'comfort is that he is not in that inferno, fighting – but being cared for in hospital . . . I think my brother must be at the front in Turkey by this time – but I cannot realise it.'[100] Another mentioned that 'Roy goes into camp next month I think: he has been devoting all his spare time to military studies for some time.' Gracie Derham observed that

> Almost every day we hear of fellows who have felt or are leaving shortly that we know. Eric Gibson was accepted with the Canadians & is now at Salisbury – Arnold Baker is going from Sydney as an X-ray expert it seems he has done a good deal in that branch . . . If wishing could give you a swift victory & safe return you would be here very soon however women must always play a waiting game so we wait on & send love laden wishes.[101]

As one soldier reflected, 'We often say amongst ourselves, that the war has done one fine thing in that it has brought our brave womenfolk into a closer and fonder relationship. I know my dear wife has through its agency found many many true friends.'[102]

This spirit drew women together, where they could share their anticipation of possible death.[103] Ellen Derham's letters to her sons Alfred and Frank suggested the way in which she shared her anxiety with others. 'A great many mothers have had cables from their sons', she wrote in December 1914, 'so I can only hope that all is well with you. Even as you have sent word to us, there is great delay, no doubt.'[104] Knowledge, information and fact were in short supply as word travelled about others' grief and soldiers' whereabouts:

Mrs. Henderson's son sent a cable from Colombo & she only received it two days ago (after you had all landed in Egypt) – Mrs H asked the postman if there were any letters from the troops from Colombo and he said that all the soldiers' letters were to be sent straight to the Postmaster General, so we shall have to wait a long time before we receive any news from you.

As she articulated: 'it is all uncertainty and in the dark as far as we are concerned at any rate'.[105] Similarly in November 1915, she wrote of delay and anxiety:

We are still anxiously awaiting letters from you as we got no mail from you last week at all. We think the Gallipoli and Lemnos mails missed the mail from Egypt as we can hear of no one who received any letters from the Front . . . Mrs Forsyth rang me up & (asked) if I had received any letter from you as she had none from the general. She was going to the Post Office, and enquiring for any letters that might be for me.[106]

Alfred Derham's sister, Ruth, spoke of the pity and anguish of other women. It was no less painful for the sisters of soldiers. She wrote to her brother that she had seen Susan Martin:

It was sad her brother dying wasn't it? Another brother who left home some years ago & has never been heard of has just left notice for his money to go to his mother while away . . . they think he must either have sailed or is going to sail for the front shortly but . . . they don't know. So Susan is trying to find out where he enlisted from . . . What worries people have. Poor Susan looks thin and old & worried.[107]

Women bonded in a collective identity. Enid Derham wrote to her brother Alfred after he arrived in Egypt in 1914. She shared his excitement – 'fancy you being in Egypt! . . . I'm dying to know exactly where you are, & what you're doing' – but was especially keen to link herself with her brother through others. 'Have you met Cyril Clarke of the Light Horse?', she inquired, 'he's Ethel's brother. Do look him up if you get the chance, & tell me something about him, so that I can tell Ethel you're met.'[108]

Letters replaced loss and precipitated a kaleidoscope of emotions, for the content of letters could be fragmentary, tentative and unresolved. Frances Anderson, then the fiancée of Alfred Derham, expressed her frustration at the confusion and uncertainty of the mail. In September 1916, she wrote in exasperation, 'I do hope for a letter this week – I have a mail-day ache very badly!'[109] 'Addie has heard from Frank two mails out of the three so we know the letters are not being delayed', she wrote. She observed that his last note was written at the beginning of April, and thanked him for his last cable. 'It is dated 6th whether April or May is uncertain', she wrote with some concern,

> but I suppose April, since I despatched the cable on the 31st March – and I believe all cables were delayed for several weeks. But perhaps it was May & *my* cable was delayed! But whether April or May it would be later than this last mail so we aren't worrying ... only I do [hope] no letters have been lost – specially if you have written to the family. It's a fortnight till next mail – oh – I do want a letter.[110]

'It's strange', she noted, 'how your letters follow on mine – or are coincident with them – and often if not with what I have written, with what I have thought.'[111] Letters were markers of time. Rereading became a way of filling the void. 'I reread some of my old letters you returned, last night – Are those discarded ones or are all my letters as empty as they? – not so much *empty*, perhaps, as constrained and badly expressed.'[112] Between some women, letters and privileged knowledge become a source of tension and resentment. Anderson told her fiancé, 'I rang your mother as soon as I got your letter – I think she was glad as she had only a p.c. of 29th July. I have not been shown your letters for months now – I was told of your asking for news of ME – and tho' she made a joke of it I think your mother was a teeny bit hurt.'[113] But Frances and her fiancé's mother also read avidly together.[114] In October 1916, she wrote: 'I received your letter of 30/8/16 two days ago(!) and shall take it to Hindfall tomorrow night to read extracts to your mother – I rang her when I got it.'[115] The desire to number the letters and so contain and structure the emotions came in 1916 when she announced she would 'start numbering my letters, as Addie and lots of other people do – this is No. 1'.[116] The numbering of letters helped recipients to keep a record of which letters they were answering because of the delays of war postage.

This ordering of emotions was a way of dealing with absence, but it could never completely assuage the pain. The official announcement of death arrived in the form of a telegram, delivered by a clergyman. It was formal and official; in its telling, it robbed the tragic event of any emotion. In contrast, soldiers transmitted the news in a personalised form, exposing their vulnerabilities and sharing their anguish with strangers as a way of dealing with their guilt as survivors. Through the letters they wrote, and the grief they experienced, their identity shifted from warrior to nurturer. As they shed their military persona, they eulogised it in the deceased, using glory to disavow their loss. In this process, they willingly became surrogate sons of the parents whose sons had died.

Back home, the recipients of these letters formed a collective identity of potential mourners as they rehearsed the experience of grief. In anticipating death, they created another layer of bereavement, which could be as emotional and dislocating as death itself. Letters and newspaper lists became precious and sacred, for they not only documented, but also ordered and defined, the volatile emotions of their readers.

How men and women dealt with grief in this sea of shifting emotions is explored in the following chapters. A collective identity based on perpetuating a memory was forged by those who suffered loss. But this was a fragile unity, for after the war, these groups tussled for the privileged status of primary bearer of memory and sacrifice. Their strategies shifted dramatically over time, for grief and loss, like sacrifice, have a history.

2   The Sacrificial Mother

> This awful war is hard on all of us but on none more than the mothers of our soldiers.[1]

Immediately after the war, mothers of the dead were in favour. In the early months of 1919, during the first time in four years when they would no longer be waiting for news of their sons, mothers were honoured with a badge which bore one star for each son or brother who had died.[2] In announcing the release of the badge, Senator George Pearce, the Minister for Defence since 1914,[3] proudly declared that, while the badge would be 'simple in design but chaste', it would be 'cherished by the honoured possessors who have specially earned the sympathy and admiration of their fellow citizens'.[4]

Such symbols of honour and sacrifice were appreciated by mothers at the time, but they soon came to be seen as hollow recognition. It was universally acknowledged that, in offering 60 000 lives to the imperial cause and in suffering another 150 000 injured, Australia had made a significant impression on the course of events.[5] After the war, however, an unspoken but underlying question gnawed at the minds of those who struggled to gain compensation for their bereavement: whose sacrifice was to be deemed the most worthy among the living? In peace, a crucial subtext emerged in the campaigns launched by returned soldiers, mothers and fathers of soldiers deceased and alive, widows and wives: to what extent should these familial groups be honoured in recognition of their loss? However repugnant such questions were – for they established an artificial hierarchy of sacrifice, a taxonomy which compared each to the other by an arbitrary judgement – it was within these terms that the families framed their demands for financial assistance. Those family members of the deceased who bonded not with other blood relations, but with strangers, sought not only affirmation, but protection from neglect. They campaigned for preferential treatment on the basis of degrees of sacrifice, and insisted that the legacy of war was being carried unevenly.

All agreed that the state should take responsibility for their pain in times of peace as well as war.

But who was to be more or less worthy of remuneration remained a thorny point. To insist on this, however, was to challenge the moral ambiguity of war. Deep resentment and fierce anger were aroused because in wartime those who had suffered loss were the 'winners', but with the onset of peace they had become 'losers'. Their pain had been denied in being renamed as glory and honour.

In an effort to resist this loss, widows, fathers and mothers attempted to articulate a language of grief. In voicing a protest against the authorities, mothers made 'public criticism' and 'complaint'[6] to express their anger and their unresolved loss. Culturally, maternal love was not considered to be 'true' love and therefore could never attain the status of 'true' loss.[7] An important paradox in this was that, although mothers were complicit in sustaining the memory of war and its celebration, their demands and campaigns for remuneration revealed their attempts to shape an expression of grief which the mythologies of war attempted to obliterate.

In these shifts we can also see how ideas about 'sacrifice' have a history. Historians of war have perceived 'sacrifice' as an overarching category, and, in doing so, have treated the representation and experience of mothers' grief as unchanging. But such a perspective ignores the shift in the grieving mother's role in the public domain: from active participant to the frustration and sadness of ignored bystander.

In the immediate aftermath of the war, the sacrifice of mothers was publicly acknowledged. But by the 1930s, the identity of the sacrificial mother had been conflated with the generic category of 'woman', thus denying mothers' entry into the public memory of war through their maternal sacrifice. Once the mother's active role of giving was superseded by a sense of 'intrusion' by women, their contribution to the memory of war diminished, and was perceived only in terms of remembering the sacrifice of their sons.

Mothers and Sons

Richard White has noted that soldiers formed an intimate relationship with their mothers, 'as intense a focus for sentiment as mateship, and a closer, more established, more emotional and even more romantic tie than many marriages'.[8] A son's death could cast a long dark shadow, as one woman claimed in 1922: 'my mother died of a broken heart six months after the death of her only son'.[9] This maternal bond, where soldiers were often infantilised by their mothers, was not severed but strengthened by absence in wartime.

Soldiers addressed letters to their mothers in loving terms. A son who enlisted could create anguish for his mother. In 1915, Malcolm Stirling anticipated his mother's response to his desire to enlist. In doing so, he approached Edward Segden, the warden of Queen's College at the University of Melbourne, for advice. Segden wrote to Stirling's mother, claiming that he felt 'torn asunder' by the conflicting demands of maintaining his own self-respect, but understanding 'how great a trial it will be to you and his father'. Segden advised that she 'dare not refuse to give him to his country'.[10] Stirling was not alone in having to wrestle his desire to enlist and the anxiety it created for those he loved. In 1915, 'Sid' wrote to his mother in anticipation of her pain and resistance to his intention to go to war:

I have been doing very little writing of late, but have been doing plenty of thinking. No doubt mummie [this] will give you a little start when I say I'd like, with your permission to be able to go to the war. Now go steady mum, I haven't only just thought of it today, or yesterday, but for the past two or three weeks ... Now you understand mother, I'm no kid, and I believe now is the best time to go. Now mother, don't be too hasty and say no! but think it over ... I know it would come hard of you mother, but think of the thousands and thousands of other mothers who feel it the same.[11]

A belief in patriotic duty eased the pain of separation for some mothers. George Doig's mother wrote with a mixture of loss and pride, when her son departed. Their relationship was shaped by a strong maternal bond:

you will understand how very hard it is for mother to write to you for the very thought of your leaving me, and of saying goodbye ... I cannot tell you how very proud I am ... three such dear boys who heard the call of duty and obeyed. I trust we will be spared to greet my three daring boys and keep the home fire burning till you return, don't forget to read your testament ... attend all church parades and let others see by your conduct that our christian life is the best. You know how we mothers are suffering just now ... I'll miss your little homecomings, I'll miss your kisses and ... smile and miss your ... everything dear ... as we have been as close as friends and companions, as well as being your own mumsie ... Now dearest don't think mother has said enough. I could keep on only I must see to other things.[12]

Earlier she had written:

my heart yearns for a glimpse of my three dear brave boys. I can do so little for you, and say so little that I feel ashamed at the very little part I am doing in this great war. There is one comfort ... I hope and trust if it pleases God to send you all back safe and well after a glorious victory. That will be the honour that I will rejoice in.[13]

Charles Murrell was one of those who wrote consistently and lovingly to his mother. He addressed her as mummie, and wrote in November 1915, that he 'wished was home to have a bath and a "good tuck in" ', as 'it's a terror, cold and windy and the main object to keep the tummy full if you can'.[14] Ellen Derham wrote affectionately to her son Alfred, offering 'love and kisses [to] my soldier boy. I wish I could have one peep at you now. All these snaps of you and us all are splendid.'[15] Mary Alice Higgins received intimate details from her son Mervyn while he served overseas. 'I have just come back from a bathe,' he wrote, 'before which I had a tooth stopped. My teeth have hung out very well, biscuits having only accounted for two.'[16]

But we should not romanticise the relationships sons may have had with their mothers. Alfred Derham was critical of his mother's opinion of his fiancée, Frances, and was frustrated with what he regarded as the idle, domestic talk in her letters. His mother reported that his last letter 'hurt me a little tiny bit', because he accused her of jealousy. 'I hope my dear son you are not so small minded to think such a thing of your mother ... God only knows it is only your ultimate happiness which influences me in anything I may say.' Alfred had evidently claimed that her letters were not welcome, and also that the differences between his mother and his fiancée were petty, given other issues. She replied: 'As you say the whole thing seems so senseless when there are shells bursting around you day and night. God knows we realise *that* here to the full; but we must write about frivolous things comparatively or not write at all. You evidently find my letters absolutely unwelcome.'[17] The distance heightened these tensions: 'You say I do not mention Frankie in my letters. Well my son I cannot fill my letters about her – you know I love her very much but of course she is not the perfect angel to me which she is to you ... Now this letter is all about Frankie. Are you satisfied old stupid.'[18]

The Sacrificial Mother

Mothers were expected to disavow these primary bonds, without a sense of grief. 'We know', confidently asserted *Our Empire*, 'of cases where mothers whose sons are at the war are in a lesser state of health owing to a condition that is best described as war strain.' It was claimed that in 'a lesser degree than mother, father also feels the strain of suspense'. Whether experienced by mother or father, it was a condition which 'should be fought, for no purpose that is any good to ourselves or to our boys is served by any weakness or despair'. Such an attitude of weakness by mothers or fathers was a 'nerve-wearing corrosion of national fibre that ... would ... form one of the important influences to determine victory'. Women should be encouraged to resist such emotions. They should 'steadfastly refuse to entertain thoughts that depress them'. The sentiments of mothers affected those of their boys, for such negativity would erode the morale of the troops. Mothers 'should resist with their will power any suggestion of depressive thoughts, just because by doing so they are not playing the enemy's game for him'.[19]

These repressions would later be projected as anger and resentment in resistance against the loss of memory of their sacrifice. Motherhood had attained a prized status during the war, but the eulogy of the 'sacrificial' mother did not endure in the collective memory. Women giving their sons become the quintessential emblem of feminine sacrifice; it was used shamelessly for propaganda purposes by those for and against the war. This was nowhere more stark than when the government of William Hughes moved swiftly to introduce conscription after the numbers of volunteers had plummeted. Men between the ages of nineteen and thirty-eight years of age were eligible to enlist. By the end of 1914, 52 561 men from about 820 000 eligible men had signed up.[20] But this enthusiasm was not sustained and although the number of volunteers was maintained throughout 1915, by 1916 there was a steady decline, from a very high 22 101 in January to 6170 in August.[21] The press began a renewed recruitment drive in 1916 as numbers plummeted from 11 520 in October 1916 to 2617 in December.[22] The conscription referendums of 1916 and 1917 failed to endorse compulsory recruitment for overseas enlistment; instead, they crystallised the economic and social tensions which had been escalating since the outbreak of war.[23]

In light of these developments, the *Argus* newspaper began a series on 'Mothers of Men' in 1916 which elevated the heroism of mothers. It was argued that the 'sacrifices made by some women in sending their sons to serve their Empire are so notable' that their contribution should be made known to readers of the *Argus*. The paper published a photograph of mothers who had sent three or more sons to the front and a brief description of the boys' military activities.[24]

The portrait of Mrs Annie J. Williams was typical. Williams had four sons on active service. They had all served at Gallipoli, two of them invalided and another two wounded.[25] The reportage of the 'sacrificial mother' aimed to boost morale, support the war effort and allow mothers to share the honour of their sons: mothers gained status and respect through an association with their men. Women's stature increased with the number of sons they had serving at the front. As 'sacrificial mothers', they were given a role into the public world of action and battle, elevating this generation of mothers to a new status.

Those for and against conscription turned to mothers for their respective causes. The anti-conscriptionists, who rallied around the pamphlet 'Blood Vote', urged mothers to resist voting yes; those who voted yes were issuing the 'grim death-warrant of doom' and 'smugly [sentencing] a man to death'.[26] Others such as Eva Hughes, the president of the conservative, pro-conscription and pro-Empire Australian Women's National League,[27] argued that it was incomprehensible that women should stop men from volunteering to assist those who had already gone to the front.[28]

During the conscription debates, mother's sacrifice was understood by pro-conscriptionists to be synonymous with citizenship and patriotism. 'Vesta', writing in support of conscription in the 'World of Women' column in the *Argus*, perceived it to be 'the test of courage and patriotism', where the 'last argument against the suffrage will have been answered. No statesman, the world over, could devise a more searching test. It is ... the final and supreme test of our right to citizenship.'[29] For those mothers who had sent their sons, 'there is no further need of a test. They have proved themselves already by their devotion and their sacrifice and their votes are bound to be on the right side.' It was those women who had not yet 'faced their full responsibility, or have faced it and have been found wanting, are the women who have now to search their hearts'. The final call was to a heightened imperial supremacy: 'if we honour the ideals of our Empire and our race, then we must put the last ounce of our strength into the contest'.[30] This connection between citizenship and nationalism was made explicit elsewhere. In the United States, Piehler has noted that the 'official memory of war ... stressed the role of the good citizen as mother'. The civic role for mothers was that they 'gave up their sons to the nation'.[31] It was thought that women would exert considerable influence on the final decision on conscription, so politicians and radicals were unusually attentive to their opinions. During both campaigns, Eva Hughes addressed thousands of women in capital cities, urging them to be 'the proud mothers of a nation of heroes' and not 'dishonoured ... mothers of a race of degenerates'. As citizens, they must 'prove that they were worthy to be mothers and wives of free men'.[32]

Within this context, grief was rewritten as pride and sacrifice. Mrs Clara Nitchie of Geelong, Victoria, had six sons on active service. Her sons were described in patriotic but unemotive terms:

Corporal H. N. Nitchie and Private James L. Nitchie were in the 8th Battalion; and took part in the landing at Gallipoli on 25 April 1915. Corporal William C. Nitchie, Driver Harry G. Nitchie [machine gun] and signaller Leslie H. Nitchie are at present in France. Corporal H. N. Nitchie has since transferred to the 6th Battalion, and Private James Nitchie is suffering from concussion, which caused blindness and deafness. Seaman Rudolf Nitchie is a present coastguard.[33]

Similarly, Mrs S. A. Ross, it was reported, had 'altogether over 30 relatives on active service'. She had three sons:

Private T. E. Ross ... was at the landing on Gallipoli, was wounded. A month later, he resumed duty, and took part in the evacuation. Driver F. N. Ross volunteered from New Zealand, and left there with the first reinforcements in the Army Service Corps. Corporal R. L. Ross ... is on active service. A brother of Mrs Ross, Trooper W. H. Sheills ... also served at Gallipoli.[34]

But not all mothers had so many survive active service. Mrs D. Hamilton of Brunswick 'has five sons and a son-in-law in the service of their country. Three sons enlisted at the outbreak of war, one died of wounds at the outbreak of war, one died of wounds received in the landing, one had been returned invalided, the others are now on active service.'[35]

The sacrifices of other mothers were described in similarly patriotic terms. Mrs M. A. Lofts had four sons serving 'with the colours': 'Sapper C. Lofts is now in Belgium, Private Alex Lofts and Private A. L. Lofts are both with the A.I.F. and the address of Private W. F. Lofts is unknown'. Mrs George Melbourne of Yackandandah has 'three sons and eight nephews on active service': Private William Robert Melbourne, twenty-three years of age, and Private George Melbourne, nineteen, were both in England, while Trooper Leslie Melbourne, twenty-one, was in camp in New South Wales.[36] The press could not resist promoting the cause through novelties: Mrs W. J. Heath sent three sons, who were triplets. The reportage adopted the style of a boy's adventure story, full of dashing officers, danger and romance. Mrs M. E. Gwyther's four sons were serving and their commitment was reported as a daring enterprise:

Bombardier L. M. I. Gwyther joined in August 1914, was at the Gallipoli landing, was seriously wounded, and, after 11 months in hospital, is now unfit for further service. Lieut. L. P. Gwyther was at the landing and evacuation, joined as a private, won his commission by superintending the taking of the first gun up Gallipoli heights, and is now in the firing line in France. Corporal R. P. Gwyther aged 21 enlisted in Queensland in June 1915, and is now in France. Gunner E. C. Gwyther, aged 19, after going through the school of gunnery ... is now at a naval base in England.[37]

Such celebration of the sacrificial mother was not confined to the *Argus*. The *Daily Telegraph* visualised it in a series of photographs of women and the sons they had given to the Empire, within the rubric of heroism and patriotism.[38]

Death notices, too, also carried the message of duty and heroism, paradoxically denying yet elevating loss. The death notice gave meaning and purpose to the trauma of the death and, as others have argued, assisted the bereaved to sustain a continuity with the deceased:[39]

WOOD – Killed in action, in France, on the 23rd August 1916, Leslie James Wood, fourth son of Henry and Helen ... Duty nobly done.[40]

CHALMERS – In loving remembrance of my dear friend, Private D. A. Chalmers [Alex], who gave his life for his country, in France ...
COPPIN – In loving memory of Corporal W. H. J. Coppin, who was killed in action in France ... Greater love hath no man than this, that he lay down his life for his friends.
FITZALAN – In ever loving memory of my dear Donald, who was killed in action ... A hero and a man (Inserted by one who knew his worth, May Hood.)[41]
GELL – Killed in action, May 5th–8th, 1917, in France, Private Francis Gell, dearly beloved husband of Ethel, and father of Beatrice and Albert. 'In a hero's grave Frank is lying/Somewhere in France he fell/Little we thought when he parted/It was our last farewell.
HAY – Died of wounds in France ... Private Clarette Hay, aged 29 years. Inserted by his loving mother, sisters and brother, and grand parents. A young life, nobly sacrificed.[42]

Occasionally, more emotive terms were used:

LEE – Killed in action, France, 16 August, Norman, beloved husband of Madge and father of Norma, brother-in-law of the late Sergeant Gilbert, beloved son-in-law of Mrs Gilbert ... Oh for the touch of a vanished hand. (Inserted by his sorrowing wife.)[43]

This was the language of pride and worth, expressed in celebratory tones which reverberated throughout the halls, the theatres, in the streets and in conversation. Yet to deny the carnage required weaving an elaborate defence and constructing a fragile edifice of dignity. Emotions were channelled into formal language which ordered and contained the pain and shock of loss. The enunciation of civic pride and patriotism could not allow for the disarray of emotions.

This is not to say that mothers were unconditional in their support. Even the most devoted mothers were ambivalent about the meaning of wartime sacrifice. Ellen Derham supported her son, Alfred, in his enlistment for the war. 'I want no Victoria Cross – I want my son', she insisted, but claimed that she was 'thankful that my son is not and never has been a coward and I know you will do whatever you consider your duty'.[44] She hoped for a happy ending, 'but it is still a nightmare to me & it will be until I hear that you are coming home again'.[45] When her second son, Frank, enlisted, she expressed a particular anxiety:

Frank's brigade marches through town tomorrow. Frank wants me to go & see it, so I must nerve myself & go ... My heart is ... full of tears all the time; but I am only one of [a] million of other sad mothers. If I could only fire myself instead of my sons! I am weeping now for you both but oh my son I am proud that my sons are to be of so much use to their country.[46]

And, in exasperation, she wrote in December 1915,

Frank is gone!! That is the chief event looming large with me at present ... my mother heart does not alter in its feeling towards my boys nor will it ever no matter how much your attitude may change with change of circumstance towards me ... I am proud that my sons are doing what alas is their duty and God has spared you for a year ... I am trusting that you will both return to me again.[47]

Pride sustained her. 'Not many mothers can be so proud of her sons as I can', wrote Ellen Derham. 'Proud of their uprightness and goodness & I have faith in them both.'[48]

After the war, the 'sacrificial' mother took on a different status, in ways which suggest that ideas about 'sacrifice' are dynamic and everchanging. Mothers and wives participated in public commemorations within certain designated spaces. In the 1920s their sacrifice had been perceived as patriotism by which freedom had been won; by the 1930s, the memories had become less immediate. The very act of remembering the 'mothers of men' had itself been sacrificed, as it became conflated with a more general perception of women's memory and mourning.

During and immediately after the war, women's sacrifices captured the imagination of the press. In 1918, it was reported that Anzac widows were clad in the deepest mourning, 'with eyes wet with tears, brave smiles forced upon grim set faces. Many wore photographs of their dead ones upon their breasts. In every face lurked the sadness wrought of the memory of one they had held dear ... Brave women!'[49] In the 'March of the Men' celebrations during 1919, while the procession was in progress, 'the widows and orphans of fallen soldiers were being entertained at the Town Hall'. The hall was full, 'the black garments of the women, pathetically pronounced massed together, were relieved by the bright dresses of the children'.[50] In 1920, mothers occupied a central place in the country's memory but, by the eve of the next war, the remembrance of their sacrifice had been shifted to the periphery. In the Armistice Day commemorations of 1920, the Centre for Soldiers' Wives and Mothers organised 'the route of the procession, which extended for a mile and a half and was crowded throughout, particularly with widows and bereaved mothers'.[51] Soldiers' wives and mothers were especially addressed by chaplains:

The mothers and widows of those men bowed their heads as the chaplain spoke. The tears rolled down unrestrained. All days were days of commemoration to them. They wouldn't forget. There were well nigh 60,000 of our men who have fallen on the fields of battle ... A day like this brings your sorrow back afresh again to you. While you mourn there is a spirit of gratitude and pride in your breasts that you are associated with such men ... It was a sad sight this glimpse into the mothers' hearts.[52]

The memorial gates at Woolloomooloo in Sydney were an important site for women's loss. The laying of wreaths here was a ritual which had been initiated by the Centre for Soldiers' Wives and Mothers in 1918,[53] an event which celebrated the heroism of their men. Each Anzac Day, mothers and widows would gather to remember and commemorate the deaths of their sons and husbands. 'Wives' and Mothers' Tribute' was the way in which the Anzac commemorations of 1924 announced the service to be held at the Woolloomooloo gates, where 'wreaths and beautiful blossoms . . . covered the gates'.[54] In 1925, the identity and the memory of the 'mother' was writ large in the commemorative celebrations:

One could not study those sacred emblems and their messages without a lump rising in the throat. 'In memory of my only son', and 'In remembrance of my two sons' were samples of many similar tokens from 'Mother' . . . floral emblems nestled beside those of many brave-hearted mothers.[55]

Two years later, it was noted that it 'was an occasion of remembrance' undertaken by old ladies, 'dressed in black, who needed no adventitious aid to memory', where a

profusion of wreaths, of white, purple, and red flowers, rioted on the gates; and the fountain opposite, erected by the Soldiers' Mothers and Wives' Association, was dressed with soft foliage and flowers. Time may have softened the sorrow, but it has not lessened the love for those who gave their all.[56]

By the 1930s, mothers had lost their distinctive contribution to these public commemorations. On Anzac Day, the annual public commemoration of Australia's involvement in war, women's rituals became universalised as one, thus negating the specific contribution of mothers. The *Sydney Morning Herald* noted in 1930 that the Gates of Remembrance showed how war had brought a 'spirit of sacrifice' in men and women, but this was understood to be remembering men's sacrifices.[57] The economic hardships of the Depression inspired a rhetoric of unity; the demands and needs of particular groups were regarded as divisive. There was a need to 'bury differences of class' in the face of 'economic danger' which was 'no less urgent than war'.[58] The *Daily Telegraph* claimed that the Anzac spirit should, during this time of adversity, 'spur us on to becoming a united people'.[59] Mothers' contribution to public memory became domesticated; they were perceived to honour men's sacrifice. 'Women' – both mothers and wives – were onlookers to the broader drama, and the public memory of war was to be that of men marching to war.[60] In 1933, the *Daily Telegraph* wrote of women being 'haunted always by the memory of something they have seen only in visions – a grey dawn of death'.[61] Women's role seemed to be honouring the sacrifice of others rather than their own. In public remembrance, the earlier eulogising of mothers as active 'sacrificial' participants in the war was superseded by domesticating women's role and rewriting their part as a passive one. Such a shift coincided with broader changes in perceptions of women's role in society. While the modern woman symbolised the new, the 'domesticated mother' was an attempt to return to prewar assumptions about women's role.[62]

By the 1930s, the categories of 'mother' and 'widow' were conflated into 'women' and they became marginal to the memory of war because they were no longer defined by their 'sacrifice'. Women's need to resist this found its most forceful expression in the efforts of women to participate in the Anzac Day dawn service.

This became a particularly sensitive issue in Melbourne in 1938, when mothers and wives were reported to have 'intruded' into the dawn service. Towards 'the end of the procession', 'nearly 100 women joined the double file of returned soldiers, and walked past the Rock. A few women and children have joined the pilgrimage in the past, in spite of requests from the Returned Soldiers' League, but there have never been so many at the ceremony.'[63] The *Age* reported the dawn service of 1938 in terms of a sacred site, which was a male preserve where women had no right to be:

Women have invaded walks of life, manners and customs that once were thought the sole preserve of man, and man has been the last to question their right. There are times, however, when he feels impelled to voice an objection. Such an occasion was the Dawn ceremony at the Shrine of Remembrance yesterday. In spite of many requests that the observance should be inclusive to men, several hundred women, singly, in groups and with male companions, attended an observance that is peculiarly that not merely of men, but of returned men.[64]

In drawing a clear distinction between the right of certain men to march as well, the *Age* was outraged that these women 'sought to pass through the Inner Shrine after the service had closed, but were firmly, though courteously, refused admission until the last of the Diggers and their companions in arms had paid their solemn respect to departed comrades'. It was asserted that if 'ever womanly presence could strike a discordant note it was then'. The Victorian secretary of the Returned and Services League (RSL), Mr Joyce, agreed that 'this intrusion tended to break down the spirit of the occasion'. In the future, it was suggested, it is 'likely that the possibility of excluding these intruders, by other means than unheeded appeals, will be sought before next Anzac day'.[65] This became an important issue for the league to consider: 'The league would also consider the exclusion of women from the dawn pilgrimage, and also the practice of leading children in the march itself. These incidents totally destroyed the significance of the occasion.'[66]

N. Osborne wrote to the *Argus* asking why it was that 'women will persist in being present at the Dawn Service at the Shrine on Anzac Day, after being publicly asked to stay away'. The rationale for this was that 'sad memories crowd in upon the hearts of the soldiers, and mothers or wives cannot possibly enter into those tragic experiences. Men do not go to mothers' meetings or to a Y.W.C.A. rally!'[67] Others agreed. 'Brightonian' claimed that a 'class of women lacking good taste will always intrude themselves in men's gatherings, even though advertisements make it clear that women are not wanted'. As an 'old digger' he claimed that he had 'decided not to attend the dawn service again until women are prohibited from entering the area until every man has left'.[68]

Women disagreed. Margaret Groom claimed that it was lacking in chivalry of the men to hold such an attitude. She too had suffered pain and attempted to gain some recognition of her sacrifice: it is '20 years since my brother was mortally wounded in France, and another one wounded. Why should I be "not wanted"?'[69] Others, such as 'A Mere Woman' agreed with their male counterparts that 'their memories cannot be shared by anyone who was not one of those millions who lived and fought together, each day not knowing whether they would be spared to see another dawn'. Women should avoid 'desecrating holy ground' when suggestions are made to join the men 'in a service in which we have no part'.[70] The parts women had played had been rewritten. Twenty years after the end of the war, it was true that women's memories were filled with the sacrifices of their men, but their own sacrifices had been lost from the collective memory. While there was a furore at attempts by women to 'intrude' on the dawn service, their wreath-laying was seen as the acceptable form of participating in remembrance. Beyond that, women's place in the memory of war remained marginal to the sacredness of male sacrifice. The 'womenfolk of the men who are honoured in Anzac day always find touching expression on Anzac morning', reported the *Argus*, 'when they meet to place their wreaths of remembrance at the Shrine'.[71]

For questions related to mourning and memory, 1938 proved to be an auspicious date. While the sesquicentenary celebrations proceeded apace with the themes of nationhood, white supremacy and progress, memories of another kind could only find a voice through protest. As the ships sailed into Sydney in January, re-enacting scenes of British triumph, dispossessed and disenfranchised Aborigines declared a Day of Protest and Mourning in memory of the sacrifices of their ancestors. Memories of warfare were embraced again months later, but of a very different nature. Anzac Day was another salute to British supremacy when the sacrifices of white Australians were publicly honoured. A voice of disaffection was heard at this event, too, when women who attempted to participate in the dawn service, in an effort to claim the legitimacy of their own sacrifice, were named as intruders onto the sacred male site of mourning and ritual. Memories of war jostled and competed for legitimacy as each group clamoured for recognition against public neglect.

Financial Loss

In the case of mothers, public neglect of their loss was compounded by the devastating financial impact of the war. The economic status of mothers has rarely been considered historically, partly because we have understood the family as an economic unit comprising a male breadwinner and a dependent wife. One area where the economic predicament of mothers has come into focus has been in relation to motherhood endowment.

During the 1920s and 1930s, when the political landscape for another war was being forged through the rhetoric of nation-building, technological power and racial supremacy, feminists and labour activists agitated for mothers to be granted a maternity allowance granting them economic independence and citizenship status. As Jill Roe and Marilyn Lake have argued, mothers, like soldiers, risked their lives and gave their services to the state.[72] It was also at this time that white motherhood was being elevated to a new science, with the introduction of 'experts' and medical expertise directing mothers to rear their children in a regulated way. It was impressed upon them that – in accordance with the modernist tendencies of the day and in response to the broken bodies which had returned – a regulated and scientific approach to childrearing would produce a healthier and more robust population.[73]

Australian politicians of all hues had been supportive of producing the new-born when allocating pensions and social welfare provisions. The maternity allowance of £5, which had been introduced in 1912 by the Labor Fisher government, was granted to both married and unmarried mothers upon the birth of a child. Only one allowance was paid where a multiple birth occurred, but there was no means test. However inclusive this policy attempted to be, the politicians responsible could not overcome the prevailing racial beliefs of the day. While white mothers lamented the loss of their sons in an imperial war, Aboriginal mothers continued to mourn the forcible removal of their children.[74] White motherhood was given priority at a time when indigenous families were being decimated, and the grief of black Australians was ignored by governments which made the denial of motherhood to these women official policy.[75] Asiatic, Aboriginal and Pacific Islander women were ineligible for the allowance.[76] The 'baby bonus', as it came to be called, remained in this form until 1931 when, following the economic strains of depression, the Lyons United Australia Party government made it no longer uniform, subject to a means test, and variable in relation to family size.[77]

Welfare payments, however, could never adequately cover the loss of a breadwinner. This became apparent financially as well as emotionally, as the response to inadequate financial remuneration soon turned to anger.

Policy-makers were unprepared for the complex and wide-ranging repatriation programme that war conditions demanded. Stephen Garton notes that in the first three years of the war there were three Pension Acts, and from 1917 to 1921 there were four Acts, each 'amending the former'.[78] Both Nationalist and Labor governments moved speedily to establish a war pensions scheme.[79] It was universally acknowledged that it was their responsibility to offer a 'fair and reasonable' pension. Public charities and philanthropic organisations also rallied, as it became evident that government resources could not accommodate the full extent of repatriation claims. The basis of the Repatriation Acts from 1917 was thrift and independence, not idleness and charity. Widows and mothers of soldiers were eligible for war pensions, but their eligibility was based on their economic dependence and on the number of children they had to support.[80]

The women at home were handed an amount from the soldiers' pay. A private serving in the AIF was given 5 shillings when he enlisted and 6 shillings a day on embarkation. A sum he nominated, usually 2 or 3 shillings, was paid to his next of kin.[81] Pay varied for the other ranks. A sergeant was paid 10s 6d, a lieutenant 17s 6d, and a major 30s.[82] The soldiers' 'dependents' could include his wife and his children; in the case of an unmarried son, his widowed mother; 'the parents, if without adequate means of support; and such other members of his family as were wholly or in part dependent upon his earnings at any time within twelve months prior to his enlistment'.[83]

The loss of a son who was a breadwinner left many mothers destitute. In June 1919, it was estimated that there were 6839 widowed mothers economically dependent on their unmarried sons.[84] Mothers whose sons were killed were caught in a contradiction: they wanted symbolic recognition of their contribution in monetary terms, but they felt that their sacrifice had been sullied by material remuneration. In a letter to the *Argus* in 1921, 'An Honorary Worker' noted the dilemma of one mother. The author cited a case of a widow with six children, the three eldest of whom were boys. Two of them had died in the war, the third returned disabled. The pension she had received for the first two was lost, because it was claimed that 'they were not maintaining the home prior to enlisting', and her application for assistance for the third had been rejected on the basis that 'he is not totally and permanently incapacitated within the meaning of the Act, although he is bereft of two legs'. The writer claimed that 'all three boys kept the mother and family prior to enlisting'. Such a case, it was asserted, 'is bringing the scheme of repatriation into bad repute'.[85]

The absence of a son's financial contribution had a far-reaching effect. Mrs Mary Watson was the mother of Edward Watson, a private, who sailed to the war in April 1916. Four months later he went missing and was later reported killed. Watson had been widowed for fifteen years and with the outbreak of the war had lost all her breadwinners. She had four sons, two of whom were married; one had been killed and another was at the front. Watson was wanting 'assistance, looking for work this morning and cannot obtain any [and was] quite without funds this week. Second son (18) enlisted without Mother's consent.'[86] Mrs Skow, the mother of Edgar Skow, a private, who was killed in July 1916, claimed she could not manage on her son's pension because her husband, aged sixty-five, was 'unable to get regular work'. She 'had two sons killed in France' and was receiving a pension for both of them.[87]

The mother of Sydney Rowland Forrester, a private who enlisted in 1916, 'was not apparently quite dependent on her son when he went away. She was able to work; before he enlisted he sent her money regularly – now she is not able to do much work suffers from rheumatism . . . he wanted to leave her his pay but she was not in Brisbane when he sailed.'[88] Mrs A. Chandler already had two sons at war when her third, Harold, sailed in June 1918. This created a financial crisis because he was her 'main support' in working in the orchard she ran, as her husband, at the age of sixty-five, was 'unable to do all the work'.[89] Mrs Kate Griffin, a mother of four, also lost an important source of income with the absence of her son. She received an income from her son, a labourer, of 30 shillings per week. He was still at war, under medical treatment in England, and another younger son was still in the firing line.[90]

Financial support from a son's pension could be crucial. Mrs Annie Clarke reported that 'one son – Sydney George Clarke – is being returned being under age and his allotment . . . has been cancelled leaving mother rather distressed to enquire if above regulation has been altered re stoppage before return'.

Taking care of their disabled sons was another burden for mothers. Mrs Fanny Lager, a widow of sixty-seven, had a son who returned

shell shocked [was] 3 days in France only in and out of Hospital – Discharged yesterday. Left Hospital last Thursday 35 years single. Would not go into convalescence in Hospital ... suffered greatly and could not stand further treatment at Randwick so got his discharge. Was a particularly strong man and is now quite a wreck and in very difficult circumstances.

She was dependent on him, as were her widowed daughter and her child, who lived with her.[91]

Mary Nestor, aged sixty-one, was the mother of Cleveland Nestor, a butcher, who sailed to the war in May 1916. He had given his mother 10 or 20 shillings per week before he joined the forces. On his departure, however, he had 'left her without any support; has no other income; husband alive in hospital an invalid; not able to earn anything; does not know why son left her without any allotment; not able to work suffers from rheumatism'.[92]

A disavowal of maternal loss, and a prevailing sense of grievance that remuneration was both inadequate and inappropriate, led to a public expression and a politicisation of the mothers' grief.

Expressions of Grief

Mothers and fathers yearned for their loss to be recognised and revered. In April 1920 General William Birdwood, the highly decorated officer and leader of the Anzac campaign,[93] who had corresponded with families during the war, addressed mothers and fathers at a gathering in Sydney. His speech affirmed and comforted the parents who had assembled; he acknowledged and legitimised their pain and anguish. In sacrificing their sons, he intimated, they too were heroes:

'My comrades and I sympathise with the parents of those boys who are not returning – sons and brothers who have gone. I believe that not one of those men gave their lives in vain. They had voluntarily left this country with one object of fighting for Australia, which to every brave lad was dearer than life itself.' ... He had done a good deal of letter writing to parents out in Australia, and a good many of those letters were of a sad nature ... To those mothers who had written to him about their boys he had told them all he could.

He wanted to shake the hands of the mothers and the fathers present, and told them 'of the whole-hearted way in which the men and women of the Old Country regarded their boys'. Birdwood finally instructed them 'to live up to the ideals that had been set them by the boys who had fallen'.[94]

Parents responded to this exhortation. J. M. Sandy, from the Fathers Association, claimed that: 'They would agree with him that the name of their distinguished guest would be immortalised ... All the mothers loved him, and the widows and fathers loved him, too. [Hear, Hear] They all knew of the sympathy and kindness the General had shown towards their boys while fighting shoulder to shoulder on the battlefield.' Mrs H. Connell of the Soldiers' Mothers Association said that Birdwood always 'remembered his men, even when things looked blackest'. While Birdwood privileged their loss, he denied its pain by framing it as the cost of freedoms won.

Mothers yearned to share in this collective grief and belong to its public memory. Some of those who had lost sons in the war were not prepared to continue to be stoic and forbearing. Many of them had fulfilled this expectation in an exemplary fashion, as they stood in horror witnessing the slaughter secondhand, but with no less pain, as the casualty lists mounted at an alarming rate. During the war, as Raymond Evans has pointed out, the public display of violence by patriotic women who had lost sons at Gallipoli against those women who opposed the war revealed a fleeting but clarifying moment of repressed grief.[95] After the final bugle call, mothers continued to be comforted and sustained by the rhetoric of honour and duty, but they were not prepared to endure in silence.

Many of the protests by mothers regarding their adversity were channelled through the Sailors' and Soldiers' Mothers, Wives and Widows Association which was formed in 1918. In the years immediately after the war, before the ascendancy of the RSL, women's groups and ex-servicemen's organisations flourished; as the league gained its monopoly, women's organisations were subsumed into it, losing their autonomy.[96] Women in the association organised hospital visiting, and 'comforts of all kinds and literature . . . to be distributed in the various military hospitals'. Soldiers' dependents had been assisted through the funds. The association operated in New South Wales and Victoria; there were local branches in Coburg and Williamstown in Melbourne.[97]

Mothers' resentment was expressed through their grievances. They took to the defence of their boys and channelled their loss through this defence. In November 1920, at a public rally in Sydney, May Mercer, the honorary secretary of the association, announced that 'some of our boys did not come back to speak but we will speak for them . . . It was the duty of the mothers of fallen soldiers to take the place of their boys.' Responding to comments by one Alderman Farrell which had referred to 'damned soldiers', Mercer was alarmed at the slanderous way soldiers had been spoken about. Another member of the association claimed that 'the men whom Ald. Farrell called "damned soldiers" were the men who saved Australia for him. He would not have been a free man now only for those boys.' She hoped that Farrell would not be a member of the next

City Council. 'If you men have not got the pluck to take action', said Mrs Doherty, 'we women have.'[98]

In terms of remuneration, critical voices had begun to unsettle post-war peace. In January 1919, at a meeting of 'local committees' of the association, delegates protested 'strongly' against 'the departmental practice of waiting for applications before paying the new scale of living allowances to soldiers' widows or dependent mothers'. It was pointed out that

> through ignorance of the new regulation many deserving women were not receiving what was their due. The widow of a deceased soldier who has no children is not necessarily entitled to a living allowance. This may, however, be granted by the state board, provided that body is satisfied that special circumstances render the applicant a fit subject for the allowance.[99]

The rates were 42 shillings weekly for a widow without children, and up to 65 shillings for a widow with five or more children. The same scale applied to widowed mothers of deceased unmarried soldiers.[100] The *Age* argued that this was inadequate and that 'it would be well if the authorities considered the position of the widowed mother'.[101] A meeting of Legacy Clubs in 1926 asserted that the 'devoted manner in which the widowed mothers were bringing up their children, caring for them, and training them to be good citizens, could not be too highly praised'.[102]

Widowed mothers attempted to claim a legitimacy for their grief. In November 1928, the Sailors' and Soldiers' Mothers, Wives and Widows Association of New South Wales passed the resolution that

> so far Mothers of Fallen Soldiers have been overlooked, considering that in the month of August 1928 the Federal Government passed a Pensions Act which provides the sum of £2 per week to Soldiers' widows and also single young women without children who had Soldiers Allotments designated to them ... While [some] deceased soldiers Mothers ... received 7/6 the other remainder 12/6 they received from the Old Age pension total £1.

The association claimed that: 'Surely the mothers who gave their sons to defend their Country are as worthy of the same consideration as those wives defacto and in justice to them, something should be done to place them on the same footing with regard to pensions.' Every mother of a fallen soldier 'should be on equal pension of £2 per week'.[103]

Women who belonged to the association were indignant at their neglect and they felt 'unwanted' and 'unrecognised'. In November 1928, it was reported that there was 'much indignation ... at the action of returned men's organisations in not having invited a representative of the association to take part in the public ceremonies connected with Armistice day'. May Mercer, the honorary secretary, claimed that

the sacrifices made during the war were made by the mothers of the workers who went to fight yet, because we have no high public or social position, we are unwanted and unrecognised... We look upon [it as an] insult... not being asked to attend the demonstrations at the Cenotaph...[104]

A resolution was sent to the New South Wales Premier, Thomas Bavin, claiming that members of the association 'are of the opinion an injustice was done [to] them on Armistice Day as no representative of the association was invited to the public meeting, especially as that meeting was in memory of fallen sons'. It was also decided to send a letter to the Prime Minister, S. M. Bruce, asking 'that pensions for all mothers of fallen soldiers, whether they were widows or not, be raised to £2 a week'.[105]

In October 1928, following the decision of the Bruce government to include provisions for widows and orphans and for the granting of a marriage allowance – but not assistance for mothers – in its social reform provisions,[106] it was decided to make an appeal to 'widowed mothers of fallen sons throughout the States to support the candidates who were in favour of increased pensions'.[107] The ways these mothers compared themselves to war widows remained striking. May Mercer claimed that 'if a soldier's widow receives two guineas [42s] a week, a widowed mother should receive the same amount'. They felt slighted at not earning just recognition. 'The question of whether the association should assist with the sale of poppies on Poppy Day ... was debated, members expressing surprise that their assistance had not yet been sought.' It was decided that the association would not take part in the sales unless 'they were granted a stand near the Cenotaph'. There appeared to be 'much indignation at the alleged "slight" by the RSSILA [later RSL] in not having forwarded an invitation for a representative of the association to be present at the AIF reunion dinner'.[108] The tensions between mothers and widows, hinted at here, suggest how they projected this anger onto other groups.

By the late 1920s, some of the mothers of dead soldiers had become even more aggrieved. In a letter to the *Argus* in 1926, a 'Widowed Mother' encapsulated their feelings of neglect and rejection, exacerbated by a sense of injustice, when she asked,

why war widows' pensions are increased and an increase is denied to widowed mothers? Which of the two classes needs it more? Most war widows are young and strong, and have the world before them, and in these days of high wages they can easily supplement their war pensions by earning another pound a week. The widowed mother, particularly the widowed mother of only one son, has nothing to look forward to.[109]

At one time, the sacrifice of mothers had been appreciated in both the public and the private arena. In 1915, Isabel Williams wrote to her friend Ellen Derham that she could

> realise so fully how very anxious your mother heart must be over your wounded soldier-laddie ... Have they not been wonderful under their baptism of fire, and have they not given us reason to be proud of them? I am very proud of them, and equally so of the brave, unselfish mothers who have spared their sons to fight for King and Country.[110]

Another friend, Annie Robinson, also wrote, 'I often think of you as one of the mothers who has sent her son to fight, and I know it means a strange mixture of pride and anxiety in your heart.'[111] But how this ambiguity was remembered later created a lingering pain for mothers.

'The paradox of nostalgia', Adam Phillips notes, 'is that it always tries to recapture a world without loss.'[112] Mothers attempted to sustain this world, but they also tried to find an expression of grief within it by voicing discontent, anger and resentment at their unacknowledged pain. On the eve of the Second World War, when mothers would be called upon to part with the next generation of sons, mothers' sacrifice was understood not as a unique contribution, but in generic terms as women's memory of men's heroism.

3 A Father's Loss

> How shall we ... look the bereaved parents in the face and try to soften their grief?[1]

In April 1921, when the volunteer army, the AIF, was demobilised, a father whose son had returned from the war was moved to write of the profound sense of loss he felt at its passing.[2] For this father, the AIF had come to symbolise more than a civilian voluntary army of men, with no military training or experience, who had freely given their lives to nation and empire. The AIF was a pervasive presence in the emotional lives of those who followed its progress. 'With its fortunes our lives were bound up, with its units our home ties thrilled', he confessed. The AIF was a benevolent force, 'a gallant host', as it carried, he recalled, 'in its arms the lives of our Sons ... Its personality obsessed our thoughts, day and night it was ever with us.' It shaped the emotions and carried the pain of those parents who waited:

We visualised more or less successfully, its trials, and its trials we felt as only mothers and fathers could feel, the hardships, and the dangers in which our Boys stood. We scanned the casualty lists of the dead, of the wounded, with mingled feelings of hope and of fear. Those were the days of anxiety, of poignant grief, softened today, but in many cases not yet healed for those whose Sons were numbered among the dead.

To this writer, it seemed incomprehensible that the AIF would 'itself die; that it would melt away', 'almost without a sigh or a reflection for what it stood for when the world was in its arms'. This was also a plea to remember the fathers' anguish and to resist the end of that memory: 'When I read the statement that the AIF was dead', he reflected, 'my soul cried aloud that it was not true. It rings false. I feel in my bones it is not true.' 'I think', he claimed, 'every Dad will agree with me when I assert that the AIF was personal to us. To me it was a solemn thing, a shrine of national greatness, full of sad and proud memories, of deeds of heroism, of bright lads gone, or sorrowing parents.'[3]

Fathers and War

Fathers' loss in war has not been examined in our histories. Discussion about fathers and war has centred on their absence rather than on their presence. The fatherless family was a source of great concern and alarm for both authorities and soldiers' organisations after the war.[4] Social anxiety about the absent or incapacitated father found expression in many sex manuals and eugenicist writings of the 1920s and 1930s which emphasised the importance of virility and strength of manhood. 'Good parenting' was preparing the next generation of sturdy, virile white Australians. With this emphasis on the social roles of postwar fathers, rather than on the emotional responses of those who lost their sons, the psychological experiences of earlier generations of fathers have remained unexplored.[5]

The paternal has been discussed in other contexts, especially in relation to the protective attitude shown by returned men through the organisations they formed. The organisation Legacy gave expression to the chivalrous role many returned men adopted towards the wives and children of dead soldiers after the war. Begun as an association for returned servicemen to meet and consolidate their wartime business and political contacts in 1923, it changed into an organisation which aimed to protect the dependents of deceased servicemen.[6] By 1928, Legacy had established branches throughout Australia. The Deceased Soldiers' Children Welfare Committee of Legacy assisted the children through social occasions and camps, gymnasium classes, boys' and girls' classes, and an overt recognition that legatees should 'stand in the place of children's fathers providing them with "chances" they would have had if their fathers had lived'.[7] Legacy was active in war widows' efforts to attain an increase in the pension from 1926 to 1928.[8] Legacy was benevolent, and chivalrously paternal: women's role was as recipients of men's protection.[9]

A similar protective attitude was adopted by the Returned Soldiers' Association (RSA) formed in 1916. The RSA, later to become the Returned Soldiers' and Sailors' Imperial League of Australia (RSSILA) and then Returned and Services League, emerged from clubrooms that had been established to assist men who had been invalided from the war. The organisation decided that the best way to meet the needs and demands of returned soldiers was to organise as a non-party political pressure group. The issue of repatriation for returned soldiers was to be their main priority.[10] Members assisted many widows and their families through their perceived role as providers.

Fathers who had lost their sons in the war shared this paternalist responsibility, but they were born of another era. Many of the middle-class fathers who encouraged their sons to fight in the war were shaped by the ethos of duty, self-restraint, courage, and perseverance, in what became known as the Victorian 'sense of character'.[11] This emphasis on the formation and moulding of manly character was a rhetorical device used by politicians to mobilise their armies, but it also provided a moral and ethical code of conduct. By the end of the nineteenth century, these moral teachings included an imperial and military aspect which emphasised patriotism and chivalry. The romantic and idealistic glorification of the imperial soldier hero emerged from these concepts of manliness.[12] There had been a long association of manliness with the military scout and colonial hunter, which had become a part of the British national heroic tradition.[13] It is easy to see how these colonial ideals of the Victorian and Edwardian era would shape the soldier of the First World War, although there was nothing in the rhetoric of chivalry or in the sporting practice of hunting which would prepare them for its brutality.[14]

The spheres of paid work and male fraternities shaped the masculine identity of late Victorian fatherhood. Fathers were not expected to be the primary emotional supporter within the family unit and, by the turn of the century, it was commonly assumed that emotional expression should be frowned upon in men.[15] Perhaps this is why it is overwhelmingly the case, in Australia at least, that the correspondence from soldiers was to their mothers rather than to their fathers. As Pat Jalland has noted, men of the Victorian period found it more difficult than women to express their emotions and document their feelings. There were different understandings of how men and women were permitted to mourn, as the rituals and etiquette for them demanded a different response.[16]

The war, however, shattered the public stoicism that fathers were expected to show in emotional crises. It completely overturned previous rituals of mourning, changing Western understandings of death forever. There was scarcely 'a family in Britain which, by 1918, had not suffered the loss of a father, a son, a brother, a cousin or an uncle'.[17] The mass slaughter and incomprehensible violence and destruction led to a growing sense of futility, which altered meanings of death.[18] The war brought all those who lived through it an unfamiliar set of circumstances, and premature death on such a scale tested the faith of even the most devout Christians. There were no models to follow which would give clarity or meaning to the slaughter. In his observation of this confusion, Freud wrote in 1915 that the 'individual who is not himself a combatant ... feels bewildered in his orientation, and inhibited in his powers and activities. I believe that he will welcome any indication, however slight, which will make it easier for him to find his bearings within himself at least.'[19] Part of this dislocation was the rupturing of the life-cycle which the war created. Sons predeceased their fathers, overturning the logic of reproduction. This was especially hard as, before the war, there had been declining infant mortality.[20]

David Cannadine has encapsulated this disorientation among upper-class British fathers when they heard of the death of their sons. Sir Harry Lauder spoke of the 'agonies' that 'cannot be written about'; Harold Macmillan recalled how the 'shadow of death had begun to darken all our young lives'. Rudyard Kipling and Lord Rosebery expressed numbness and incredulity at the loss of their sons.[21]

A common response to this emotional challenge was to contain and channel the pain into affirming the values of heroic sacrifice and pride. In Australia, loyalty to Britain was a fundamental principle that many fathers upheld.[22] In a letter to his uncle, describing the death of his son at Gallipoli, Edward Bechevaise expressed his feelings in terms which glorified his son's heroic stature. He focused on his son's sense of duty in volunteering, unlike 'many others who are shirkers and slackers'. He 'did his duty for King and country and made the supreme sacrifice. He was only 22, a fine steady young fellow of a religious turn of mind ... He was one of the first to enlist when war broke out, and did it from a stern sense of duty and as an example to others.'[23]

In other instances, this patriotism was expressed with some ambivalence. One member of the AIF recalled that when he asked his father for

> his consent to enlist, the day I was 18, I found that my father considered me strong and able enough but his concern was that I would become dirtied by the bad company I would be amongst. I assured him that ... we read and talked a lot about women, Drink and Gambling but that none of it had become my way of life.[24]

Gilbert McDonald's father was delighted when he enlisted, although he intimated the pain he had felt in the process. 'Just a word to say that I think you are doing the right thing in offering your self in the service of the empire', he wrote proudly in June 1915.

> I am proud to know that you are a man, and not a verandah post supporter. I think Murray will be going with you, and if you do both go, try and arrange with the authorities to be tent mates ... Gib I am like you, my feelings do not lie on the surface, but you boys will be sadly missed, and I sincerely trust that it will be the will of the all disposer of events that you return safely.[25]

In this interplay of patriotism and pain, McDonald's father received a letter from another father:

> My own youngest son is in ... Hospital [in] France his horse killed under him and I am waiting patiently to get further news from Base records ... Side by Side old friend as it were our sons faced God daily in this awful war. Shoulder to

Shoulder ... you will always have my sincerest friendship and my prayers that the great God of Battles will tenderly lead [to] comfort you and yours in this sad trial.[26]

In grief, fathers searched desperately for more information of their sons, as if in the elusive details the riddle of the meaning of their sons' deaths would be solved. Alexander MacDonald was killed in August 1918 at the age of twenty-seven. His father, J. R. MacDonald, wrote to the colonel of his son's battalion of his frustration and disappointment at missed opportunities. He remarked that the telegram he received of his son's death

is bald of all other info and I take the liberty of addressing you as the Colonel commander of the 24th battalion AIF of which my son was an officer, to ask if you would kindly give me particulars with reference to his death ... [I] am very anxious to learn all I can of my son, and of his conduct both on and off duty ... He was very reticent in all matters military ... Instead of explaining anything to me, he would simply say 'and when I return I will let you know some surprising things' ... hoping that what I have asked of you as an anxious father, will not give you much trouble ...[27]

It was not common for soldiers to comfort the fathers of dead soldiers in the same ways they did mothers. Writing to the father of a soldier, in one unusual example, Lieutenant John Archibald noted how 'keenly I realise the terrible sacrifice that you have been called upon to make for our Empire'. He spoke of their relationship:

I realise how deeply you were attached to each other & how beautiful the comradeship between you. He used to speak of you so often to me. Your consolation must spring from the fact that he died for all that we believe to be Right & True & Honourable; that he gave up his life for the defence of his fatherland, & for the protection of those he loved & 'Greater love hath no man'.[28]

For some fathers, grief at the loss of a son brought physical consequences. The brother of one deceased soldier wrote to his brother's soldier friend, observing that his brother's death in May 1918 'has completely broken my father's health of course he has passed the allotted span being 81 years of age. Such a great shock.'[29] For other fathers, it was an imagined future which was lost. The judge Henry Bourne Higgins had opposed the Boer War; at first he supported the First World War, but became desolate and disillusioned after he lost his only child, Mervyn, in battle in December 1916. He wrote:

> What has he lost? Mayhap, some fifty years,
>   The joy of children – work, success, defeat;
> The sense of failing strength, corroding fears,
>   The sense that age makes not the life complete.[30]

As a result of Higgins' son's death, in the words of his biographer, 'a void ... now opened in his life. For Mervyn was not just his son, but his future as well.'[31] This was encapsulated as the first year without his son dawned:

> The pain is of the living, not the dead ...
> For us, in age, a childless home – and tears.[32]

Whereas some families built defences to resist the anxiety of grief, others formed organisations which assisted parents through their bereavement and provided a supportive social environment.[33] The intimate relationships which formed within a group, drawn together through loss, fostered a collective identity.[34] Both fathers and mothers of deceased soldiers sought to create relationships where mourning would be facilitated through the support of others. These groups served the purpose of legitimising their identity, allowing people to grieve, and even encouraging them to do so explicitly.[35]

These groups operated differently for men and women. Unlike the maternal figure, which quickly faded from public memory, the paternal authority of fathers was legitimised through their association with masculine organisations. While their loss was not exalted or idealised like that of mothers, their immediate connection with such organisations allowed them a place in the arena of public, masculine commemoration. Another difference was that fathers were less reliant on their soldier sons for financial support. Many women who had lost their husbands and sons faced dire economic circumstances, a complication not encountered by fathers, for whom employment was more readily available, and was an acceptable part of their social role.

Fathers did, however, share with mothers a fear that their sons' sacrifice, and by association their own, would be forgotten. As one father wrote when he read a letter from a mother who had lost her eldest and youngest sons: 'I felt kin with the brave mother, and saw the same light as she ... We feel that we have been privileged to share the sorrow with one who is unknown to us, to have had a sacred look into the sanctuary of a mother's heart.'[36]

It must also be remembered that, while the rhetoric and values that patriotic fathers had grown up with pointed to devotion and duty to Empire, they had missed the opportunity to elevate themselves through patriotic glory. They achieved this vicariously through their sons. Hector

MacDonald, whose son was serving, wrote to Thomas Derham, after news that Derham's son had survived in battle. He expressed this lament at the failure of their generation to attain heroic status.

> Forty-five years ago we too would have responded just as rapturously to the trumpet's call as our sons today – But our generation fell upon an unheroic time and we have only the reflected glory of knightly deeds done by our own boys ... Any day may bring me similar news to that which you have received, but as I have from the first regarded my son as a 'dedicated spirit' as I feel sure you have regarded yours I hope to be resigned whatever may happen.[37]

Regional conflicts throughout the Empire did not carry the weight of significance of a world war, and their experience suggests another loss that fathers endured – that of being unable to demonstrate in the most glorious fashion those values which formed the essence of their identity as men. This lack they would displace onto their sons, by helping to keep alive the memory of the sacrifices of those in war. One soldier recalled how his paternal grandfather, a Crimean War veteran, had 'played on my emotions', and there 'is no doubt that I enlisted for the adventure ... and to gain the approval of Boer War and Crimean veterans who had fed me with too much glory rubbish. I know they were all proud of me.' Young men who had grown up in an army family felt the pressure acutely. Another soldier noted that his 'motive for enlisting in the 1st A.I.F. on August 10th 1914, was that being born and living in the army atmosphere, I thought to then make the Army my career.'[38]

The Sailors' and Soldiers' Fathers Association

The Sailors' and Soldiers' Fathers Association was an important group in affirming the fathers' paternal role. It provided a forum for fathers to grieve by allowing overt expression of anguish, as well as of anger, both inevitable responses to bereavement.[39] In this way, the association operated paradoxically, to allow fathers to relinquish their repressions, while at the same time it gave them a means of voicing their commitment to Victorian values of self-restraint.[40]

Formed in May 1918 in Victoria by a group of middle-class fathers, the association's purpose was to promote the interests of all sailors and soldiers who had been on active service. 'Our sacred duty, as fathers of sailors and soldiers, and as citizens of the Commonwealth', its first journal proclaimed, 'lies clearly and insistent before us.'[41] The association became an active and energetic social organisation which drew together a community of fathers who shared a passionate conviction about their duty to returned soldiers. Local branches organised musical evenings, for the purpose 'of meeting together of Dads and Diggers', their wives, daughters and sweethearts. There were also social cricket matches between 'Dads and Diggers', and evening events were held where various military figures addressed families.[42] These occasions were held to commemorate those who had died, and recount the 'many deeds of valour by Australian troops'.[43] Fathers also met at 'smoke evenings', addressed by a speaker and accompanied by a musical programme, which usually concluded with a rendition of 'God Save Our Splendid Men'.[44] A male fraternity was forged through the 'Diggers and the Dads' association.

In its early years, the Fathers Association was a thriving group. Its membership increased steeply in its first few years. In June 1918 it had 1023 members, with representatives from about eighty districts outside the Melbourne metropolitan area.[45] By August there were 2340 members.[46] In March 1921, the association in Victoria reported a membership of 11 393, with ninety life members and eighty-four branches throughout the state. There were also branches in New South Wales, South Australia, Queensland and Tasmania. It ran its own journal, *Our Empire*, and held quarterly meetings, and branches held monthly gatherings.

As the immediate memory of war faded, so did this initial burst of enthusiasm. By 1937, membership of the Fathers Association had declined to 1300. The president, W. J. Basham, claimed that, despite this drop in numbers, it was 'still necessary to consider soldiers' problems'. Promises had not been fulfilled. It was unacceptable that preference was not being given to soldiers by some municipalities and corporations, and it was incorrect that soldiers were keeping other men out of work; women were responsible for taking men's jobs. This had been a significant issue in 1926, as 'the principle of preference to qualified returned soldiers' was the cornerstone of the association's platform.[47] At its annual conference in 1937, more than ten years later, it remained a concern, and a resolution was passed that 'all returned men who were working in Government positions as casual employees should be given permanent employment after two years of service'.[48] The association attempted to extend paternal protection to returned soldiers and war widows. In 1926, it resolved in favour of 'a widow [to] be provided with at least enough to live on in comfort. At present there was the ever constant dread of a decrease in the pension already provided ... something should certainly be done to ensure a measure of independence for war widows.'[49] In 1929, it was reported that the increasing distress among returned soldiers, because of sickness, unemployment and poverty, is 'making the work of the ... Association of Victoria more onerous every year'.[50] Other concerns had remained with the fathers, such as attention to war graves, and a 'restoration farm, for the maintenance and welfare of subnormal and derelict ex-servicemen'.[51]

Fathers were proud of these links to the war. In retaining them they separated themselves from other ideological currents of the day. In some quarters, the mass-cultural ethos was to moving away from the patriotic and dutiful call to arms which had formed the essence of the bereaved fathers' identity. In some respects, they were caught in the unexpected dislocation from the Edwardian to the modern era. Australia did not lose dependence on the imperial connection; this was to take the full drama of another worldwide conflict. But the shift towards disarmament and the strengthening voices of the peace movement confronted the uncritical patriotism and militarism of the war years. The establishment of the League of Nations in January 1919, and moves towards internationalism and settling disputes by arbitration, introduced a new method of diplomacy.[52]

Not all fathers responded with nostalgia and lament. Some, like H. B. Higgins, embraced the disarmament cause. 'Now, now is the time to act; now lest we forget', he argued on the tenth anniversary of Armistice Day. 'Now before the generation passes which felt what modern war means ... Let us unite to save from the horrors of war that which is the most precious asset of the world – human life.'[53]

But just as mothers and widows felt excluded from the national landscape, some fathers expressed a wish for the virtues of manliness to be maintained amid the shifting values of the 1920s and 1930s. Fathers' feeling that these virtues were threatened was revealed in the anger they expressed towards the authorities. The very meaning of their Victorian character seemed potentially to be lost. Fathers spoke of exalted citizenship and duty, but they drew on ideals from a prewar era. In these circumstances of grief, the bereaved had to deal with social and psychological environments which were changing as a result of loss. In the new world, fathers grieved for their loss of status as well as for their sons.[54] Their aim, then, was not only to foster 'a closer union between the fathers of sailors and soldiers' but also to 'help returned men to carry out in civil life the high standards and ideals that dominated them in the field of war'.[55]

The badge of the Fathers Association became a marker of collective identity, and a symbol of attachment to an earlier era. One father wrote that it had been an advantage wearing his badge, for 'when I meet someone who is wearing one I immediately feel inclined to acknowledge him, for I then know he has his boy or daughter taking an active part in the war the same as I have'.[56] The badge was a treasured possession. 'The feeling of pride which members have in the Association badge is akin to that which the returned soldier has in his military decoration or Association badge.' In 1918 *Our Empire* exhorted readers to wear their badges, because 'the father of a son or sons who have voluntarily given their best services, and, in many instances, their lives, for King and Country, has much to be proud of, and is it not a duty that the badge should always be worn in honour of those sons'.[57] After the war ended, the badge was an important symbol of fathers' connection to the war. 'It is their silent tribute to their sons' courage and loyalty', it was claimed in 1920, and 'puts to shame the shirker and the cold-footer'.[58] In March 1921, it was reported that a total of 11 205 badges had been issued by the association in Victoria. While it was a form of recognition of support for returned soldiers, it also unquestionably represented their own dignified association.[59]

Fathers craved a part of their sons' glory. When the first Anzacs returned, it was observed that 'no one in the dense crowds had a better claim to welcome the boys than the Fathers Association; the "Dads" were in full force, waving our famous flag of "Carry On", and shouting themselves hoarse with enthusiastic cheers'. The Fathers Association's so-called 'Strong Post' had become a 'strong rallying centre' and their cheers were the most 'inspiring and noisy' of 'Well done! Welcome Home!' given to the troops. At a later march, the 'fathers formed up like veterans as if for a route march'. Out they stepped down Collins Street, to be cheered themselves by the crowd as fathers of boys who had 'played the game'.[60] Fathers would gather when ships sailed into port. Every time soldiers returned, fathers occupied a 'post' to 'give them welcome, and the last gathering brought back memories of joy, tinged with sorrow in welcoming so many of our wounded and maimed men, and ever present was the thought with many that for their boys there was to be no homecoming'.[61]

The fathers considered themselves to be the 'representatives of those gallant boys'.[62] Fatherhood in this context carried with it particular responsibilities. The Fathers Association did not claim that 'fatherhood of a soldier must be a qualification for membership of their state or local repatriation committees', but it did stress emphatically that fatherhood of an eligible shirker or slacker 'shall be a fatal disqualification for membership of any State or local repatriation committees'.[63] Like mothers of soldiers, the fathers embraced the cause of their soldier sons, creating a new identity as fathers of soldiers and sailors, and committing themselves to the memory of their sons. 'We ... exist for those who have fought for us in foreign lands and on foreign seas, and upon many of whom are those honourable scars which make their claim upon us all greater', declared the first issue of *Our Empire*.[64] The association undertook a responsibility to remain 'faithful stewards' of returned soldiers' welfare, and through this their status as citizens was enhanced. The objective of the association was 'in a straight line to the activities of supreme citizenship'. This was to elevate their sons, to whom they owed a great debt. 'The glow of enthusiasm we feel for our boys', *Our Empire* claimed, 'must be kept warm at the fires of doing things that count ... If we slacken in our purpose to secure the best Australia can give the sons of its inheritance, we are defaulters and cowards who have betrayed our trust, fathers who have strained their manhood with indifference in the day of great things.'[65] Fathers were expected to use their contacts and connections to promote the cause of returned men. 'It behoves every father to think what can he do either in connection with his own business or the business of someone else to secure for the son of some other Father such a position as will enable him to "make good", and in which he would like to see his own son placed.'[66]

Fathers did not direct their emotional energy to an analysis of the values which, for some, the war had shattered and exposed as shallow. Instead, they criticised the authorities for not upholding the values for which in their opinion the war had been fought: honour, a sense of duty, integrity and courage. For this reason, the issue of repatriation aroused great indignation.

From the end of the war, the Fathers Association attempted to improve the rehabilitation provisions available to soldiers. The association perceived it as an opportunity to settle soldiers on the land and utilise 'our waste [sic] fertile spaces'.[67] For Aboriginal groups of course these were not wasted or empty spaces. The requests for reserve land from those who had fought in the war seemed irresistible to the political authorities. Soldier settlement brought new pressure for Aboriginal land to be relinquished. The result was further dispossession. In New South Wales, for instance, by 1927, almost half the Aboriginal Reserve land had been lost by revocation.[68] At the time, it was considered legitimate to dispossess Aboriginal groups in order to compensate for the sacrifice and loss endured by returned soldiers. The memory of sacrifice of the soldiers could be upheld only by repressing the memory of earlier black wars of the nineteenth century.[69]

Despite repatriation initiatives by governments, by the 1920s an aggressive and hostile mood had mounted within groups such as the Fathers Association towards the repatriation authorities. 'So scandalous has this repudiation of the policy of preference become', declared *Our Empire* in February 1920, that 'some employers have refused the reinstatement of their old employees.' Despite the law 'that such employers were liable to a fine of £100', *Our Empire* found it an outrage that such men were not reached by the law. The fathers aimed to achieve their target by moral pressure, causing 'remorse and shame' so that even 'deadened consciences' who were guilty of 'backsliding' would repent.[70]

In 1921, there was a 'fire of hostile criticism' when the mayor of Prahran in Melbourne, who was also the president of the Prahran branch of the Fathers Association, gave his casting vote against the employment of a returned soldier. The president subsequently resigned from the branch. Anger, outrage and a sense of betrayal swept the association. One member said that 'the repudiation of a returned man in the circumstances was bad enough in a father, but it was a hundred times worse in the President of the Branch'. It was claimed that another councillor, whose name was cut in the foundation stone of the Soldiers' Memorial Hall, 'should be chipped out of a stone as unworthy to appear in such a place ... The Soldiers and Fathers would not forget these things.' The motion to accept the president's resignation was 'carried unanimously with prolonged applause'. A new president was then appointed, Mr McGregor, 'a very worthy Father', who 'lost both of his boys at the war within a month'. It was also decided to oppose those councillors who had voted against the returned soldier when they came up for re-election.[71]

A public meeting was held to 'serve as a sharp lesson to other defaulting councils, and remind them that the ratepayers are their masters'. It was claimed that councils were in a position of public trust, and when they betray that trust 'in such vital principles as preference to the men who fought for the Empire, they must expect public indignation meetings'.[72] Memories, it was firmly argued, should not be lost. One councillor who supported the soldiers noted that it must be remembered what men had gone through in the war, and it could not be expected that they be 'equal in health to the man who stayed at home'. Sir John Monash, who addressed the meeting, was 'horrified and saddened' to see the service of professional men forgotten, when they returned to 'find their practices gone and gobbled up by men who stayed at home'.[73] The fathers interpreted this as a slight on their grief, as well as on the memory of their sons. 'God help the nation that forgets its heroic dead!', *Our Empire* announced in March 1921. 'This generation of parents is still very close to April 25 1915, and to those who lost their home lights in the great host that perished it is a sacrilege that Anzac Day should be observed otherwise than in a reverent manner.'[74] Memory of men should be sustained in a variety of ways. Missing soldiers should also be remembered, for it was considered a sacred duty 'that the feelings and the wishes of the parents of missing soldiers should be considered in every way'. It was considered imperative to consider the 'danger of "slacking" in this direction as the days of the war grow more distant ... such forgetfulness would be little short of a national crime'.[75]

A Father's Loss

Memory and remembrance in private offers a glimpse into the ways in which fathers dealt with grief outside of public debate, and how individuals ritualised and memorialised it. Jay Winter has examined the symbols which sustain a bereaved culture, such as memorials and monuments, in his outstanding study of mourning and memory.[76] On an individual level, the war redefined the rituals and etiquette of mourning and people developed their own personalised ways of memorialising the dead. With no body or funeral, families often resorted to other forms of ritual to commemorate death. As others have noted, the lack of a place of mourning can prevent resolution of grief.[77] It can also create an obsession for detail, a voracious appetite for information, and a relentless quest for an identification and attachment to the lost soldier. The psychological desire for presence produces an obsessive impulse to substitute for the internal loss.[78] This was often combined with a routine of personalised rituals.

We can see how one father dealt with his son's death through the case study of the diary of John Roberts. Roberts, an accountant with the Melbourne Tramways Board, lost his son, Frank, aged thirty, on 1 September 1918, at the battle at Mount St Quentin in France. Frank had served with the AIF for two years and four months. At the age of fifty-eight, Roberts was the father of three children, and a grandfather. He inhabited the world of the public service, finance and business; his life was imbued with the Victorian culture of respectability. His male pride and honour sustained him throughout the immediate period of his son's death, but his response was a kaleidoscope of emotions: from pride and anger to calm resignation. Roberts was governed by a sense of duty and a stoic self-restraint, and he channelled his emotional response away from any doubt of the prevailing values.[79] Instead, he reaffirmed the achievement of his son in attaining the highest level of honour and duty. In his diary, we can see how he developed his own rituals and patterns to structure and contain his deepest emotions.

Roberts records receiving the news of his son's death on 13 September 1918; it was the 'most awful day in our lives when we received word of our dear gallant soldier son Frank's death killed in action in France on Sunday 1st September'. On the day, Roberts felt the intense force of the loss, writing, 'I felt very much upset positively sick with grief.' His initial response was to perceive Frank's sacrifice as heroism, a brave gladiator who has helped to save the world: 'I had to tell my brave son's brave mother that our first born had died a hero's death in France to help to save mankind. We were both distressed but proud of our son.'[80] This was an initial displacement of loss.[81] The news of Frank's death shattered his wife, Ruby:

During the morning Berta and I went on over to Warwick Farm to see Ruby who was in bed feeling her grief terribly. We tried to comfort the poor girl the best we could but it was a distressing time ... Ruby greeted me with, 'It isn't true father, is it?' and I had to reply, 'yes girlie it is', and she cried, 'Oh! my Frank my little Nancy will never see her father' . . .

The pride of Frank's heroism overshadowed all other emotions and expressions during the early stage of Roberts' bereavement:

I read Frank's letter to Ruby delivered to her yesterday how his platoon salvaged a German gun after being in the trenches following an attack for two days and nights and beat off two German counter attacks . . . 'Death has lost a lot of the terror and mystery it had for me. I've seen too much of it over here: it is those behind that I think about.'

There were also regular visits to Ruby and a bonding with his son's widow, as, in the face of death, he clung to romanticised memories:

I told Ruby that as long as I had a roof over my head and a crust she and Nancy should share them for my dear son Frank's sake and how proud she should be of her soldier husband and that the memories of their happy days and dear associations amongst the beautiful scenery around us . . . the horrors of war might have sent him back home in a condition worse than death with brain gone or so mangled that he might be a wreck only of his fine old self.

Roberts assumed the reassuring stance of the patriotic father, 'I believed in his marrying [and] having to go away to fight for the empire's cause . . . that her home could always be with us if she wished.' After the first week, he described the last six days as the 'worst days of my life and yet the proudest'. Despite this pride, the legacy of war for Roberts would not be peace, but the perennial darkness of loss. In October, near the end of the war, he reported that 'Great War news today but our dear old Frank is out of it all now'. Later, with a more resentful tone, he recorded that peace will not bring joy: '*Herald* . . . came out with news of peace. Felt upset at the prospect of it at the present stage as if Frank's life would have been sacrificed in vain.' In the midst of peace and victory celebrations, he sought distractions: 'Today I read more to keep from thinking of dear old Frank's death.'[82] Other fathers recognised that this mixed blessing of anger and guilt could be so emotionally charged that it could be contagious. 'They would come back', observed H. B. Higgins, '– thousands of boys to their mothers – but never our boy. But I have no right to infect others with our grief.'[83]

Roberts developed his own private ritual of recording and documenting his son's movements and treasuring his possessions. Letters arrived after his son's death. Parcels of clothing, newspapers and other gifts were returned untouched by Frank, whom they had been meant to comfort. Roberts became a fanatical collector of such items as he attempted to relive and recreate his son's pain, his triumphs and his battles. This collecting became ritualised. 'Some cards arrived to-day from dear old Frank 39 days after his death & to Bert to Gwen and Nancy. He appears to have got them in vacated houses.' 'Today', he wrote on 11 October 1918, '3 parcels arrived from Frank for Bert containing Belt and clasp [German] water bottle. 2 for Ruby ... Letter from dear old Frank for Ruby arrived.' Throughout December 1918 parcels and letters kept arriving from Frank, and at the end of the month Roberts wrote: 'we saw the old year out – the year of trouble and affliction beyond all others ... dear old Frank's body lying in France'. 'Parcel from Frank with date 20/8/18 came for Ruby containing ... pouch for Bert B Kaiser Cigarettes for Berta and one of two German shoulder straps for her also clips of ... shoulder straps for Ruby.'[84] The return of their own letters was also noted: 'One of my letters and one of Ruby's sent to Frank returned.'

Roberts began obsessively amassing information about his son in a scrapbook, assembling the missing pieces of Frank's death. Losing his son also meant losing an established social pattern which he replaced with a diligent compilation of cuttings and mementos.[85] He took the time of 'an evening ... pasting cuttings in record books'. This became a ubiquitous diary entry. In the evening he would pore over Frank's old letters, and copy out portions of them. 'In evening I copied part of Frank's letter of July 9th to Ruby received on 13th September the day we got word of his death in action.' He sorted through newspaper clippings, and 'Finished in evening making out itinerary of Frank's movements in France and Belgium and I made out list of official photos AIF to illustrate Frank's itinerary'. After breakfast, he resumed making 'extracts from Frank's diary [from] 30 April 1918 [until] 2 days before his death', and he 'Copied Frank's letters from Geelong camp and Duntroon'; in the 'evening read over more of Frank's letters ... took 41 leaves of Frank's letters [for] typist to copy'. He wrote a memoir of Frank's life, which ended with the deceptive line of closure, 'faithful unto death, Sunday 1/9/1918'.

The memorial card was a particularly important symbol in remembering Frank's death. Four hundred copies were made of the card, which elevated Frank's memory to a heroic ideal. In a similar response of elated pride, Roberts was thrilled that the monument which was to be built at Mount St Quentin would be based on Frank's appearance. The headstone inscription was detailed, reading 'Not Lonely with the Boys – I'm One of the Aussie Family Here'. The letters Roberts chose to insert into his diary were those of Frank enunciating his commitment to the war effort:

I've had a lot of pals killed and wounded, good fine fellows who paid the price. By God, Sweetie, I wouldn't be a slacker who has to look the men of Australia in the face when we march home. I consider myself a man, Darl, I've faced death with the fine lads of Aussie, done my little bit to the best of my ability, and I'll be proud to be one of them to the finish.

Sixteen months after Frank had died, Roberts was still obsessed with his relics. In January 1920, Roberts compared 'some of Frank's letters to Ruby with copies'. Mementos of any sort were cherished as a reminder of Frank's personality. 'The silver Wristlet watch that I gave Frank before he sailed and the gold ring that Lucy Roberts gave him when he visited her in Ireland were received by Ruby today from Sgt E. E. Edwards . . . They had been handed to him by his brother Sgt V. J. Edwards . . . who was with Frank when he was killed.'[86] Others have noted the ways in which a supportive network can facilitate the mourning process. Roberts' family was a great support to him, but it was the interest and care others also showed which allowed him to deal with his grief, especially in channelling his attachment and identification with Frank.[87]

In an attempt to create sustaining relationships in the absence of his son, Roberts befriended soldiers in Frank's battalion. As women built a collective identity in the absence of men gone to the war, fathers gained legitimacy by being drawn into the male fraternity of the army. The male camaraderie which developed between Roberts and these soldiers – some of whom he adopted as surrogate sons – was noted in his diary entries. He recorded that in January 1919, Sergeant Morphett, an Anzac, 'had a talk with me he was at the attack on Mount St Quentin when Frank was killed in afternoon'. Later that year, he took Alf Fox out to lunch, an old chum of Frank's 'who was badly gassed a few weeks before Frank was killed'. Another friend, 'R E Hilliard called and spoke of his associations with Frank', while 'Les Baker called to see me one of Frank's old chums of the A.I.F.' In August 1919, he wrote how G. F. Dobson, 'one of Frank's . . . comrades' also called on him. In the following year, 'Sgt Lawerson late of 21st Battalion . . . an old comrade of Frank's who won the VC at Mount Quentin came to see me . . . he had afternoon tea with me'. On the anniversary of his son's death, Roberts recorded how 'Frank's old Sgt Wignall called to see me today he was fearfully wounded in stomach near by where Frank was killed at Mount St. Quentin.' Roberts was haunted by the details of Frank's death, and he keenly sought information about it from other soldiers. Private R. J. Knight wrote to him that he 'did not see [Frank] killed but said he buried him in a military cemetery on Mt St Quentin on 2nd September and placed a cross on his grave. He was killed by concussion.'

Roberts made contact with other bereaved families, and in this exchange began a path towards writing a different memory and constructing a new sense of himself. Soon after Frank's death, others gathered around: 'Gwen and Will and Edie came and we talked of Frank and Len our eldest ones killed in battle as gallant soldiers. Frank in France and Len in Gallipoli and by such deaths is freedom won.' In December 1918, Roberts wrote to J. A Blackmore, 'thanking him for photo of his son buried in same grave as Frank'. He retained links with the Blackmores. In August 1919 he noted that he had lunched with 'Mr and Mrs Blackmore parents of the soldier buried in same grave as dear Frank'. The sister-in-law of 'soldier buried near Frank called and I gave her 2 photos of grave'. A Miss Edith Alston called at his office in March 1920, 'and left with me to read Frank's letters to her after his visit to Paris two years ago'.

Constant contact of this sort helped in the path towards an acceptance of Roberts' loss. A fraternity of grieving fathers began to figure in his diary. 'Jack Meagher said that his son [Lieutenant] had written "that he had seen Frank Roberts going into action and did not expect any of them to come out alive", or words to that effect.' Soon after Frank's death, Roberts recorded 'Joe Rowles came to see me re: Frank's death his son was killed about 9 August.' A month after Frank's death, 'Walter Leckie (with one son killed and another Captn Peter at the war) Rev. A. J. Wade (son killed) both old school mates of mine called to see me.' In the same entry, 'a man with father's button on coat seeing mine stopped me and said "that's alright I've had one son killed and another with a leg off"'. 'Mr. Dickson ... whose son was a Lieutenant in 21st Battalion [Frank's] and was also killed the same day 1st September 1918' visited Roberts in early October. Dickson said that General John Monash had ordered 'an attack but not in sufficient strength'. Ruby's brother Ted sent a letter 'written in France Sept 23rd re his having visited Frank's grave and he enclosed list of those other soldiers buried in the same grave or near him'. In December 1918, Roberts received a letter from Mr W. E. Thompson with a photo and cuttings of his 'dead soldier son buried in same grave as Frank'. The visits continued throughout January 1919; 'Mr. Staff of Echuca whose son is buried close to dear Frank on the slope of Mount St Quentin called to see me.' Near the anniversary of Frank's death, Roberts 'Took to lunch at the Australia Hotel Mr Dowell father of one of the boys buried with Frank'.[88]

Warm nostalgic memories of family life with Frank seep through Roberts' writings. Nostalgia and sentimentality protected Roberts from despair in the interplay between absence and presence. Frank's death rekindled family memories. At a time when his death created such a loss, Roberts' family stories provided a strong connection with the past, a sense of continuity, 'of rootedness and family tradition'.[89] On the day they heard the news, 'my old wife and I talked of old memories of our son and how proud we were of him and what a fine dear son he had been'.

A fortnight later, 'We lit fire and talked of our dear brave son that is gone'; and again, 'thought of our dear old Frank [who] would get up sometimes and give me tea ... in the early morning before I started. A lonely dawn and morning many of which Frank used to see in the hills and will now see no more.' Later, at Sunneyside, where Frank had spent the last five years of his life before the war 'clearing the ground planting trees ... building sheds ... and his joy in the country life', his parents reflected on his life. In October 1918, Roberts wrote: 'I went for a stroll in afternoon ... and had many recollections of dear old Frank and child, boy and man the walks we had on the neighbourhood his attending Camberwell State School.'

Roberts' entries on anniversaries suggested his desire to retain a continuity with his son's memory. Anniversaries formed the basis of his memory. 'Anniversary of Frank's and Ruby's. Married two years ago. A sad journey this time.' 'Nancy's birthday 1 year old another dear father who never saw her is dead 2 months'; 'A year ago Frank left England for France and now his body lies in French soil'; 'a year ago since Frank arrived [in] France and he was never to leave except for the time he was in Belgium'. On 1 March 1919 Roberts wrote, 'This day a year ago old Frank was on Paris leave – this day six months ago was killed. This day 34 months ago joined AIF.' On 23 July 1919, 'This would have been Frank's birthday', and on 1 August 1919, '11 months today since dear old Frank was killed.' He recalled, 'A year ago today since my fine dear gallant son was killed in the capture of Mount St. Quentin between 1 and 2 o'clock in the afternoon ... A great feat of arms.' 'A year ago I got word of the death in action of my dear gallant son Frank', he wrote, its legacy being that 'I feel his loss greatly and always will.' 'Dear old Frank would have been 32 years old today', he noted in 1920, 'if he had lived. I gave some toys to Nancy for the day.' On another anniversary, he relived how he had 'received the fearful news that my dear old son Frank had been killed in action'.

Almost two weeks after John Roberts' son was killed in the war, the burden of grief was already beginning to take its toll. In September 1918, he wrote with a sense of weariness, 'Oh this damnable war is taking our best.'[90] Two years later, the Fathers Association journal, *Our Empire*, reflected upon the dilemma confronting those left to deal with the loss: 'human nature is a frail thing in sorrow, with hearts swollen in grief. Our tears will fall, though we try to be brave'.[91]

Courage in adversity was part of the repertoire of Victorian fatherhood, but an uncompromising belief in rigid stoicism could only be enforced if it were not really tested. The war offered such a test. Fathers gained some vicarious glory through their sons, as the young men marched off to prove their manliness in ways not available to the older men. But fathers suffered a dual loss in this process. Their sons had gone, but the values which had given meaning to the sacrifice and which had shaped their own masculine identity were now being transformed. In this shift of values they often felt they had lost their own self-worth, which fuelled further anger and resentment. To rob them not only of their sons, but of much of what they believed, was to leave them 'without honour, without memory, and without heart'.[92]

4   The War Widow and the Cost of Memory

> In most cases the home has to some extent been broken up as the result of the enlistment of the husband.[1]

One week after the announcement of the outbreak of the First World War, Frances Anderson, who was then engaged to be married to Alfred Derham, wrote to her fiancé after he expressed a wish to join the procession of men who clamoured to enlist. 'I know it is no passing enthusiasm', she claimed with a degree of certainty.

> And altho' your going will hurt me as it will hurt Ruth [his sister], I wouldn't say – don't go . . . even if the worst came to the worst I think you are right to go . . . For myself I enjoy physical risks more than nearly anything! and I honestly don't believe I am afraid of dying or death – tho' I find it hard to extend this feeling to the people I love.[2]

The lure of adventure soon dissipated for Anderson as the numbing brutality of war began to impress itself onto the consciousness of those awaiting news on the homefront. Within two years, Australian losses were to reach 5000 a day on battlefields such as Pozières in France, which became a plateau of death.[3] As early as November of the first year of combat, Anderson no longer offered unconditional support for the war. 'Alfred it seems to promise to be a long war', she wrote with alarm; 'in one way, one thinks it would be impossible to go on at the rate of the last two months . . . Dear Boy, when I think of that and other things, I bitterly regret your going, and yet I know that if you were here now, or a year hence you would feel as you did, again, & so would I.'[4] But a heavy dread had already set in:

> I was in town today when the troops marched thro' the division that is to go in about a week. Frank [Alfred's brother] with it. I only saw the tail end of it, I am glad to say – I have missed all of the processions of that kind. I suppose this sounds . . . cowardly, but I don't think there are many women now who can watch troops marching, unmoved. It's not the glad sight it once was.

The war, she predicted, 'seems to look longer every day; everyone needs and will need an awful lot of patience while it lasts'.[5] In public, there was a collective, supportive spirit of grief, but ironically, it also bred selfishness. In 1916, she wrote, 'Oh Alfred – it is a sad world at present – nearly everyone is being hit by these last casualty lists ... They say love is selfish as I begin to believe it when at every gush [of] grief I hear of – I pray a tiny prayer for *my* soldier boy.'[6] And finally, with sheer desperation she pleaded, 'I can last out alone till Christmas ... but *please* not any more.'[7]

The correspondence between Derham and Anderson conveys the intimacy which characterised many letters written between couples during the First World War.[8] On the eve of the war, white women of all classes were expected to find gratification and fulfilment through motherhood and marriage. Although various alarms had been raised since the turn of the century at the declining birthrate and the rising numbers of middle-class single women who eschewed marriage, it was considered to be a cornerstone of Western civilisation.[9] For women, as well as for their partners, letters such as these at once accentuated and replaced intimacy. 'You asked me [in your] last letter', Anderson noted,

did I remember the night you came and patted my head in bed on the verandah ... I did long that night to draw your head down close to my breast ... D'you remember the day war broke and we were putting the tyre on the motor bike all wrong? You shouted Kipling like a ten year old – and I couldn't say a word.[10]

'At present', she wrote in 1916, 'I cannot write any of the things I long to be able to whisper close to your funny old ear.'[11] She recounted that 'there's not an hour of my everyday life that passes without some thought of you – I find "Alfred said" – "Alfred thought" – "Alfred would say" has crept everywhere, and it is often quite hard to refrain from quoting you to folk who do not know us both'.[12]

In letters to each other, it was common for soldiers and their partners to record past and present conversations as a way of recreating a lost intimacy and a familiarity. But the men who returned were not always the same men to whom women had waved goodbye with tearful farewells along the streets of every capital city and country town in Australia. Returned soldiers often did not resemble the men who had proudly marched off with great fanfare, because the war did not end for many of them when they disembarked and re-entered civilian life. As many historians have shown, by the 1920s, frontline soldiers around the globe had 'returned home in a violent frame of mind'.[13] They were restless, uneasy and directionless. A community which had wanted to honour the soldier had become increasingly disturbed by drunken riots and violent outbursts as peace brought its own dislocations and challenges.[14] The fragility of ex-soldiers was not lost on psychoanalysts. Jung noted that 'the war, which in the outer world had taken place some years before, was not yet over, but was continuing to be fought within the psyche'.[15]

The trauma these men endured can be glimpsed in an account of behaviour in the Soldiers' Club in George Street, Sydney, which offered a resting place for returned men. The club had been established in 1915 by the medical practitioner and feminist Mary Booth, who set up several centres during the war to assist the war effort and its victims.[16] The club was one of these, offering assistance to soldiers. 'Being in the heart of the city', Booth wrote proudly and maternally in 1917, 'it exactly suits the needs of the men. Those on leave from camp rush in, deposit their kit in the cloakroom, book a bed, have a hot bath, light refreshments etc ... and then set out to their different businesses or pleasures.' It was with a sense of accomplishment that she claimed that the 'Committee has had the pleasure of watching many of these men, highly strung and over-wrought, gradually regaining health and self control and settling down to civil life again'.[17] By 1921, it was claimed that over 1000 men used the club daily and 'its 100 beds are usually fully occupied'.[18]

Booth had intended the Soldiers' Club to become a resting home and a recreation centre for those whose lives were in transition. Instead, it became a refuge for many anguished, disturbed and restless men. Throughout 1918 and 1919 there was a high incidence of suicide and attempted suicide. The porter was moved to write in June 1919 that 'this suicide mania seems to be on the increase as this rules the second tonight'.[19] Sleeplessness among some soldiers suggested that traumatic memories of another time and place lingered. 'Returned soldier A. Dean [who had been staying at the Club for eleven months regularly] ... was in such a state when he came back from the front that he could never sleep till about 4 in the morning and then went off into such a dead sleep that he would not wake till late in the day.'[20] The increased incidence of drunkenness and violence tarnished the efforts made by the Soldiers' Club to present a wholesome image. In September 1919, Charles Wilson was found by the porter,

> rolling about on the floor, very violent, and some of the men vainly trying to hold him down ... I sent an urgent appeal to the civil Ambulance to come at once, which they did, and the two men with it had great difficulty, even with the help of ... some of the soldiers, in overpowering Wilson who was eventually got onto a stretcher and tied on with a rope.[21]

The disruptive behaviour of other soldiers made nonsense of heroic myths. J. Lawson had made 'vile and insulting remarks to the girls in the

Refreshment Room, used filthy language, created a disturbance in the Hallway and had to be twice put out', while Archer Blackburn came 'in very drunk, for his money, was most abusive and insulting in the office. Given his money and sent out.'[22] The porter claimed this was no 'wholesome resort' and accurately predicted that the 'public-house would probably claim many victims'.[23]

Mothers and wives endured the indelible marks of warfare carried by their husbands and sons.[24] Most men who volunteered for the army were young and single, so mothers faced a lifetime of nursing and caring for those who returned physically or emotionally damaged. Of the 330 770 men who joined the First AIF, 57 496 (17.4 per cent) were married.[25] Of these recruits, 91 per cent were under forty and 52 per cent were aged under twenty-four.[26]

In recognition of these marital obligations, Australia started early in devising a war pension scheme. 'It would be an eternal disgrace to this young and rich Commonwealth', asserted the Minister for Repatriation, Senator George Pearce, in 1914, 'if any of the relatives of those who are going to the war had to beg for a living.'[27] The welfare state was to be protective and paternal. 'The State', claimed the president of the Sailors' and Soldiers' Fathers Association, Mr J. Clayton, 'should take the place of the dead fathers.'[28] A separate welfare system for soldiers and their dependents was devised under the Australian Soldiers' Repatriation Act, which was administered by the Commonwealth Repatriation Commission established in 1920.[29] Garton has estimated that during the 1920s and 1930s, between 70 000 and 80 000 incapacitated soldiers received a pension each year; this number rose to a quarter of a million when war widows and children were included.[30]

The war widow was granted the same pension as the totally incapacitated serviceman, which was based on rates authorised under the Workers' Compensation Act. In 1920 the basic wage was 73 shillings, which was considered necessary to keep a man, wife and two children. The incapacitated ex-serviceman and war widow, without dependents and up to the rank of lieutenant, was on a general basic pension rate of 42 shillings. It remained at this level until 1943. The war widow with children received 10s for the first child; 7s 6d for the second, and 5s each for the others.[31] Widows, it was alleged, suffered no incapacity and could earn a living. Women's welfare rights were understood in terms of their relationships to men.[32] Citizenship assumed a new connection to war service which excluded not only women, but all Aboriginal people who had not yet attained citizenship rights.[33] Financial assistance was also provided by organisations such as Legacy which gave relief payments to war widows and assisted them by alerting them to their pension entitlements.[34]

The war widow's pension, introduced in 1914, brought a new dimension to the welfare system.[35] In June 1919, 9000 wives or widows and 6839 widowed mothers of unmarried soldiers received a welfare pension. For caring for incapacitated soldiers, 23 200 wives and 1200 mothers received welfare payments.[36] In material terms, the state recognised the right of women to be remunerated when a male breadwinner was removed from the family unit. This represented a dramatic shift. From the nineteenth century, widows had been financially aided by philanthropic and benevolent societies when the loss of their husbands created economic hardship for themselves and their families.[37] The civilian widow's pension, which was premised on the same financial argument, was not universally introduced until 1944. The New South Wales government took the initiative in 1925 when Premier Lang introduced a means-tested pension for widows with children under the age of fourteen.[38] There had been several proposals for a national benefit, such as insurance proposals in the 1920s, but social welfare provisions remained woefully limited for widows.[39] The committee set up in 1936 by the Victorian government to investigate establishing a widow's pension had recognised that the 'lack of assistance for widowed mothers in poor circumstances is the cause of much hardship and privation in this State'. The evidence presented before the committee, it was noted, reflected 'some remarkable cases of courage and resource on the part of these women'.[40] But widows had to await the arrival of the next war for the introduction of such social reforms. This suggests that the state only recognised such a responsibility when the men had been killed or maimed in its service.

The cost of memory appeared in a dual guise for war widows: they carried its financial and emotional burden and, as we shall see, often endured social disgrace. When they challenged these mores, they found another expression through which to articulate their grief – the voice of protest.

Morality and the War Widows

The sweeping claims that soldiers' widows and children would never be impoverished, and the unshakable conviction that the widow should be compensated for the sacrifice of her soldier husband, dissolved as soon as financial realities began to test patriotic exuberance. A widow had lost her financial supporter, but the cost of maintaining his memory was not only an economic one. In addition, she was expected to live by morality and etiquette appropriate to those deemed responsible for perpetuating a sacrificial memory.

In the reordering of gender roles after the First World War, the place of the widow was ambiguous. In welfare administration the term widows 'includes widows of soldiers who have died whether whilst serving or often after discharge. The term . . . should also . . . be given the same wide interpretation, and . . . includes mothers of Australian soldiers, provided that they were dependent on the soldiers prior to [their] enlistment.'[41] Although a widow was eligible for assistance within seven years of the soldier's discharge, she had to prove that the soldier's death was due to army service.[42] This had been a source of tension between military widows and the army even before the war. In 1914, Mrs Mary Skinner applied for compensation on account of her husband's condition, which had come 'from a disease, which I humbly submit, was contracted during the performance of military duty or if not actually contracted, then I submit, his death has hastened by performance of military duty'.[43] Proving this was not a straightforward issue, and the application was rejected; her 'application for compensation cannot be entertained on the grounds that . . . Skinner died from cancer of the stomach, which was neither caused nor accelerated by his military duties'.[44] The army was stringent in investigating this, and other claims made by widows.

The expectation that the state would be paternal in its dealings with those in need of welfare payments did not always translate into practice. At the same time, women's prospects of entering employment remained limited and restricted to certain industries. Although the end of the war saw a period of expansion which provided employment mainly for women without dependents, this was relatively shortlived. It has been estimated that the influx by women into the factories had been so significant that the 'proportion of women among factory workers grew steadily so that by 1923, according to some estimates, men constituted only 48.3 per cent of the factory workforce in Australia'.[45] The incessant demands by returned servicemen to reclaim their jobs, and the onset of the Depression which threatened the status of the male breadwinner, created resistance to extending women's employment opportunities.

Like the male recipients of war welfare, widows wanted 'reasonable assistance', but not on 'humiliating conditions'.[46] Welfare pensions were paid to women because of their relationship to deceased soldiers. But unlike mothers, whose claim to the memory of 'sacrifice' carried more weight because they literally 'gave birth' to soldiers and thus could claim maternal citizenship, the widows had no such indisputable ties to their dead men.[47] The scrutiny of their moral conduct revealed an anxiety about the ambiguous place they occupied in postwar Australia. Surveillance was conducted by the Commonwealth Investigation Branch (CIB), formerly the Counter Espionage Bureau, which had undertaken political surveillance during the war.[48] The branch used the same strategies adopted to curb communist and radical behaviour, by following them, observing and noting their behaviour and passing judgement on their activities.

Although the state claimed responsibility for providing for widows, in some cases it forced women into worse economic difficulties. The personal and public campaigns launched by widows reflected their resentment that the pensions they received were not adequate, or equal to the living standards they had lost. At the same time, like mothers, widows felt that monetary compensation sullied their men's memory. In Britain, the socialist and suffragette Sylvia Pankhurst recalled that poor widows referred to such remuneration as 'blood money'.[49]

The 'war widow' did not fit into emerging postwar understandings of femininity – that of the single modern girl, or of the protective maternal figure. She could not be characterised in ways which were familiar to a postwar society – either as sexualised object, or as married woman. Widows had been perceived in these ambivalent terms before, but the war opened new challenges to such cultural perceptions.[50] The war widows' sacrifice was framed by their ambiguous sexual position. Although moral surveillance of welfare recipients had been prevalent before the war, war widows were scrutinised because of their association with the reverent memory of a nation's manhood.[51] Widows have evoked ambivalent cultural responses from society: either they were understood to be chaste, or their unmonitored sexuality evoked fear and unease.[52]

Judgements of women's character were not exclusive to Australia. In Europe, war widows who were not perceived to have upheld the memory of their husbands in their moral conduct were vilified.[53] The war had left some 600 000 widows in France,[54] 200 000 in Great Britain,[55] over 500 000 in Germany,[56] while 200 000 were recorded in Italy.[57] Although widows' pensions were introduced in Germany and France rather belatedly, there were strict controls on the private activities of aid recipients, to ensure they would be 'dutiful widows'.[58] In Germany, they remained the war's 'neglected' victims,[59] while the British policy of family welfare was based on the model of the male breadwinner.[60] During the inter-war years, those war widows who did not remarry were dependent on limited state pensions and low-paid employment that kept them on the lowest rungs of the socio-economic ladder.[61] Italian war widows were similarly under examination for their moral behaviour. In a predominantly Catholic culture, they occupied an ambivalent status after the war, as either victims of war or a threat to social harmony.[62]

The conditions on widows' rights to the pension were strictly applied. Whether pensions should be given to women who had been married to soldiers who deserted was one point of contention. Private Daniel Williams of the 16th Battalion enlisted in the AIF but deserted in a detention camp in Britain. He worked in the coalmines in Wales where he had 'the misfortune to meet with an accident, causing his death'. The decision taken was that

> a soldier who is a deserter, and whose desertion is not the result of ... insanity brought about by war service, should not be considered as eligible for any benefits ... but when as a result of desertion those dependent upon him, [as in this case] ... are left in a position of complete dependence ... the community might feel under some obligation to make some provision for such cases so that they may not be left in a state of destitution.[63]

Illegitimate children posed another problem for the granting of pensions. Trooper C. J. Seton died in February 1932 as a result of an injury sustained on military duty. Approval was given for the payment of £546 4s as a compensation to his widow and three children of twenty-two, nineteen and fourteen years of age. In April 1930, an order was made that an amount of 10 shillings per week be paid for the maintenance of two illegitimate children, born on 16 February 1929 to one Mildred May Teresa Conlon. The question arose whether the Defence Department was liable for payment of compensation to the illegitimate children. The act stipulated that the persons to whom compensation is paid were those whose husbands had died as the result of an injury sustained on military duty. The Crown Solicitor stipulated that the word family, 'in so far as a man with children is concerned, ordinarily means his children, but only his legitimate children ... the ordinary policy of the law is not to recognise relations created through illegitimacy'. Furthermore, it was noted that 'the illegitimate children of the deceased were not so treated or recognised by him'. Another area of contention which arose was that of compensation to adult children. The definition of 'children' was debated for it was stated that 'in so far as married children, whether sons and daughters, who are living in their own homes are concerned, they are not members of the family within the meaning of the relevant section'.[64]

De facto relationships and the remarriage of war widows further challenged the assumptions of the welfare system. Provisions were introduced which granted a pension for a de facto widow or wife, and stipulated the right of a 'dejure widow to continue to receive a pension for the two years after remarriage', which assumed that after that time, her new husband would support her. With the onset of the Depression, such provisions were considered a luxury, and the clause was abolished in 1931.[65] A 'morality clause' was introduced in 1942, during the Second World War, where a 'war widow who "misbehaved" was threatened with the loss of her pension and the withdrawal of allowances for her children ... A preoccupation with "morality" by some community elements ensured constant reports of "suspicious behaviour" which had to be investigated.'[66]

The War Widow

Widows were under the roving scrutiny of the welfare eye well before their 'misbehaviour' became enshrined in legislation. In the discussion of the introduction of the widow's pension in New South Wales, the only state where non-war widows did receive the pension during the inter-war years, a particular role for women was encouraged and promoted. The main purpose of the legislation was, claimed Premier Jack Lang, to 'keep homes together and allow the mother to keep her children with her ... [and] to enable the mother to devote the whole of her time to her home and children'.[67] In a commonly expressed view, it was considered a danger to the community if children were not reared with the full attention of the mother, and it was deemed the responsibility of the state that 'the environment ... shall be the best possible; that the home life shall be attended to by the mother'.[68] Even the Victorian Committee on Widows' Pensions, which firmly recommended the introduction of an allowance to widows as soon as possible, did so on moral grounds. It was unfortunate, the committee observed, that mothers who needed to supplement their income by working left their children unattended; the children then 'play in the streets, where they often contract undesirable associations'. If these women were economically secure, they would maintain 'decent home surroundings' and such things would not occur.[69]

Women had to justify their claims and, in some instances, prove their *moral* worth as welfare recipients. The type of surveillance endured by welfare recipients was not new, but the category of war widow was, and it precipitated a range of assumptions about how women who were receiving a war pension should behave. In 1926, Mrs Vera Hayes, the widow of Private Leslie Hayes, had her pension reviewed. Her finances came under scrutiny by the South Australian police, and her assets were meticulously documented. It was noted that:

(a) Her Pension is her only income
(b) She worked for her father at Berri, picking fruit last year and earned about £30 out of which she paid £12 for lodging
(c) She is at present paying 30/- per week for board and lodging and has been doing so for about 3½ years
(d) She has £42 in the Savings Bank of South Australia (Book no 9741)
(e) She owns furniture valued at about £50 (no other property)
(f) She has no assistance from any other sources.[70]

It was desired 'that *discreet* enquiries should be made as to her mode of living and habits, to ascertain whether she indulged in alcohol and with whom she resided'.[71] Police officer W. H. Lindsay subsequently reported: 'I have made discreet enquiries re the character, and mode of living of Mrs Hayes, and have been informed that she is of good character, clean living, and industrious.'[72]

Not all women received such a positive assessment. Mrs Agnes Hollway, the widow of Edwin T. Hollway, who received 84 shillings per fortnight, was investigated in 1926. She also received 30 shillings on behalf of her son, Evan, an 18-year-old student at the School of Mines in Ballarat, Victoria. An application was made by her son for his allowance to be increased and for 'his personal collection'. This came about because, 'owing to ill health', his mother was forced to give up her home and it 'is now necessary for him to provide his own board and lodgings'. During the course of these investigations, 'it has been alleged that his mother's conduct and mode of living is not all that might be desired'. The CIB was instructed by the Repatriation Commission to 'treat this matter as especially urgent and cause discreet inquiry to be made regarding the conduct and mode of living of the widow, and also the true facts of the circumstances of the son'.[73] The Ballarat police undertook the task in July 1926. Senior Constable Elliot reported that he had

made inquiries into the conduct of Mrs Holloway ... She is no doubt a woman of loose habits, and I should say she is not a fit person for her son to reside with. She has been renting several homes in different localities at Ballarat, which she has been forced to leave on account of her conduct which is very bad ... I strongly recommend that the son be given an increased allowance, and that it be paid to him or some other persons on his behalf, and not his mother.[74]

This sort of attention also followed Mrs L. Caroline, the widow of Clement Moors, who was killed in action. Although her application for financial assistance was refused on the basis that she had already been granted a loan, a personal evaluation had been made to assess her suitability. Police judgement of women's 'character' focused on predictable areas; Mrs Caroline's 'cleanliness' measured up to the level expected of a 'good' woman. Inspector McCarthy's report stipulated that 'her shop is attractive and neat and the premises clean ... Her character is good as far as the committee know.'[75]

Surveillance by welfare authorities could assume ridiculous proportions. Mrs Amelia Lyne, a widow, was seen 'at a Picture Show a few weeks ago in the company with [sic] a young man', and it was shown that she had not collected her pension.[76] It transpired that another widow, Mrs Amelia Black, who was deemed 'a very respectable person',[77] had collected the pension on her behalf because Lyne 'was ill in bed, and unable to collect it herself'. Surveillance such as this made it difficult for widows to remarry or to court men, despite the social pressures on women to marry. Widows were placed in a bind: if they attempted to remarry, their conduct was scrutinised and disapproved of by both the authorities and other widows who had not remarried; if they remained widows, they were destined to be poor.

The living arrangements of widows could also throw into question the continuation of their pensions. Mrs Annie Kirkwood was the recipient of a war pension of 84 shillings per fortnight as the widow of William John Kirkwood, AIF. It was noted that in June 1924, she was living in South Melbourne and had one lodger, who paid 20 shillings per week. The CIB sought to establish her exact relationship to the boarder.[78] Subsequent investigations revealed that Kirkwood was living in 'South Dandenong with a man who goes under the name of Kazan Champion, and is also known as "Tomahawk Joe". She is known, and addressed by him as "Lone Star" the snake charmer.' These people were identified as 'side show people, following Country Shows' and it was believed that 'except for an occasional local person, to whom they demonstrate their prowess in snake charming, throwing tomahawks, etc. no other persons visit the place'.[79] In light of these developments, the CIB was instructed to undertake 'discreet inquiries ... for the purpose of ascertaining her conduct and mode of living in recent months'.[80]

When citizens believed that widows were receiving payment unfairly, deep feelings of resentment developed.[81] In July 1918, an anonymous letter arrived at the North Melbourne police station about Mrs Morrissey, the widow of the late Michael J. Morrissey of the AIF. In an aggressive tone it expressed vitriolic resentment that Morrissey was receiving payments for funeral expenses. The writer asked whether it was fair for her

to be getting so much money for the death of her husband ... [because] her fancy man went up and buried the husband and now they are taking up a collection for her which she does not deserve for the disgraceful carryings on. She has a child to this man ... she does not deserve a penny of that money of his – other women who need the money don't get it and have three and four children to keep on 5/- p.w.

The letter asked the police to look into the case, as Morrissey went under the name of Mrs Staff and had made a false declaration about her baby 'to get money from you', for the baby belonged to Mr Staff. The writer was an embittered war widow who felt she was acting justly in informing on Morrissey: 'I think I have done right in informing you, as I am a soldier's wife myself – and there are other women who need the money more than this disgraceful frauding woman.'[82] Inquiries revealed that this was the case, and Morrissey's rental allowance of 12s 6d for three months was cancelled. It was observed that she had also 'openly boasted of the liberal consideration with which her application had been met at the hands of the Department of Repatriation'.

Allegations of misconduct by other women were often proved false and malicious. In April 1926, a letter was passed to the CIB which falsely accused a war widow of fraudulently accepting benefits. The letter began by claiming that the writer had been 'approached by various people in the neighbourhood requesting me to write to you concerning an individual who is in receipt of a pension for her two sons'. The letter continued:

R. P. Laurie who was supposed to have been killed returned home to find his wife married to another person, she [his wife] although forfeiting her claim after two years still continues to draw a pension for two boys although their father was discharged without a pension. I feel justified as a taxpayer in resenting the payment of pensions to those who are not entitled to same, especially this element who spends the major portion of their income in drink.

The CIB decided to investigate whether the father had returned home.[83] Inquiries showed that the soldier Laurie had indeed been killed on active service, but the identity of the author of the letter could not be established. Following the 'investigations which the Police have made, they believe the story is untrue, and describe it as likely to be a cruel frame-up'. As for the claim that

Lynch and Mrs Lynch are addicted to drink, the Police say that this can be emphatically denied. During the past twelve months, for which period the reporting officer has been stationed at Allansford, Lynch has never been seen the worse for drink. He is described as a hardworking individual, and the same may be said for Mrs. Lynch. Their children are always clean and a credit to them.

The letter was thus judged 'a malicious one, to which no further weight can be attached'.[84]

Women's 'moral' character was an important consideration when they applied for remuneration or when others complained about their eligibility. Mrs Lydia Young wrote to Senator Millen in November 1918 with the following complaint. 'My dear husband, Private George Young was killed in action on May 3rd 1918 and if you have had anyone killed you will quite understand my feelings when I received this terrible news.' Her daughter had been staying with her, 'but now that the war is over . . . she will be going into a home of her own and then I shall be absolutely alone and have 16 shillings for rent to pay out of a pound. Could anyone . . . pay rent and live on a pound a week?'[85] Her complaint then focused on another soldier and his wife who, she believed, received a more generous payment. She thought it unjust that

when a soldiers widow tries to get . . . things to keep the little home she . . . is turned down and insulted. The only excuse they have is that I have no young independents [sic] . . . I ask you is this justice that they take my husband and then will not see that I am looked after. I would not care if I were young and had not been so ill but it is not fair . . .[86]

Young assumed she had a right to a living allowance: 'I do not think it fair I should have to go to work after all I have suffered [and] giving my Husband's life for Country [sic].'[87] Her application was refused.

Resentment was directed against other widows, especially when they remarried, rather than the authorities. Witnessing other widows build a new life and still being paid accentuated some women's own vulnerability and inflicted a deep hurt. Vitriolic outbursts such as those outlined above must have been, in part, motivated by the impression that those women who had remarried were less constrained by the legacy of war, while those who did not remarry remained in its shadows, destined to be blighted by its memory and burdened by its sacrifice. An attitude of envy and scorn from women who had lost husbands towards women who had them was not an unusual response. Often, they idealised men because they remembered the life they had had with their husbands as perfect.[88]

Divisions also emerged within groups of widows who perceived a hierarchy of sacrifice in giving their husbands. This tension found its most explicit expression in public, when women projected their grief as anger. In 1920 there was a 'lively' debate over whether an officer's widow was entitled to a higher rate of pension than the widow of a private. A heated and rather rowdy exchange between widows took place at a public meeting when Mrs D. R. Thompson, the president of the Commissioned Officers' Widows Association of Western Australia, attempted to form a similar body in Melbourne. She claimed that when the pensions were increased, 'the widow of an officer with dependent children benefited very little. Her pension was that of a private's widow.' Her argument was that war rates for widows should have been increased proportionately. The Fisher government had supported a higher pension for officers' widows on the grounds, as Pearce, the Minister for Defence, claimed, that 'a higher rate of income deserved a higher rate of pension'.[89] But other widows took exception to Thompson's position. One questioner from the assembled crowd claimed firmly that:

The widow of a private has made the same sacrifice, and suffers just as much hardship as does the officer's widow. Today ... all these orphan children are treated alike, and each can receive a good education. If you wish to do good, madame, try to get the pensions for the children increased. The war is over now, and there should be no distinction of rank amongst the widows.

Thompson explained that she wanted others to appreciate the fact that men had given up 'good positions to serve, the rank they had qualified for in times of peace should be kept'. She asserted that if the men had thought that their children and wives would not be adequately looked after, then they would not have gone to war. This claim inspired a chorus of commentary. One woman exclaimed that then 'they would have been cowards, and have shirked their duty', and added proudly: 'My husband did not wait 24 hours.' Another interjected: 'My husband sank his rank as an officer, and enlisted as a private in order to get to the front.' Another woman, wearing a 'widow's costume', exclaimed dramatically that her husband had gone to France 'and was killed the next day'. After the meeting was reduced to such a rowdy exchange, the chair suggested that, 'as it was evident that the meeting was not altogether in accord with Mrs. Thompson's proposals, there was little use going on', and closed the meeting.[90]

The Politics of Grief

Widows wrote letters and submitted applications for funding to charitable bodies and to government authorities to gain financial support. These documents were written for public scrutiny but were of a personal nature; in them, women made themselves vulnerable in exposing their emotions. In the language of entitlement, they attempted to forge new identities as breadwinners of fatherless families. The letters, petitions and applications that widows wrote show how women came to see themselves as 'war widows'.

These texts also reveal the way loss was tied to the development of a *political* identity. Widows united to resist what they perceived to be attempts to marginalise them. Although they carefully avoided criticism of soldiers' entitlements, war widows wanted economic independence and tried to articulate a notion of 'sacrifice' in their own terms. This became a way of politicising their grief. Another point which emerges in these letters is that these women had internalised the belief that they were entitled to be supported by the state, by virtue of their marriage. Unlike single women of the period, for instance, who accepted that they had to earn a living, war widows expected to be provided for in the same way that a male breadwinner would support them.

Women voiced their complaints directly to politicians in impassioned expressions of anger. In November 1916, Maud Whittle wrote to Senator Pearce pleading for support. Her husband Albert had died in December 1915, leaving her with one child and 'entirely unprovided for owing to [his] death'. She requested the £33 due to her and asked for

that money for Xmas as I am badly need[ing] it. By my husband's death his child and I are left unprovided for – I don't think I have been waiting in patience as it is eleven months since he died. I have several times been to the Barracks here but they know nothing about the money. I am sorry to trouble you in these troubled times but there seems no one else who knows anything about it but you.[91]

The secretary of the department noted with sympathy that 'the dependents of the late Sergeant Whittle are in destitute circumstances in view of which it is suggested that pending the final decision in the case, it might be possible to make an Advance to Mrs. Whittle of a portion of the amount – say £10'.[92]

Mrs O. Reynolds, comparing herself to others with fewer children, wrote to Prime Minister Hughes in 1920, complaining of the difficulty of rearing several children. How 'can a soldier's widow and 2 children live on £2/14/6, and pay rent out of it', she wrote. 'The widow with one child', she claimed, 'is not so badly off. She gets her £2/10/0 and I can manage comfortably enough, but we with two children are expected to keep an extra child on 4/6 per week.' Her effort to keep her children respectable was being compromised and, while she agreed with a rise in the pension for returned men, widows deserved more payment. 'I see by the paper the returned men are to have their pensions raised (and rightly too)', she observed, 'but no mention is made of the widows.' Her efforts to be a responsible mother were being stretched to the limit. 'I have always tried to keep myself and children decently clothed, but it's getting beyond me now. I have two boys, one five years and the other nearly nine years old, and I can assure [you] they take as much to keep [as] a man.' Her plea was for assistance: 'I would be so grateful, Mr Hughes, if you could do anything for us, as we are truely hard pressed. I have struggled on for two and a half years, but I simply can't carry on any longer. I often see in the paper where they take up subscriptions to help soldiers' dependents, but nothing ever comes my way.'[93]

The employment of war widows became a delicate issue when returned men demanded their jobs back and assumed a natural right of preference over women. In June 1919, Nellie Strutt wrote to her local member expressing concern that widows would be removed from their positions once the returned soldiers had been given their jobs. 'Of course', she wrote, 'we are temporary employees [and] we cannot expect to have the same privileges as permanent hands, but if we are kept on for an indefinite period as the soldiers are, we will be very thankful.' The need to be the breadwinner made her own situation desperate. 'My term of six months will be up very shortly (next month)', she claimed,

> and if I am discharged I have nothing in the world to turn to and I know most of the widows are placed the same as myself... Our officer-in-charge is well satisfied with our work and says it will be to his advantage if we are kept on, as new hands have to go through the same routine and it takes a good while to get accustomed to the work.[94]

It was decided to keep the women on, partly because they were satisfactorily performing their duties, but also for fear of unnecessary agitation by those who would use 'the subject of political agitation ... for their own advantage'.[95] In recognition of these difficulties, schemes were established in Britain, for instance, to assist in the training of war widows. The schemes resembled those arranged for disabled men, but sharp distinctions were made between the two groups. In the case of the disabled soldier, 'the state deemed that it owed a duty to the man to provide him with the means of regaining the highest measure of industrial capacity that his disablement allows'. In the case of the widow, 'the state is not replacing an earning capacity which has been lost in its service, but offers to assist the widow to add to her income'.[96]

The Sailors' and Soldiers' War Widows Association also sent several deputations to Prime Minister Bruce. In one of these, they requested 'a more generous pension for war widows who are without children, or whose children have passed the age of sixteen'. The association observed that the pension was 23s 6d per week, with the full amount of 42s being paid only when a widow is 'in ill-health and unable to work'. The war widow was in an invidious economic position in the absence of a breadwinner and a decision had to be made

whether it was the wish of the community that the widow of a soldier should rear the soldier's children until they reach a certain age and then be thrown upon the labour market, or whether it is desired that the widow should receive the same care and freedom from having to earn her own living as would have been provided by her husband had he not given his life in service.[97]

When they petitioned politicians, widows drew on both economic and moral arguments, to resist forgetting their sacrifices. As early as March 1919, a group of war widows from Western Australia petitioned the Minister for Repatriation, Senator Edward Millen, complaining of the inequities of a system which privileged some widows over others. 'We, the undersigned,' the petition began,

wish to draw your attention to the unjust treatment by some of the widows under the new scale of living allowances which have been granted to them. Under the new regulations only those widows who have been in receipt of rental allowance from the Repatriation department are entitled to back pay ... The widows who had tried to struggle along on their pension without help, and many did not know that they could receive such help, only receive payment as from the date of their application.

This situation, they declared, divided widows. 'To us, it seems very unfair, that those who had done without should get no back pay, while those who had been receiving help should get an extra cheque.'[98]

Another petition signed by a group of war widows was sent to Millen in February of the following year:

We ... wish to bring before your notice the struggle we are having in trying to live on our pensions. It is true that we were granted a living allowance in Oct 1918 but the cost of living has greatly increased since then and the price of food and clothes continues to rise. We feel that if we are to pay our way, feed and clothe our children decently, we must have help. We would suggest that we be granted a temporary rise in our living allowance until such times as the high cost of living is reduced and things become more normal. We respectfully ask that you give this matter your earnest consideration at once as we need help now.[99]

The women from the west were not alone in airing these complaints. In 1920 New South Wales widows expressed their discontent and dissatisfaction. In February 1920, a 'large meeting of Manly War Widows was held at the Town Hall ... in reference to living allowance'.[100] The meeting passed the resolution that: 'we, the War Widows of Manly and District, labouring under the excessive costs of living, respectfully request the Prime Minister of Australia to make a substantial allowance to meet the extra demands which at present time are causing general hardship'.[101]

Sites of Loss

Women's applications for assistance to the Anzac Fellowship of Women offer some glimpses into how women publicly framed their private loss. Women made themselves extraordinarily vulnerable, as they exposed their personal details for public scrutiny. The fellowship was founded in April 1921 by Mary Booth. A committed patriot, Booth answered the call to arms in the only way a single, educated, middle-class woman could in 1914: by forming several charitable organisations. Marginalised by a war which denied a role for women who had not mothered a son or nurtured a husband, Booth claimed a role for single, childless women at a time when their status was devalued. As well as being the driving force behind the fellowship, she formed the Babies' Kit Society for the Allies' Babies, and, as we have seen, in 1915 she opened the Soldiers' Club to cater for returned men. Her other wartime activities included an active role in the pro-conscription Universal Service League and the Centre for Soldiers' Wives and Mothers.[102] The Anzac Fellowship, of which she was president until 1956, allowed her to continue an involvement with the war and foster 'the spirit and traditions of Anzac Day'. Its key aims were to 'promote the comradeship of women who were engaged in war work during the Great War' and 'to have regard for the welfare of the soldiers and their bereaved'.[103] Activity in a range of war-related organisations enabled women such as Booth to claim a public place in the memory and sacrifice of war.

Several cases came before the Anzac Fellowship from widows seeking assistance. In 1925, Mrs L. A. Adams, the widow of J. J. Adams, was rendered destitute when the death of her husband left her in a 'very distressing position'. She had no money or property. The money she received from the Children's Welfare Department, for the maintenance of her four young children whose ages ranged from six years to ten months, was 'barely sufficient to maintain her children'. Adams was not in a position to pay her husband's debts, and her limited assets were either 'broken or worn out, and even those enumerated are practically valueless and of very little use'. The CIB observed that the furniture she owned was 'worthless', and 'it would be a mercy to write off and let the poor woman make what little use she can of it'.[104] The police report concurred, claiming that 'This unfortunate woman has no money or property whatever, and her only means of existence is an allowance paid to her by the Children and Welfare Department for the maintenance of her four young children'.[105]

Mrs Catherine Eadie, the wife of the late James Eadie of the British Army, who had enlisted in January 1915 and was killed in action in September 1916, was similarly plunged into a desperate state. She had a five-year-old daughter and she was in 'a very precarious state of health, and living with her parents', having suffered from 'a nervous breakdown and being subjected to asthma of a chronic kind'.[106]

Mrs M. E. Gapper's husband, Private F. C. M. Gapper, was a butcher prior to enlisting in 1915. After contracting 'gastric trouble', he died in 1918. His wife experienced 'constant strain night and day for twelve months lost one stone in weight – now unable [sic] to do only bare household duties – granted pension of 3/6 per week for herself and 2/6 per week for boy 10 years of age'. The letter, lodged by one R. Richard, argued that the state should ensure 'fair and liberal treatment for those who are left belonging to those who sacrificed their life if not on the battlefield, from causes contracted on the battlefield'.[107]

Other organisations appreciated the difficulties that war widows faced in making themselves vulnerable through the exposure of their distress. Legacy offered its support during the inter-war years, as did several other groups.[108] The Centre for Soldiers' Wives and Mothers, begun in February 1916, was another organisation which aimed to care for soldiers' dependents. It organised entertainments, picnics and social outings for children, and a furniture outlet where 'soldiers' dependents would be enabled to procure necessary household furniture at a reasonable price'.[109] In 1921, at the meeting of the branch delegates of the Housewives Association, it was resolved that the association

> desires to enter an emphatic protest at the meagre allowances given to the widows of those men who paid the supreme sacrifice for their country during the war, and we claim that better consideration should be given to them, and at least a

home provided, rent free, which is the only possible offering that this community might afford them in honour for their great loss.[110]

The League of Loyal Women 'offered themselves in the welfare of war widows in this state [South Australia]' because they believed that 'war widows are among the dependents who require special consideration and there is no doubt that the co-operation of this ladies' committee will prove exceedingly helpful to the Repatriation Committee and beneficial to the widows'.[111] The Returned Soldiers' Association worked in tandem with the War Widows and Widowed Mothers Association.[112] In 1923, the president of the Melbourne branch of the RSA, Mr J. McKenzie, echoed the chivalrous view of many returned men when he claimed that in the 'early days of the war any man who said that the widows of deceased soldiers would some day be unable to secure medical treatment would have stood in danger of lynching'. There was also recognition of the 'nervous strain' which many women endured and which made them more susceptible to illness 'than those who had a more detached interest in the war'.[113] In September 1920, the Voluntary Workers handed over two cottages to two war widows, Mrs Holt, widow of Private Henry John Holt, who was killed at Pozières, and Mrs Moran whose husband was killed at Villers-Bretonneux. The ladies were going to occupy the cottages, 'which had been erected in recognition of the way in which the men fought and died for us'.[114] Even so, the plight of widows could never rival that of returned men. During the Depression of the 1930s, the RSL attempted to have the pensions of widows reduced so that repatriation payments could be maintained for returned men.[115]

Mrs Corkett ran a small business in 1920. She wrote to the Repatriation Commission seeking financial assistance. Her husband had been killed at the war, and she had 'three children to keep and it takes something to keep them at the present time'. She related that her creditors were demanding their money, and the

> small business I have is just a living and that's all ... one keeps these children in boots and clothes to school there's nothing to save we had plenty when I had my husband to work for me and his little children but now we have to struggle on what we get and Xmas coming and no further only worry through such a dreadful war so trusting to hear from you at your earliest and that you will try and do your best for me as everywhere else homes are handed over to a soldier's widow and there is no convenience about mine.[116]

Her application was rejected on the grounds that she had received a 'considerable increase in pension'.

War widows endured the private grief of having lost their husbands. They also had to negotiate the complex paradoxes of their status as public relics of the short lives of the soldiers who did not return. The cost of sustaining the memory of war sacrifice was endured in two respects by war widows.

First, war widows were caught in the paradox of being neither fully provided for, nor permitted, by the conventions of the time, to be providers. The promises of the authorities, that they would not endure hardship, were broken, but widows also found it difficult to make themselves into breadwinners. Many felt they should not have to, as their applications for relief show, considering that their sacrifice of their husbands warranted continuing support for themselves and their children.

Second, the new identity of war widow, which gave them a place in the public commemoration of war, carried with it a high moral and economic price. They were obliged to carry the memory of war losses, but only in terms that enforced acceptable standards of womanhood. Widows were, of course, complicit in such enforcement, often lashing out at other widows, and taking out a sense of lost entitlements and disregarded sacrifices on women even less fortunate than themselves. They unleashed their wrath, feeling no shame and no desire to shield their agony. Both these paradoxes, and the complex ways in which they were negotiated by women, can be seen in the politicising of grief that organising as war widow entailed.

5   Returned Limbless Soldiers: Identity through Loss

> to see our brave soldiers boys back from the war wounded and maimed for life ... [who] have to be cared for. But they are a cheerful lot of fellows mostly and they will tell you they think themselves lucky if they only lost a leg or arm we think a lot of our Australian boys ...[1]

Writing to his mother in 1916, Lance-Corporal Hislop described how he came to have his hand amputated:

> [My] left hand [was] so badly shattered that the doctors had to amputate it a little below the wrist. This was only as a last resource as they tried to save part of the hand but failed. You must not let this worry you at all as there are other cases here where men have had to have both legs amputated so I do not complain.[2]

The comparison Hislop drew with other disabled men who were worse off was a common device by which disabled soldiers defined a sense of identity based on their distinctive loss, a physical absence which, unlike psychological loss, could not be repressed.

Physically, the disabled soldier was a disturbing presence in the social and political landscape after the war. Amid the celebrations, the disabled soldier, who had seemingly diminished in size and become distorted in shape, assumed a grotesque presence larger than life, offering an ironic comment on the desperate efforts of those around him to wrestle free of the horror of war. The shattered heroes hovered on the margins, defying easy categorisation.[3]

The adventure and excitement of a new era allowed little room for expressions of regret, lament, or even nostalgia.[4] Disabled men had to find another language of self and identity, one which would expose but underplay the extent of their wounds and afflictions.[5] They found this language in their plea that their difference be seen as positive rather than a disadvantage, and in their claim to a heroic citizenship where their disabilities would be honoured. Their claims for preferential treatment were underpinned by a lingering resentment. Financial assistance would never extinguish their mourning, observed the *Limbless Soldier*, 'for [while] the pension and monetary aid are good in a way, they will never stop the brooding and the bitterness of those who gave up their best energies forever in the prime of their youth'.⁶ A focus on the ways in which limbless soldiers attempted to translate this grief into political expression distinguishes the perspective from other studies that have largely focused on medical and surgical aspects of the limbless soldiers' experience.⁷

Identities of Loss

Several associations were formed during the 1920s to protect the interests of disabled soldiers, deprived of their limbs, their eyesight or the full use of their lungs through war service. A generation of soldiers carried injuries so permanent and stark that their visibility unsettled even the most ardent patriot. The soldiers themselves were clear about adequate levels of compensation for the damage caused by their patriotic service. Through their repatriation claims, they attempted to rewrite their loss as a gain, worthy of elevated respect. They did not expect that such deference would have to be earned.⁸ As the 1920s drew to a close, these demands of the disabled soldier could not be met in the modern era, but the returned soldiers' voice continued to echo through public forums with as much impatience and restlessness as the lingering memories of fallen comrades.

Such a view was unthinkable when the war ended. Although the larrikin element among returned soldiers had disrupted social harmony with public displays of drunkenness and violence in the streets, those who returned from war were greeted with hushed respect. Initially, governments provided assistance through soldier settlement programmes and an elaborate scale of pensions, all of which were, by the end of the decade, dismissed as hopelessly inadequate.⁹ Even before the cessation of hostilities, the medical profession warned of insufficient services for returned soldiers. In early 1918, the *Medical Journal of Australia* foreshadowed that 'despite efforts to introduce a properly equipped orthopaedic service and ... a properly adjusted neurological system ... there has been no serious attempt to create a proper service, which would offer our soldiers the best chances for a profitable and useful life after the war'.¹⁰ The same problems were identified internationally. In the last year of the war, at the second annual meeting of the Inter-Allied Conference on the After Care of Disabled Men, one participant, Sir William MacEwen from Scotland, suggested that the shortage of professional limb makers and the men's lack of knowledge of how to use artificial limbs would both be significant problems.¹¹

In this early, optimistic climate, when peacetime was expected to bring comfort and safety, the limbless spoke with hope of the rewards that would be bestowed upon them in deferential recognition of their enforced disability. A mounting resentment came from others in need of repatriation benefits, but also from civilian recipients of welfare, who felt marginal to the new type of citizenship based on war service.[12]

First, limbless men had to convince their fellow soldiers of their worthiness for special consideration. In Victoria, the limbless soldiers came together initially as a sub-section of the RSL, but then broke away because members felt that a recognition of difference through preferential treatment was not being accepted by the league. In this mood of defiance, in December 1920, a group of men who had 'lost a limb in the service of the Empire during the war' formed the Limbless Soldiers Association. Their goal was primarily to obtain employment, for the loss 'of an arm or a leg does not make a man mentally unfit, and these amputation cases desire something better than caretakers' or liftmen's positions'. Another aim was to encourage men who had once been proud and even arrogant in the display of their bodies in their full splendour to make better use of artificial limbs.

The impulses which bonded these men were often at odds with the modern desire to valorise, to celebrate, and to live for the present rather than the past which surrounded them at the beginning of the 1920s.[13] While they may have come to symbolise for some the ethos and the excesses of an era best forgotten, it was by firm recognition and remembrance of their efforts in another time and place that they aimed to reorient themselves into civilian life. The move to form an exclusive organisation was a part of this process, and the former soldiers were unequivocal that 'the interests of limbless men could best be served by restricting membership to limbless soldiers only'.[14]

A competitive spirit developed between soldiers' organisations. In response to these manoeuvres, the president of the RSL, Mr A. M. David, said in September 1921, that he did not know whether to 'regard the decision as a "licking" but time would prove whether the course adopted was the right one'.[15] It was no doubt a positive decision for those 945 returned soldiers who had, by 1926, joined the Limbless Soldiers Association.[16] The association saw its role as aiding a 'body of returned soldiers who lost one or more limbs in the war, and [it] was formed with the object of looking after the interests of those who have suffered in this way, and more particularly those among the sufferers who have found it difficult, if not impossible, to make a fresh beginning in life'.[17] The perception that the RSL could not further the distinct demands of men who were now disabled came from a profound sense of neglect and disrespect, one which the RSL did little to allay.[18]

The early success of the Limbless Soldiers Association was impressive. In December 1924, when it held a 'smoke social' in Melbourne,

200 limbless soldiers met in the upper Town Hall to welcome Mr B. W. Bagenal, the first president, back from abroad. 'As a result of his travels', noted the *Argus*, 'he had come to the conclusion that the Limbless Soldiers' Association of Australia was the finest in the world.'[19] As early as 1923, branches had been established in the major capital cities and a federal body, the Commonwealth Council of Limbless Soldiers Associations, was formed to lobby politicians.

The badge adopted by the Limbless Soldiers Association became a symbol of new identity that demanded public respect.[20] In 1921 a design was adopted which 'was recognisable from a reasonable distance without having to read the inscription on it'. An 'innovation of this badge was the remarkable coloured centre to indicate whether financial or not'. The association suggested that a badge, 'a triangle surmounted by a crown', be procured for members in order to distinguish the 'limbless soldier from his more fortunate brother in trams, trains, etc., where the public do not now realise his disability and leave him to stand while sound men sit'.[21] Bagenal asserted that 'just as schoolboys who receive books of tickets are recognised by their caps, so the limbless soldier could be recognised by his association badge'. A badge would identify the returned man in public. 'CMB' observed in February 1922 that the thoughtlessness of 'young, healthy "conscientious objectors"' was undeniable when 'a returned limbless soldier has been permitted to stand in a railway carriage all the way to the city'. While most recognised the badge, 'there still appears to be a large percentage who [did] not'.[22] Association members demanded that their distinctive status be recognised by all, and set about making that happen.

The public presence of limbless men was a delicate matter which sometimes inspired an emotional response. According to *Our Empire*, 'The sight of boys minus a leg or an arm in Melbourne melted women in the streets to tears',[23] and many disabled soldiers expected that their public presence would command such instantaneous respect. But this expectation was not always met, and some soldiers were reluctant to wear their badge of sacrifice in public because it also on occasion elicited a hostile reaction.[24] While the Limbless Soldiers Association encouraged a high profile for respectable limbless men in public, it was opposed to street mendicants, and was committed to putting down 'this practice of limbless beggars'. Such a public display would 'poison the public mind against limbless soldiers' and it aimed to eliminate the need for begging in the streets.[25] The association warned against canvassers and was 'strongly opposed to this practice'.[26]

The public presence of limbless men could be softened with the employment of men at street fruit barrows. This was the 'greatest effort of recent times by the Association in regard to the absorption of our unemployed'.[27] By the late 1930s, this had become a most effective means of employing men, some returned soldiers having occupied a kiosk for more than ten years.[28] Such employment minimised their disability. In the Martin Place kiosk, in Sydney's central business district, one such occupant, Mr Trice, had suffered the 'amputation of two legs and loss of an eye'.[29] His condition, at least partially hidden from view, was not an affront to the public.

The haunting spectacle of the disabled soldier was unsettling in the new postwar world, because it was the fully able body which shaped the advances of modernity in the 1920s and 1930s. The antecedents of the modern period were formed as early as the seventeenth century, but by the early twentieth, technical change, scientific developments, the integration of time and space, and the fragmentation of work came to symbolise that which marked the years of civilian life after the ravages of war. Modern inventions refined understandings of space, time and technology.[30] Cultural and political developments were shaped by advances in movement, with the automobile and aviation. Fashion and art emphasised the streamlined and the sanitised. For the middle classes, modern life was a quest for consumer pleasure and desire, the nature of which changed greatly in the postwar years. To some, this flighty indulgence showed a disturbing indifference to the ideals 'which were enshrined in the word Anzac'; they were being perverted 'by the petty social distinctions and little cruelties of peacetime social life'.[31]

In this landscape, the returned disabled soldier was caught in a paradoxical position. His body, which in wartime had been heralded as the icon of nationhood and manhood, exalting Victorian values of heroism, chivalry and glory, was now considered an anachronism, belonging to a premodern world. Modernity was associated with a particular form of masculinity, one of rationalisation, industrial productivity and repression.[32] These maimed men were connected to the advances of the modern era by the promise held out by science and technology of constructing artificial limbs, which would allow them to retrieve what they had lost.[33] But this was a tenuous connection, for the premise of modernity and modern identity was based on a denial of loss. The injured and the limbless became invisible in the masculine rhetoric of heroism and sacrifice.

In order to retrieve this, the disabled soldiers' organisations cultivated a rugged masculine independence and a defiant self-sufficiency in their attempt to 'help men to help themselves', not to 'give charitable doles'; the aim was to train and employ men so that each man could 'make a livelihood for himself and his family'.[34] As early as 1916, this ethos was a fundamental part of the soldiers' return and their repatriation. It was hard not to be impressed, noted W. Fitzpatrick, author of *The*

Repatriation of the Soldier, 'by the sturdy independence of the majority of these men, who are seeking any work they can get, and the cheerful way they are facing a fresh start in life'. Humbled by the experience, these 'men are simply asking for a helping hand to earn their bread, and to rest content ... with the consciousness of having done their "bit" ', and 'having the proud memory of their military achievements to brighten the rest of their way through life'.[35]

The interplay between independence and dependence would pose a perennial problem for returned men attempting to claim a new identity. They were outspoken in their demand for assistance, but refused what they perceived to be charity. In arranging functions to supplement their incomes, the Blinded Soldiers Club, for example, insisted that this was 'not in any sense an "appeal" for money'. The word 'appeal', it was said, had given offence to many blinded soldiers and they were insulted by the stigma of charity. It was difficult for public fund-raising activity not to adopt a charitable flavour, but it was equally difficult for disabled soldiers to assume an infantile and feminised dependency.

This tension was apparent in the countless fund-raising drives and appeals arranged for disabled men during the inter-war years. Well-known celebrities such as Dame Nellie Melba actively supported their cause. In December 1925, the Red Cross had thrown a party for the Lady Helen Club for Blinded Soldiers, where 'flowers and shaded lights made a pretty sight ... every soldier received the special Red Cross present box. Dancing and a fine supper provided by the Red Cross and served by VAD [Volunteer Aid Detachments] helpers dressed in their picturesque uniforms brought the evening to a happy close.' Social functions remained an important part of the activities of these groups and, by the 1930s, had become a central preoccupation. The Blinded Soldiers Club organised monthly entertainments which were financed by the Red Cross, and the club also functioned as a depot for 'the sale of blind soldiers' work such as baskets ... mats, and woodwork of various descriptions'. Women – as ever, the chief voluntary workers of philanthropic and charity organisations – generously offered their services. When the partially blinded soldiers organised a fund-raising campaign in 1927, it was noted that for 'weeks women connected with the appeal have been working every day at Anzac House, checking buttons, boxes, permits and arranging various gatherings to assist funds'. It was not only women who assisted in this way. The president of the Sailors' and Soldiers' Fathers Association, John Clayton, claimed that 'any man who was the father of a soldier would always be willing to do his utmost for "the boys" '. But organisations like the Limbless Soldiers Association attempted to discourage men from relying on these benefits – as women needed to – and insisted that the returned man do 'his full duty to his country, as befitting a soldier and a man, that he will make an earnest effort to fit himself for the position of interdependency and self support'.

The arguments for a new identity based on preferential treatment on one hand, and manly independence on the other, drew on comparisons with others. The disabled body, which would signal difference and preference, became crucial in shaping new, postwar identities. These groups had to retain their distinctiveness, and not to be conflated in the generic category of the 'disabled' soldier, in the way that a notion of 'mothers' sacrifice' had been lost. Each group of disabled soldiers claimed a distinct contribution and a special place in the memory of war.

Soldiers who had lost an eye demanded equal recognition of *their* disability with other soldiers. A deputation by these men to the Minister for Defence and Repatriation in 1925 asked why should 'men who had lost an arm or a leg at the war ... receive 75 per cent of the maximum pension, while those who had lost an eye ... receive ... 50 per cent, plus a percentage of any disability existing in the remaining eye'. It was hoped that 'one eyed men be placed on a similar footing to limbless men'. Later that year, they were granted an increase in their pension.

The partially blinded soldiers – a different group to the one-eyed soldiers – were also keen to assert their distinctive identity. In 1927 it was estimated that there were at least 1300 partially blinded soldiers in Victoria, about 385 of whom had lost an eye, the sight of an eye or worse. Theirs was often a deteriorating condition. The 'tragedy of the former soldiers whose eyes were injured at the war is that many of them are gradually suffering from increasing loss of sight'. Like other organisations, they emphasised their separateness by wearing distinctive badges. In the general meeting of the Victorian branch of their organisation, 'considerable discussion took place regarding the choice of a badge to be worn by members of the association'. As a bold statement of their distinction, in March 1924, they declared that a 'proposal to admit men who had been wounded in wars prior to the Great War was defeated. It was decided to continue membership to those ignored in the last war.'

Tubercular soldiers also wished to distinguish themselves. In September 1920, the various organisations 'which have been trying to better the conditions under which men who contracted consumption as a result of warlike operations at home or abroad ... have decided to form an Australian association'. The need was acute for a 'permanent pension to enable patients to continue the treatment learned in sanatoria'. By 1928, the tubercular association had 300 members. Tubercular soldiers had no hesitation in declaring their superior need for monetary support above other disabled men. It was pointed out that men who suffered from the loss of an arm were allowed to travel free on the trams, unlike tubercular soldiers, who in many cases could not walk any distance, were compelled to pay full fare. The opinion was expressed that in the case of a tubercular soldier being transferred from one state to another, first class rail warrants should be issued.

Soon afterwards, the request was made to have travelling concessions made uniform throughout the Commonwealth and that all warrants 'should be first class'. The privileges of the Repatriation Department 'should be extended to men who contracted tuberculosis on home services'. In 1926, a deputation of returned soldiers asked Senator Guthrie for preference to be given to soldiers above ordinary citizens in the treatment of tuberculosis.[36]

In ways which mirrored the tensions between widows for preferential treatment, there were differences within groups of disabled men. In 1924, there were fifteen categories of limbless men who received different pensions. Examples ranged from a returned soldier who received 63 shillings for having his arm amputated below the elbow, to a double amputee having lost two legs above the knee receiving 84 shillings. Another who had two legs amputated below the knee also received 84 shillings. Recipients obtained more for a wife and for each child.[37] 'Wingey' wrote to the *Argus* in 1921 claiming that these distinctions were unacceptable. Those 'of us who had lost [legs] would receive free travelling on the railways ... we who have lost arms are to receive no concession'. Everyone would agree, he claimed, 'that a one-armed man is at an even greater disadvantage than a one-legged man'. He argued that he had been on the unemployment lists for over six months, 'but no one seems to want me in their employ'. He was distraught that he was classified 'as five-sixths incapacitated, and a one-legged man was classed as two-thirds, yet he will get free rail and I will not'. 'If we are not treated equally', he asserted, 'I think we who have lost an arm should be given a full pension to make up for the loss of the travelling concession.'[38] In a letter 'From One of the Boys', a one-armed man reiterated the point:

[we] have not even the same concessions as the one-legged ... we have to pay fares on trains and trams. It is a big item to some of us, who only earn a few shillings a week to supplement our pensions ... perhaps the public service will be able to find us suitable employment, or else members of Parliament may see it possible to give us a substantial increase to make things more nearly even. Many of my comrades have been out of employment for months, and some have been unable to secure employment since their discharge. I am sure Australia is able to show that her boys are not behind in fighting, so why not now give them a good deal?[39]

The campaign for concessions on public transport encapsulates the tensions. In an era characterised by vast improvements in movement and speed, the Limbless Soldiers Association was 'always on the look out for caring and bettering the facilities ... [in] regard to moving from place to place'.[40] One of the first complaints of the returned soldiers was that the artificial limb factory in Sturt Street, South Melbourne, was not on a tramway route. 'The patient who has to visit the factory to have an artificial leg fitted, or repaired', reported the *Argus*, 'must make his way there as best he can.' It was hoped that if 'a more easily accessible site could be found soldiers needing the aid of the factory would be very grateful'. In 1921, the association expressed dissatisfaction that the Victorian Tramways Board had not issued tramway passes for all the 800 men who had lost a limb or limbs. President B. W. Bagenal argued that no distinctions should be made and, though it might be thought a 'one-armed man has no call for this concession', 'there are so few avenues of occupation for him that we ask for this concession in order to facilitate him in work as a messenger or traveller or hawker, and also because frequently in carrying a parcel it is very inconvenient with one arm, and the number of men involved is comparatively small'.

The Tramways Board was not averse to the idea of assisting the men; nor was the *Argus*, which asserted that the 'cost of the war and the cost of repatriating and compensating those who suffered in the war is a national obligation and should be borne by the nation as a whole'. But if one concession was given, others would also expect exemption. Tramways policy granted

> free all-lines tramway passes to returned soldiers who have lost two limbs or two eyes as the result of active service ... Any injury to a limb which renders it useless without the aid of a surgical boot or other appliance has been considered as equivalent to the loss of the limb ... If free passes were granted to all returned soldiers who have lost one leg the board could not logically refuse similar concessions to soldiers who have unfortunately suffered other injuries which may be even more serious than the loss of a leg.

In 1921, the Limbless Soldiers Association launched a campaign to have a pension granted for life to limbless and permanently maimed soldiers, 'irrespective of a man's earnings'. In 1922 the Tramways Board had approved of the issue of about 500 000 free tickets per annum to returned soldiers suffering from injuries that 'impeded their means of locomotion'. It was, however, to be regretted that the 'one-armed men were debarred from participating in the privilege'.

These requests, it was argued, were not unreasonable. The president of the Victorian branch argued that the loss of revenue for the Tramways Board would be minimal. 'There are 440 legless men in Melbourne, and

76 who have lost an arm, or 520 limbless men altogether ... There are, therefore, less than one in a thousand for whom the concession is sought.'

Treatment of the 'maimed digger', it was observed, was generous in other states. The cost was the issue. The Premier of Victoria argued that suburban passes to such soldiers would cost the state about £20 000 a year. The Tramways Board replied to the men that

> while expressing sympathy with the disabled men ... this was more a matter for the Repatriation Department, as it was an obligation upon the nation to recognise the claims of these men, which should not fall solely upon that section of the metropolitan residents which used the tramways [and] the board had issued about 90 free passes to soldiers who had lost the sight of both eyes or the use of both legs.[41]

The pension levels were calculated on a scale of disability, which privileged certain groups of men and certain disabilities.[42] The highest rate of payment, for instance, was for losing one leg and one arm at 80 shillings per week, while the lowest rates were for losing one arm (30 shillings) or one leg (35 shillings). The classifications and categories suggested an elaborate hierarchy of severity. In September 1922, Senator Guthrie noted that there were 3779 limbless soldiers in Australia; 2636 of them were 'leg cases' and 1143 were 'arm cases'. These men had additional expenses, including higher rents to live near trams and trains, charges for luggage carriage, and extra wear on clothing. Uniform travelling concessions should therefore be applied. The difficulties of public transport travel had also forced the men who had lost one or both legs to register for 'motor cars and motor cycles'. It was claimed that 'the difficulty and inconvenience of travelling in trams and trains were inducing limbless soldiers to save for the purchase of motorcycles and light cars to convey them to and from their work and afford them recreation'.

In 1922, the Tramways Board had already 'issued free passes to about 150 returned men who had lost the sight of both eyes or the use of two limbs. As to the question of extending the concession to those who had lost one limb, ... the request of the deputation [would be considered by] the members of the Tramways Board.' A few months later, the Nationalist Party intended to urge that one-armed men be granted the concession. Other exemptions had been granted to the men, and in this climate of respect, the Tramways Board was out of step. The Carlton, St Kilda, Essendon, Geelong, South Melbourne, Collingwood and Fitzroy football clubs would also admit members to the grounds on the production of their badges.

The logistic difficulties of travel and movement were highlighted by the parent of one disabled soldier. 'Cannot the board realise', asked A. J. Day, that many of these unfortunate maimed men ... now must hobble painfully to and fro because they cannot afford the extra expense of tram fares ... I now live too far from the train to suit my son. His stump cannot stand the strain of walking to and fro ... these men have suffered and are suffering ... Surely the travelling public are not so niggardly as to allow such small cost as would be entailed to interfere with their duty to these men.⁴³

As these men grouped together, they drew on a language of privilege and distinction to assert their achievements, and to insist that their new identities be honoured in the postwar era. But fewer and fewer were listening to these proclamations in a world that was moving fast to forget the horror of the war. One of the attempts made to counter this displacement was the idea of a heroic citizenship.

Hero Citizens

The essence of Australian modernity was to be expressed in a virile body, but also in one which was white and racially 'pure'. In a climate which still embraced eugenicist ideals, laying the foundation for later persecution on the basis of race, the 'modern' citizen was understood to be white and able-bodied.⁴⁴ Citizenship in the national 'family' was premised on the idea of blood ties with British and European supremacy. As such, citizenship was based on a selective, repressed memory, in which the loss and grief of Aboriginal sacrifices were denied. This marginalisation in public memory was challenged when Aboriginal servicemen claimed citizen rights after they had defended the nation.⁴⁵

During the 1920s, disabled soldiers claimed a peacetime heroism as a way of asserting their achievements against these eugenicist currents. 'Nearly all limbless men [displayed] a splendid spirit of pluck, energy and cheerfulness', announced the Governor of Victoria, Sir Tom Bridges, in 1924, at the annual reunion dinner of the Limbless Soldiers Association. 'These men', he claimed, were 'men of grit, who kept on at it and went kicking in spite of their apparent disabilities'.⁴⁶ If the community would not elevate their achievements, then it was the duty of the association to do so. The mythologies of war sustained the memories and the identities of these men. When elected as president of the Commonwealth Council of Limbless Soldiers Associations, G. Martin Farrow was lauded as having a 'double amputation, having lost two legs in the great Titanic struggle'.⁴⁷ In spite of his disability, it was claimed, he moved 'more freely and faces the grimness of life's battles with a spirit of determination and brightness'.⁴⁸ Though this sort of heroic rhetoric was to harden during the inter-war years, some saw its futility. In 1925, one A. B. Sheldon wrote with poignancy, foreshadowing how hollow such rhetoric was to become, for 'whilst the glamour of being idolised as a wounded hero lasted he may have had a pardonable pride in his swinging stump or sleeveless arm but today he is just a man minus a leg or arm or more'. As a sharp reminder, he added the 'limbless soldier is today ... relatively better off than he is likely to be in later years'.[49]

The manly adventure which had disfigured the men was, during the 1920s, lauded as heroic and glorious. Their twisted bodies became markers of sacrifice, deserving of the adulation which would be compensation for their loss. The men's desire for affirmation and self-esteem coalesced around celebrations on Anzac Day with a recognition of their disability. The spirit of Anzac, claimed the *Limbless Soldier* in 1927, was of men at night 'turning their faces to the wall and weeping, in the day facing the care and toil of life bravely and without murmur'. The heroes were those who transcended their physical handicap, putting to shame 'many who are now unemployed without injuries of any kind'.[50] The reception the Anzac heroes received in Melbourne that year confirmed a positive response. It was reported that during the Anzac Day march comparative 'quietness reigned for about a quarter of an hour until the fleet of motor-cars bearing military hospital patients and limbless soldiers came into view. The occupants of the cars were greeted with a continuous round of applause and excited waving of flags and handkerchiefs.'[51] Those who had overcome and survived disability were the new heroes. Senator Guthrie, a vocal supporter and advocate of the rights of disabled soldiers, pointed out that most 'of the soldiers were willing to work at anything, and he had known them to clear land and grub timber without complaint. He recalled one man in particular with one leg who had been employed clearing forests until he had broken down.'[52] Dudley A. Tregent exemplified the way in which the Anzac spirit was translated into civilian life. Tregent was a blind returned soldier who, since returning from the war, had taken out final honours in law at the University of Melbourne. He had enlisted aged seventeen, went to France and, during 'the heavy fighting along the Hindenburg line shortly before the Armistice', his 'eyesight was destroyed by shrapnel'.[53]

But by the 1930s, there was a discernible shift in the memory of the war towards honouring the bereaved and the dead, rather than celebrating the achievements of the living.[54] In 1935, the Queensland branch of the Limbless Soldiers Association observed that Anzac Day 'was a soldiers' day: it is not now ... observed with flags at half mast, denoting intense sorrow or mourning ... with the Diggers' cheerful spirit dampened by civilian gloom'.[55]

Some limbless men argued that a special sort of citizen had been shaped through a war experience where limbs were lost, and that this identity had to be sustained and privileged. In December 1926, the

Governor-General claimed that the limbless 'had received the scars. They knew that all respected them for it.' Their place would be recognised next to those who had given the ultimate sacrifice: 'Just as they had stood in silence in memory of those who did not return, the limbless soldiers were entitled to the next place in the public regard.' It was a proud thing for one representing the King 'to know that the organisation was ensuring all those things the king had most at heart ... and a place in the esteem of the nation, that it would not let them suffer want'. It was obvious how 'unequal the sacrifice had been. He would be sorry to think that the youth of the country were not trained to take their places and one reason the country was sound at heart' was because of 'the example [limbless men] ... set ... in contributing to the advancement of industry'.[56] The *Limbless Soldier* reported information regarding the 'celebrities of the AIF', documenting the heroism of soldiers who had endured physical pain and torture, claiming that the 'indomitable spirit' would carry them through the hardships.[57] Men had been elevated to a privileged position through their disability. The president of the Blinded Soldiers Association, Mr Maxwell, declared in 1921 that 'the affliction of blindness had brought to him a clearer vision of the love of his fellow beings. Affliction also seemed to have raised the blinded soldier into nobler heights.'[58]

It was from this conviction, that their loss had shaped a privileged identity, that the limbless argued for the principle of privilege in the world of work, where male identity was so fundamentally formed and, after the war, needed to be retrieved.

Labour and Loss

In the years immediately following the shortlived boom of the 1920s, returned men believed that the spheres of manufacturing and commerce had benefited from their participation. The inter-war years saw a brief prosperity and enhanced employment opportunities, and these men asserted a right to privileged access to new opportunities.[59] Yet these requests were not met to the satisfaction of returned soldiers.[60]

The Limbless Soldiers Association appealed to politicians to affirm a commitment to employ returned men. The chair of the Commonwealth Council of Limbless Soldiers Associations, Francis Killeen, claimed that 'work is what is needed by these men ... [they] could be given special encouragement to qualify for permanent positions, and get away from blind-alley jobs'. Their humiliation should be hidden from view: 'the public ... ought to be spared the sight of limbless soldiers rattling collection boxes on the streets'.[61] In 1923 representatives requested that limbless soldiers should be 'the last to be dismissed from Government departments, and that if their services were no longer required in one department they should be listed in other departments, if possible'.[62] The limbless men regarded the public service as a workplace where they could gain considerable privileges; in fact it was virtually the only form of employment in which the government could grant soldiers preference.[63] In 1926, there were about 400 limbless men in the public service, the majority of whom were in temporary positions, on a twelve-month trial basis, where they would be made permanent employees if suited to the job.[64] Indeed, it was stipulated that 'special examinations for returned soldiers desiring to enter the Commonwealth service should be continued to enable limbless men to qualify'. In addition, the lack of time and money for men to study at night would limit the opportunities available to limbless and seriously maimed soldiers.[65] Limbless men also insisted that 'committees assessing the earning capacity of industrial trainees should not over rate the efficiency of the returned soldier',[66] for it was the duty of the paternalistic state, rather than that of the wives and children of the men, to support them. One politician noted in 1928 that it 'was never meant that former soldiers should be supported by their wives and children because the men were unable through war injuries and disabilities to work. If the people of Australia were appealed to, they would acknowledge that the burden rested upon their shoulders.'[67]

That a case needed to be made for preferential treatment in employment was unexpected. 'It came as a great surprise to us', claimed the *Limbless Soldier* in 1923, 'when it was learned that the Repatriation Department were dismissing a number of limbless men – all of them holding excellent records of their service in the Department – and yet retaining physically fit men, who have a far greater advantage in seeking other employment'.[68] Although support for preferential treatment was not unconditional, the number of unemployed soldiers during the immediate postwar years was not large. In 1926, in Victoria, there were 945 returned limbless soldiers, 30 of whom were unemployed.[69] In 1928, of the 965 members of the Limbless Soldiers Association, only 36 were unemployed. Some politicians were supportive, and Senator Guthrie claimed that 'it was a disgrace that able-bodied men or women were employed to drive lifts while limbless soldiers were unemployed. There should be absolute preference to former soldiers.'[70]

There was ambivalence in affluent times, but public resolve against preference for soldiers hardened during periods of economic difficulty. The prosperity of the 1920s was quickly destroyed by the cruel onset of the Great Depression. Limbless soldiers still demanded preference in employment, which heightened the resentment felt by other men who were, by the 1930s, feeling equally disregarded. Tales of rejection reverberated throughout the country. In Victoria, following a number of retrenchments in government service, the *Limbless Soldier* predicted that it was going to be very difficult 'for the man concerned, for he had little hope at the present time in obtaining employment outside the Service'. From New South Wales came a report that there had been a number of redundancies and dismissals, while in South Australia, the 'unemployed list has considerably grown [and] ... the Association has tried every avenue to have them re-instated'. In the west, the unemployment numbers had become 'more acute', and the warning was issued that some had foolishly come over in search of work and had only found 'themselves worse off'.[71] Efforts to secure employment for disabled soldiers had proved futile. In 1931, at the depth of the most desperate economic depression the country had witnessed, W. Groom, the energetic, committed manager of the Victorian readaptation branch which devised programmes to integrate limbless men, wrote with the lament that 'this has been a trying year – most disappointing and unsatisfactory as far as employment is concerned. The unemployed problem is becoming more difficult as the years go by.' He was right. Employers preferred young and fit men rather than the 'disabled who are now approaching middle-age'.[72]

Women who were given positions at the expense of limbless soldiers were the target of particular resentment. Large commercial firms were accused of not exercising their responsibility: they could employ trained and competent limbless men as lift attendants, 'but they close their eyes to the sight of men having lost a limb through fighting for them, and their ears are also closed to our pleading for the just rights of our limbless members ... they employ girls as lift attendants, and insist on doing so, regardless of the bad example they are setting'. Assuming that employers would prefer men if given the choice, they argued that equal pay 'to both sexes is the only solution for such selfish motives, and every effort will be made to bring this about'.[73] By the late 1920s, the employment of women inspired intense hostility. 'We still have a few men', declared the *Limbless Soldier*,

with empty sleeves and a leg missing, who have been trained as a lift attendant ... Yet twelve lifts in our city are being worked by female attendants. Firms who could – and should – employ the broken man who fought for them. Soon all our men would be employed if they would accept the same wage as paid to these women. The employer who would pay a limbless man small wages because he is receiving a pension commits a revolting offence, and fraudulently enriches himself at the expense of the men who sacrificed a limb in order that he may still live under British rule and prosper.[74]

The issue of female employment remained a constant source of anxiety, as disabled men tried to retrieve their manliness through their breadwinner status. Ten years later, in 1937, it remained a point of contention; females were working as lift attendants, 'which is detrimental to the employment of disabled soldiers'. The *Limbless Soldier* did not advocate dismissal, but rather 'that when female lift attendants leave their positions for any reason, then the vacancy [should] be filled by a disabled soldier'.[75]

The Limbless Soldiers Association attempted to place men in positions in commerce and industry as opportunities arose in the postwar years. But the disabled body could be too easily disregarded in the reorganisation of the workplace after the war. With the spread of Taylorism – the scientific organisation of industrial work through time motion studies with the assistance of the efficiency expert – the worker's body was perceived to be 'a machine capable of infinite productivity and ... resistant to fatigue'.[76] At a time when modern industry demanded a productive, energetic body, the disabled soldier became a metaphor for wartime fatigue and exhaustion. Unlike other veterans, who could, ostensibly, be integrated into the industrial process, the crippled, the blinded and the maimed represented the antithesis of the energy, productivity and precision demanded by the modern workplace.[77] In 1923, the editor of the *Limbless Soldier* had noted the tension between finding places for 'disabled men in positions in commerce and industry where they could work with the able-bodied, and in obtaining working conditions which will not aggravate their disability'.[78] Paying limbless men a lower wage for a lower output was also 'outside the spirit of what the ... Association is trying to do'. This may have been helping men in the short term, but the best 'way is always the way by which they can be brought up to the productive par with able-bodied men'.[79] It was important to convince others that disabled men could perform a range of duties. In 1925, there was a case of a married man with two children, whose left arm had been amputated above the elbow; he had to convince his employer that he could perform the work required.[80]

The advances of science and technology apparently allowed disabled men to achieve the complete worker's body. The equipment devised and designed for the limbless men was considered a 'triumph of the mind and of the will'. Devices had assisted the limbless man to negotiate his lot through the triumph of science.[81] Scientific advances helped to negate the disability of limbless men. The construction of artificial limbs was undertaken at the repatriation artificial limb factory in Caulfield, Melbourne, established in November 1917. Other factories were eventually established in other states. The Melbourne factory moved to South Melbourne in 1919 and became the centre of limb construction in Australia.[82]

If the industrial workplace proved to be inhospitable to those who could not readily fit the model of a utopian labouring body, then the option of a rural idyll proved to be even less viable. In 1924, one writer declared that he 'can only recall two or three cases of men wanting limbs who were successfully engaged in farming'. A reliable wife was an essential asset, but in one way this defeated the purpose of obtaining jobs for disabled men, because 'where a disabled man has made good on the land, it will be found that he has been backed up by a capable and hard-working wife'.[83]

By 1929, the mood was changing, as a new generation who had not known war began to challenge claims of privilege. The Camberwell City Council in Melbourne refused a request from the RSL that the 'principle of preference to returned soldiers be affirmed'. Councillor Read noted that 'it was not fair that young men who were boys in the years of the war should be prevented by a rigorous system of preference to returned soldiers from seizing opportunities for employment and advancement'. The mayor, Councillor Mackay, also believed that 'young men should not be deprived of opportunities because they had been too young to go to the war, and he was inclined to think that the returned soldiers were pushing the matter a little too far'.[84]

By 1932, almost fifteen years after the end of the war, demands from ex-soldiers had not changed although, with an ageing group of returned men, new priorities emerged. In an address to the Limbless Soldiers Association, the Governor-General, Sir Isaac Isaacs, said that society should pay these soldiers the 'homage due to them in their lifetime, rather than provide it after they were dead'. The years were making the war a fading memory: 'The men who had fought in the war had left to those who were following them a great spiritual legacy. Their spirit of loyal service and their ready response to a sense of duty had set an example which should be, and was proving, the finest inspiration to the younger people of Australia.'[85] For this reason, efforts were made to establish an old-age provident fund to assist returned soldiers.[86] Limbless soldiers argued in 1928 that 'the age after which a man who had lost one or more limbs should not be required to work to support himself was 50 years. The association was desirous of providing for these men so that in old age they would not be forced to beg in the streets.'[87] In the ensuing years, the returned soldiers would need all of this assistance. But their campaigns gained an unexpected boost in 1939, when the outbreak of the Second World War ignited memories of past tragedies and glories. In December 1939, the *Limbless Soldier* reported with sombre anticipation that provision 'has been made in the Constitutions of the Limbless Soldiers' Associations of Australia to provide for the admittance to the Associations of any ex-soldier who may in the present hostilities suffer the amputation of a limb or limbs as a direct result of war service'. The hope that after the First World War 'the world would at last have been relieved from any future War' was dashed with the onset of the Second.[88]

Unlike the dead, who remained timeless heroes, those who returned were not immune to the ravages of time. During the inter-war years, limbless soldiers attempted to shape a new postwar identity by privileging their physical losses. By translating their loss and anger into political expression, they channelled their grief and embitterment into a form of militancy.[89] In this way they insisted that their sacrifices be acknowledged as a way of resisting a further loss – that of a revered place in public memory.

Part II

The Second World War

6   Absence as Loss on the Homefront and the Battlefront

God how terrible is this leaving all I love.[1]

When the Second World War broke out in September 1939, links between the two world wars were immediately made. The memories of the First World War re-entered inescapably into people's lives as they braced themselves for yet another conflict. Each year Anzac Day, the occasion of remembrance, provided a source of continuity with the past, for although those who participated in the Second World War shaped their own war stories, they drew irresistibly on earlier national mythologies. 'For twenty-five years', the *Sydney Morning Herald* noted in 1940, 'we have kept a day of memory, a day from which to draw the inspiration of a splendid past.'[2]

By the beginning of the next war, the meaning of that inspiration and memory had been rewritten and imagined in different ways. As the peace movement became more prominent, and isolationist voices emerged, there had been a shift in the meaning of war. But it remained central to nationalist mythologies. The instability of postwar peace created conditions which were to usher in a new war as unresolved hostilities created mounting antagonisms.[3]

The enlistment of the next generation of sons revived emotions connected to an earlier time and place. The advent of another war could still arouse immediate sadness, for a mere twenty years had elapsed since the earlier conflict. One woman remembered that her older brother could not 'wait to turn eighteen to enlist', but 'it saddened my father and mother, Dad having seen action in France in 1916–17 and carried the sadness with him, and Mum having lost a brother in France. I think now how 1939 still seems like yesterday, and ... for them it had been only twenty years of peace and now another war in sight.'[4] One observer noted that 'it was incidents like that that woke up the memory of the pointlessness of Gallipoli and the mud in Flanders'.[5]

The battles of the Second World War were conveyed to a waiting public in a less romantic way, but this did not ease the shock. The experience of an earlier conflict did not make grief any easier to cope with, or to understand. The overall impact was statistically less severe than the aftermath of the First World War. In the 1939–45 war, 540 000 Australians enlisted, as compared to 417 000 in the First World War, but there were fewer deaths: 34 000 as opposed to almost 60 000 in the First World War, when the population of Australia had been less than 5 million. But, as historians have pointed out, the casualties came from smaller families than those of the earlier war, thus concentrating the trauma.[6] The Australian response varied according to the different phases of the war. The initial reaction has been described as 'subdued'; by 1941, this had been transformed into a sense of crisis as the threat to Australia's shores became more acute. Soon, there was deep concern and, whatever the public rhetoric, the personal memories of the First World War 'left a greater legacy of grief than of glory'.[7]

Mothers and wives had lost their privileged status in public memorialising of the First World War, and this remained the case after the outbreak of the Second, despite the fact that women participated in the war effort in unprecedented numbers. The press invoked ideas of unity and cohesion which were meant to unify the nation. 'The spirit of Anzac', noted the *Sydney Morning Herald* in 1940, 'brought together a spirit of oneness that had not existed until those days.'[8] In 1941, Australia 'commemorated the heroism and victories of her sons in two wars'.[9] By 1943, the Anzac Day procession was described as a 'solemn ceremony' that united 'two generations of veterans'; as they stood 'shoulder to shoulder, united by their remembrance of good and bad times together, men of all degrees rewarded for a few hours the spirit of their soldiering days'.[10]

The Anzac spirit included Aboriginal men, although until 1942 they had been excluded. Aboriginal labour on the homefront challenged the view that they were a people doomed to extinction because of their 'primitiveness'.[11] As the war came home to Australia in 1941, Aboriginal soldiers were further involved, because of the remote location of many mission stations and the demand for labour in the north.[12] Aboriginal men who survived combat returned to the further dislocation of having their families sent off the land to make way for white returned soldiers, despite their service.[13] The hope that by serving in the military they would earn full citizenship was eventually realised in 1949, when the Commonwealth franchise was extended to those who had served.[14]

National rhetoric of unity and cohesion of purpose made a mockery of the fragmentation and dislocation that the war created. The war effort bound soldiers and civilians together in a commonality of purpose, but it also created conditions that undermined this unity by fostering resentment and anger. It was usually grief, not glory, which drew communities together.

Loss in war can take various expressions. In the interaction between the homefront and the battlefront, loss, absence and displacement were defined by physical distance. Those at home yearned for news of those abroad, and their lives became precarious and contingent, preparing for the possibility of death, or what others have termed 'anticipatory bereavement'.[15] Meanwhile, soldiers abroad longed for domesticity in surroundings which were antithetical to domestic life. A close examination of the letters of General George Vasey to his wife, Jessie Vasey, provide an insight into these processes.

On the Battlefront: Yearning for Domesticity

From the battlefields of Europe, General George Vasey wrote in frustration to his wife Jessie of their imposed separation. After being stationed in Palestine and Egypt for four months, the general declared in April 1940 that her letters were 'my one contact with a pleasant and peaceful life which seems years away at present but of which I cannot hear too much. Keep it up sweetheart – but please don't look for quite so much in reply.'[16] Jessie's letters repaid him for enduring the punishing routine of the military. 'Your letters are my reward for anything I have been able to accomplish here. When all is said and done there is not much satisfaction in just accomplishing anything – it is the appreciation of one's loved ones that gives the satisfaction and is the spur to continued effort.'[17] The consistency of her correspondence gave him a sense of a shared experience of war. 'You are marvellously regular with your letters', he wrote in 1942, and 'they are indeed the only real pleasure here. As I said before success is not in itself a pleasure: but sharing it is.'[18]

Vasey's romanticisation of domesticity and intimacy in his letters to his wife sustained and nourished him during the period of his overseas service. In the rupture created by wartime conditions and the danger of combat, he looked to the domestic realm for certainty and for security. 'I think of you daily', he declared; 'you and the boys are my sheet anchor in a crazy world.'[19] As others have shown, this 'mythic tranquillity' associated with the past and the future is often conceived of in relation to the disorder of the present.[20] The letters connected Vasey with another time and place that were less volatile and uncertain. Correspondence became the space where he could expose his vulnerabilities; anchor himself with the acknowledgement of birthdays, anniversaries and other markers of time; and give legitimacy to emotions and desires which involvement in war negated. But above all the domestic space was a place of safety, unity and containment – indeed, a haven from a heartless world. Vasey displaced his anxieties of war onto this quarantined space, which was far removed from the dislocation and fragmentation of the battlefront.

In his letters, Vasey explored different forms of self-expression. Emotional expression is, by definition, about the self.[21] Correspondence allowed Vasey to play out a variety of roles: not only that of soldier, but also of father, lover, and husband. In wartime, when the public persona of a general demanded the expression of particular leadership qualities of discipline and control, Vasey found other emotional possibilities through letters.

Analyses of desires other than love and romance remain curiously absent from histories of war. Studies of literary representations in wartime poetry and fiction sometimes offer us a glimpse of the wider emotions other than romance which emerge in wartime.[22] A few notable historical accounts have analysed wartime emotions, but in them the psychology of displacement remains unexplored.[23]

Emotions, it has been argued, are private, subjective and idiosyncratic, and for this reason are not reliable: they are not in the public, objective realm of rationality.[24] But spontaneous emotions and desires are not passive responses to the world. Too often they have been understood only as distorting or limiting observation and knowledge. Vasey's letters suggest that emotions and desires are the ways in which we actively engage with and construct the world.[25]

Wartime Correspondence

Wartime correspondence helped to nurture romance, to cement relationships and to precipitate marriage. But in most published collections, wartime letters between partners are treated as unmediated texts, compiled on the assumption that the written texts allow direct access to those who wrote them.[26] The letters of George Vasey are, uncharacteristically, not concerned with either wartime romance, passion or love – for the Vaseys had been married for almost twenty years – nor with details of the battlefront and combat experience. Instead, the domestic details in Vasey's letters show the general romanticising the private sphere, allowing him to displace the exile he endured in the emotional impoverishment of a war zone.

I take a different view from that offered by others who have considered wartime letters in general, and the Vasey letters in particular. David Horner, the editor of a selection of Vasey's letters, stresses the ways in which Vasey viewed the war from a general's point of view and explores his experience of the troops he led to battle in the frontline. In his selection of the letters Horner argues that Vasey shows himself to be a family man. However, most 'of the family matters have been omitted', he comments, 'with just enough included to indicate that Vasey was a family man with all responsibilities, worries, cares and joys ... a man's relationship with his wife and children is an important guide to his character'.[27] But to omit these parts of his life creates an artificial distinction. The 'public' and the 'private' aspects of Vasey's life were inextricably intertwined. The correspondence with his wife provided him with the emotional sustenance to maintain the public face of a war commander.

In wartime letters, declarations of affection were often restrained by the restrictions of censorship, which patrolled the borders of intimacy. On the frontline, the letters of soldiers were censored by their officers, while officers like Vasey were expected to censor their own correspondence.[28] 'There is a very definite restriction on what we can say now', Vasey cautioned; 'censorship is firmly established here.'[29] But there were other reasons for restraint: 'I don't discuss the war with you sweetheart, firstly, because if I really knew anything I wouldn't say it and any ideas I may have aren't likely to be considered and by the time you get them they are likely to have been proved wrong.'[30] Vasey's Methodist upbringing may also account for the emotional restraint of his correspondence. His tone is affectionate and caring, but not effusive or sensual. His passion is reserved for the fantasy his wife has come to represent, where he can, psychologically at least, retreat and take solace. Vasey's letters bonded him with domesticity, but for his wife they left a void, accentuating his absence. 'Letters leave so many questions in the air', she wrote in 1943; 'they bring you so near and yet leave you so far away that I am rather unbearable on that day.'[31]

The Second World War separated the Vaseys for the first time in their eighteen-year marriage. In 1921, a month after graduating from the University of Melbourne, Jessie Halbert accepted an offer of marriage from a young and dashing but rather earnest soldier, George Vasey. She was born in 1897 in Brisbane into a family of wealthy pastoralists. When the family moved to Melbourne in 1911, she was educated at two of Melbourne's elite schools for girls: briefly at Lauriston Girls School and then at Methodist Ladies College, where she was a weekly boarder. Jessie Halbert completed her schooling in 1914 and began an Arts course in 1918 at the University of Melbourne. A resident at the women's college, Janet Clarke Hall, she graduated with first-class honours in April 1921.[32]

Jessie Vasey assumed her role as a soldier's wife with confidence and ease, and her correspondence from the time the Vaseys spent in India suggests she enjoyed her time abroad while her husband pursued his career.[33] Thorpe Clark writes that she was a 'contented and complementary wife to an outstanding and popular soldier'.[34]

George Vasey was twenty-six years old when they married, but his war experience had denied him the innocence and naivety of youth. He had been recruited in his prime in 1914 to battles at Gallipoli and in France, and he returned a much-decorated soldier. After the war, Vasey joined the legion of returned men who seemed undirected and disoriented following years of harrowing combat. During the inter-war years, Vasey began to settle into domestic life. He trained as an accountant and Jessie bore their two sons, George in 1925 and Robert in 1932. But it was not the domestic world – for which he pined in wartime – to which he looked to give expression to his desires and ambitions in peacetime. His restlessness led him to serve in the army in India in the 1930s. On their return, on the eve of the Second World War, the Vaseys bought land in the Dandenong Ranges in Victoria, and a cottage, known as Tiltargara, which was surrounded by flourishing pines and gums. Jessie Vasey restored and renovated their home while her husband was in combat overseas.[35] It was to this place, where the couple hoped to plant the spectacular flowers they had discovered in India, that Vasey directed much of his nostalgia.

Apart from brief visits to Melbourne in 1942, 1944 and 1945, Jessie Vasey endured the absence of her husband for much of the war. Major-General Vasey fought in three campaigns during the time their correspondence flourished: in Libya, Crete and Greece. He sailed from Melbourne to Palestine in December 1939 with an advance party of the Second AIF comprising fifty officers and sixty other ranks. His task was to establish a 'training area, arrange administrative matters and prepare for the rest of the force'.[36] During 1940, another contingent of Australians arrived at the Suez Canal. Vasey was the chief administrative officer and responsible for providing accommodation for them.[37] In September 1940, the 6th Australian Division moved to Egypt 'to start its final training and to complete its equipment for operations'.[38]

Between January and March 1941, the Allied campaign in Libya took place. In January 1941, the British and Australian artillery of the 6th Australian Division took over Bardia and Tobruk. At the same time, the troops of the 16th Australian Infantry Brigade attacked the Italian position.[39] In April 1941, Vasey commanded defences in Greece and was central in orchestrating the Allied withdrawal to Crete.[40] In Greece, the Australians were 'hopelessly outnumbered, outranged and exposed but, in the face of mounting casualties, bravely fought throughout the day until nightfall, while their position was destroyed'.[41] Vasey was responsible for the defence of Crete and he led the Australian campaign in the region. He took charge of the administration and welfare of the Australian forces, preparing men for battle despite the disorganised force and limited resources available to him.[42] Horner concluded that in the 'defeats of Greece and Crete Vasey proved his mettle as a fighting soldier'.[43]

In 1941, Vasey returned to Palestine to retrain his brigade and then helped to defend Syria in the latter part of the year. His service in the Middle East had evidently provided 'preparation for higher command appointment'. He contributed to the establishment and training of the AIF; put training into effect in Libya; and in Greece and Crete showed a 'remarkable ability to command in war'. One diarist noted that these campaigns were 'an epic of endurance, physical and moral'.[44]

The outbreak of war in the Pacific region brought Vasey closer to home. During this period Australia was in a state of national emergency. The bombing of the American fleet at Pearl Harbor in December 1941 and the collapse of Singapore in February 1942 propelled the nation into crisis. As Australia came under the threat of invasion and attack, the tone at home became sombre and solemn. In 1942, the dawn service and the march were eliminated from the Anzac Day commemoration. This year saw two events which would be crucial to Australia's consciousness and memory of war: the Siege of Tobruk, where Australians resisted a German attack in North Africa, and the fight on the Kokoda Track, where the Japanese advance in New Guinea was halted.[45] In late 1941 and during 1942, Vasey committed his full energies to the campaigns in the Pacific. In 1942 he was stationed in Port Moresby and then sent to the Kokoda Track. In the following year, he was involved in the Gona and Sanananda campaigns against the Japanese Army in Papua New Guinea. Later in 1943 he trained soldiers in Queensland's Atherton Tableland and the Markham Valley, and during the summer of 1943–44, he was in the Ramu Valley and Shaggy Ridge. These battles stretched his stamina and strained his capacity to unify his men. Vasey experienced the vagaries of military life, through triumph and victory, frustration, disorganisation and defeat.

Vasey has been praised as a soldier and commander of men. Horner describes him as 'sensitive and intense' behind a 'brusque exterior'. In Crete, he 'came out of the campaign with an enhanced reputation for coolness and determination and with a sharpened awareness of the requirements of modern warfare, which he applied in the war'.[46] His relations with soldiers were friendly, and he exemplified 'the heroic style Australian commander and leader'.[47] Horner asserts that Vasey's great gift was that he was 'genuinely interested in the well-being of his soldiers. His tall, gaunt figure, with its dark brown hair parted in the middle, was often found in the forward areas where he could talk and joke with his soldiers, yet never lose his dignity.' He attempted to have a drink each evening with his staff.[48] But such conviviality and personable relations were not enough to sustain Vasey and it was through his letters to his wife that he attained a different type of intimacy.

Absence and Presence

Absence and presence became central motifs in exchanges between correspondents, and letters became a means of attaining intimacy. 'I have read and re-read [your letter] with infinite presence', Vasey confessed in 1941. He felt not only an emotional gap but also a physical absence: it 'will feel miserable to be moving about the city without you'. This gulf was difficult to fill. 'You speak of me being so far away and lost to you', he wrote, 'Sweetheart, I feel that is one of, if not the worst feature of all this terrible business ... I try to share things with you by my "personality" stories but otherwise it is not possible to tell you what goes on as I do at home.'

The army was, as Vasey rightly observed, an 'unnatural life'. There was much time spent waiting and absorbed in mundane activities:

It is such an unnatural life this ... there seems to be nothing but work or hanging about. The only amusements are my club and visiting in messes neither of which are very intellectual pastimes. As you know I am not a good reader and anyway with black out restrictions and the heat sitting quietly inside is not a pleasure.

The boredom was tedious and oppressive:

War has often been described as consisting of periods of intense boredom interspersed with periods of intense fight. So far we have not had the relief of the latter. Although there may be some local interest in seeing new places and so on taken by and large it is all very boring. The same people to see everyday and the same sort of thing to do everyday.

'I really get awfully bored here', he claimed in a restless mood. 'How I should love to be able to come home and blow off steam to you. I wouldn't get nearly so tired ... Letters from you are the best medicine.' The monotony was a constant source of frustration and he wrote of the 'sameness ... in the days here [where] one seems to drift into another'. The lack of intimacy he experienced in wartime made this routine even more dreary:

Sharing joys and sorrows as well as the every day happenings is a most satisfying process and really makes life worth living. To my mind the lack of that is what makes life here so tiresome. There is no-one with whom I can be quite frank. There has to be neutral reservations on all occasions and with everyone.

He was aware this absence was reciprocated. 'It must be dull and hard for you', he observed. 'For me I have varied and new interests and in between times I only live for the moment. It is the periods when I am not occupied that are so bad. Here of course with a number of us living together I am only by myself when in my room.'

Vasey was philosophical about the adjustments that had to be made. 'I suppose during this period we must re-orient ourselves somewhat and make the best of what is available.' And again,

> I know that the word happy can only be relative nowadays. Separated as we are I know neither of us are happy as we were before: but accepting that one big ache I hope both of us are as happy as circumstances permit. I'm a bit like a thermometer – up and down – I suppose one cannot be anything else in these times.

He looked to his wife to shelter him, and home affairs became a source for emotional support. 'The week has been one of work and worry except for the bright spot of your airmail of 7 Mar and [it is] marvellous of you to write all that. It put me right in the picture as regards the house and the family's affairs – all I want now are some photos. Where are the two doors onto the north verandah.' 'The worst part of this business I am on is in being away from you all – and honestly there hardly seems to be time to think of you – though perhaps that is as well in some ways.' The demand for intimacy is explicit: in 'yours of 2 Sep you said it would be a good letter if you said "I love you as much as ever". I too feel that but one of my big grouses here is that I have not the opportunity of ... really thinking about you and the boys.'

Discussing the minutiae of everyday life was not the only purpose of the letters. Intimate personal details were an important means of bringing his wife into his life. 'The news of the week is that I weighed myself and found I was 13 stone 3! Would you believe it and me and you imagining myself overworked and all that. I was in shirt and shorts so it wasn't all clothes. I don't think I [have] ever been so heavy even in the last war.' His physical appearance became the source of much commentary. His 'hair patch is as it was – I hardly think of it now ... If worry will make it worse I'm afraid I should be bald by now.' 'My hair too you can imagine what it is like. I've had the sides clipped: but the top nearly needs hair pins.' Illnesses were also commented upon.

> I am a bit concerned about your chest and cold. Your mention of it in so many letters over a period makes one wonder if it is not worse than you say ... If it has not cleared before you receive this will you promise that you get some expert advice. Mine has disappeared entirely now and I am feeling as fit as I ever have.

Vasey discussed his changing habits: 'I regret to say I am smoking cigarettes again. What a man! But I keep to Craven A – they are made specially to prevent sore throats.'[49] It was not, however, through private details alone that Vasey drew the presence of his wife into his own sphere. He did this most effectively by recreating a domestic space.

Domesticity

The 'suburban' home, it has been argued, is a place invested with particular memories.[50] The homes of returned servicemen were to be domestic havens, where the chaos and madness of war were at last to be replaced by order and predictability, by a culture of sanity. Vasey's letters anticipate this desire, for his memories of domestic life are written with a golden hue, longing for the comfort and peace of domesticity. But as both men and women were later to discover, suburban life could prove to be a shabby compensation for the emotional ruin unleashed by war.

In his letters home, Vasey looked to domestic romance as a way of displacing the experiences of war which surrounded him. This fantasy shaped Vasey's preoccupation with domestic details. He was insistent that his wife keep him connected with their domestic world, for it was one way in which he could share intimacy. 'How much I hope you will tell me of yourself, the boys, the horses, the dogs, the cats in fact of all connected with Tiltargara.'

Are you able to do anything about the potato patch? Have you considered fowls again since George was home. Eggs are becoming more and more scarce and a dozen or so fowls would provide your needs for a whole year as well as producing the odd bird for the table. I seem to be full of ideas today don't I?

He became obsessed with the renovations which his wife had undertaken on the house. 'So you have done away with the sitting room wall. What a girl! I'd laugh when I read it for haven't you been threatening to do this for months and months. What a mess the place must have been in while the job was being done!' As a way of having some control over their future, Vasey carefully followed the plans and changes of the renovations. 'All your alterations have confused me', he wrote with annoyance; 'I don't know what the place looks like now. Get George to take a photo and send it to me ... It's a great pleasure to me to know what interest and pleasure you are getting from Tiltargara. Our decision to go bush has turned out to be a marvellous one.'

Although Jessie Vasey's responses to her husband's letters have not survived, it is obvious that the correspondence was a dialogue. She kept all of his letters and would no doubt have reread them in subsequent years to relive their relationship. Vasey responded to his wife's reports of events, to her own vulnerabilities, fears and anxieties. 'Your news of the progress in the house is fine. There seems to me no doubt it really will be a house when you have finished. The painting worries me. Can you manage it. I remember how long it took me when I did it and I imagine you have got to do the whole place.' He attempted to empathise with her predicament. 'How I enjoyed reading of your doings at Tiltargara, though

I absolutely agree that, in the present crisis, it is almost too much for you. I think you are just marvellous how you are carrying on improving the place when labour is so limited and you are so tied up with your work in the city.' Vasey felt frustrated with the gender role reversal which characterised the homefront in wartime. 'It makes me wild to realise I am not in it doing it myself', he wrote in exasperation. 'But if that cannot be hearing what you are doing is the very next best.' He could not be engaged with 'productive' labour in the home, the traditional masculine domain. 'I feel awfully wild when I hear all you are doing at Tiltargara', he confessed. 'How I wish I were there to help you with your painting, bricklaying and other activities. In my depressed moments I wonder whether I would not be better employed doing these things than here.'

Nature represented not only the realm of domestic tranquillity but also became a source of security. Vasey's questions invited comment from his reader and drew their worlds together. 'This is a great Country for flowers', wrote Vasey; 'they grow well here provided they are watered. At present the fields are covered in red poppies. Our table for lunch was decorated with carnations ... a youth came in selling lovely rose buds. Talking of roses – how did ours stand the hot weather.' 'There is a bit of a garden round this cottage and I pushed a lawn mower this morning but not for long. The combination of long buffalo grass and power mower was too much.' Vasey focused on the specifics of the garden and his idealisation of it suggests the way he romanticised his wife's presence within his domestic haven. 'Imagine the whole garden must be looking very well now. How are all the iris – including the bed of babies you planted last year. Are any of them at the blooming stage. And George's gladioli are they making a show this year.' 'I suppose all the trees are showing green now', he speculated in spring. 'The wattle I imagine is over already. It is now that you will find out first what trees have died owing to the wet. Will you let me have a casualty list.' In this attention to detail, Vasey made the garden a central point of reference. 'There are quite a few flowers about here – rather poor specimens actually but flowers all the same', he observed. 'There are lots of vines, apricots and walnuts but of course all the fruit is gone now. Yesterday I saw the biggest vine I ever imagined. It was at least a foot through at the base and had branches as thick as your arm.' Horticulture became an important part of his connection with the domestic world and he noticed relevant horticultural details wherever he was. The progress of the vegetables also absorbed him. 'I was interested in the news of the vegetable garden. I was looking at a *Leader* today and saw pictures of some of the market gardens down Moorabbin way.' He was pleased that his son George shared his passions. 'I am pleased to hear [George's] interest in gardening continues. I can see George V and Son being florists when we have disposed of this swine

Hitler and his minions.' The garden also suggested to Vasey the possibility of an alternative to his career in the army. 'The way things are developing it seems more and more unlikely that I shall remain in the army long after the war and I do want to have the basis for augmenting the pittance a grateful government will give me after I have paid for it.' Vasey presented a romanticised idyll of domestic life in these letters which inspired him to look elsewhere to map his future. 'Do you wonder I want to retire to Tiltargara to live with you and grow flowers', he insisted. 'I don't think they believe me – and say they will see a truck running about with, painted on it GAV Florist.'

His sons, George and Robert, aged seventeen and ten respectively, in 1942 become a focus of concern. George would soon be of military age. 'I am disappointed that he still shows no improvement in his outlook towards everything. Actually I'm not sure that he isn't only a little worse than I was at his age. I am afraid I recognise some of my characteristics developed along a rather new line.' He had continuing conversations with Jessie regarding George's talents and abilities. In 'the ordinary scholastic sense he is not too hot is he', he observed.

I am convinced it would not only be a great waste of money; but very prejudicial to George's future to send him back to [Geelong] grammar ... Other than the education department Tech schools are there no institutions that cater for technical education ... I told George he would not be returning to Grammar: but would either go to a tech school or some jobs where he would be able to continue his education.

The impact of paternal absence concerned him. 'I do not want our boys to feel they can't talk over their troubles and difficulties with me.' 'This ... will be a great week for Rob – his first appearance at a real big school and George's too. Is he very excited about it ...?' The familial separation caused him considerable anxiety: 'I hope the upset of a very happy family will do him no harm.' He was concerned at being displaced from the responsibilities of the head of the household. 'Your recounting of the bills paid makes me quite jealous – even at this distance I get a certain amount of kick out of it. It is a great relief to me to know you are rid of all those bills and have been able to get so much done about the place.'

Mention of family anniversaries was another way in which Vasey could connect himself with the rhythms of domestic life. 'This is your birthday letter now sweetheart', he wrote in October 1940.

I had thought it would be separate ... How I wish I were with you to wish you many happy returns myself instead of writing it. For twenty years now I have always been able to do it in person. How dull and lonely is the separation business. I believe I once said I would like it. Believe me, I take it all back! Give both the boys my love sweetheart, but remember they are incidentals. You are my interest.

It was necessary to understand the circumstances. 'Your birthday and here I am miles and miles away and only able to write to you. It is dull, very dull sweetheart, but it is in a good cause and I am sure that neither of us would wish it otherwise in the present circumstances.' Christmas became another marker of absence and presence: 'This is your second Xmas with me away and may it be the last for the boys I hope it is a very happy day and for you sweetheart I hope it is a day when, in the absence of one who cares most for you, others will do their best to make it a day of happiness for you too.'[51]

Jessie Vasey's Correspondence

The correspondence between the Vaseys was also important in allaying Jessie Vasey's feelings of loss and absence. She discussed her daily routine with her husband. In particular, her political manoeuvres were of interest to him. 'I am sure your Women's Association is a worry: but it is an interest too and brings you in contact with a lot of people which I am sure you [will] enjoy as well as being good for you.' He marvelled at her success in the various organisations in which she was involved. 'I am delighted to hear of your success both at Red Cross and "organising". I have always known you were a clever woman and am pleased others are beginning to realise it.' He was extremely supportive of her:

How delighted I am at the success of your meeting, both as a personal triumph for you as well as an excellent start for a vulnerable institution ... it is a tremendous pleasure to us – at least there is some scope for your energy and talent. You are sure to have lots of troubles with some of your people, but you will overcome them.[52]

Vasey was a supportive companion for her, putting in perspective the political bickering of the AIF Women's Association. The association was formed in 1940 to bring together the wives of men on active service.[53] The organisation absorbed much of Jessie Vasey's energies and was apparently a source of much angst, as her husband pointed out:

I am afraid your Women's Association is proving too much for you. It seems to have taken you away from your beloved garden and hardly gives you time to think of yourself and your family. Further than that it seems it must be a source of mental worry for you. The bitches with whom you come in contact appear too tiresome for words ... It is definitely no good both of us becoming aged during this blasted war ...

He insisted that she monitor her activity. 'What a trial that work has been to you and most of them ... only doing it because they had to or because they got or hoped to get, some kudos out of it ... less work for you will certainly be no harm.' Vasey attempted to comfort her: 'you are having a more trying time with your association than you have admitted. Your letter is that of a very depressed woman. God knows this is a depressing time.' He gave legitimacy to her frustrations when she had complained: 'you must blow off steam too. Don't be concerned at letting me hear of your worries. We each feel better for having written of them I'm sure.' To Vasey, her experience seemed a 'very mixed blessing', but he encouraged her to be more assertive: 'Of course I am interested to hear of your AIF Women's Association – firstly to learn just how much you are doing for them and secondly to be in a position to tell you when I think you are doing too much!' He was responsive when political machinations affected her: 'From them all I gather that our own family, that is the boys, are not a source of trouble to you: but that your troubles come mostly from other quarters.' Vasey offered his advice: 'I am sorry to hear that the Association has been hanging so heavily on you and only hope that Mrs L does in fact do something to remedy the present impossible situation.' He also encouraged her to confide in him. 'Tell me just how much pleasure and how much annoyance do you get out of your association. It seems to be a very mixed blessing, though I am sure the work you are doing is a most important one and if not done by you and pushed by you would not be done at all.'

Vasey's description of a photograph sent to him by his wife suggested a nostalgia for the domestic. His observation of the detail in the photograph was a romanticised representation of the world he longed for and missed. 'I loved the one of you, Rob, and the dogs taken near the cherry trees, which apparently were in bloom', he noted.

> It is a pleasure to see how things are progressing and the one of Thelma and dogs shows how well the front verandah looks with its bricks. I like the white, pleated frock you are wearing ... the weeds on the paths are growing well: but everything else seems to be growing well [sic]. Rob looks the same dirty little ruffian as ever. The ground still seems to be his favourite seat.

The thought of returning home bolstered him. 'Believe me sweetheart the thought of having ... Tiltargara [which] you will have built and planned, to come home to as a place for being with my family is the most cheery one I have.'[54]

As for so many others before and after him, this domestic life, for which he longed so desperately, was a world which he would never know. On one of his intermittent returns to Australia, he perished. In March

1945, six months before the end of the Second World War, George Vasey died when the plane in which he was a passenger was briefly diverted and then lost its way in making the turn back to the aerodrome. The plane apparently slipped sideways and plummeted into the sea, near Cairns in North Queensland. The number of casualties was not high, just six army officers in a war which claimed the lives of almost 34 000 Australians. But it did not go unnoticed by the press; one report claimed that it was 'one of the most tragic air disasters for some years'.[55] What was significant about this accident – tragic as it was because it occurred in the calm of civilian life away from the bloodied fields of Europe – was that it claimed the lives of some of Australia's foremost commanders who had led Australia's wartime campaign. Tributes flowed from around the country. The daily papers carried lengthy and detailed profiles of the men who died, eulogising their military careers and lauding their contribution to the war effort. The *Argus* solemnly announced that Vasey's death in particular was an 'untimely accident [which] has dealt this country its most serious blow'.[56]

The mode of death, claims David Cannadine, determines the method of mourning.[57] Accidental death seems to be the most tragic of all. It provokes desperate questioning of the meaning and purpose of premature loss, and of the injustice and futility of a life robbed by chance. Vasey's death was met by a chorus of accolades from colleagues, friends and acquaintances, who saluted his full life of service, commitment and self-sacrifice. But the news was also received with a profound sense of missed opportunities, a sentiment which heightened the intensity of his loss.

Vasey's letters are a testimony to the importance of the idyllic, mythic and nostalgic view of the world of home and hearth, which he projected as a way of displacing the haunting experience of war. Jessie Vasey was fortunate in maintaining this correspondence, for it helped fill the void she was forced to endure. Others whose men were absent yearned for their absences to be filled in a similar way.

On the Homefront: Yearning for News

The rituals of death had been transformed by the beginning of the Second World War. By 1938, fewer funerals left in a procession from the house than was the practice fifty years before. The advent of the motor car meant that the tradition of the long-drawn-out funeral procession was ended, while the custom of wearing black crepe was not as prevalent, although men and women continued to dress in black.[58] Public mourning rituals had disappeared, to be replaced by a less public display.[59] This led, as others have noted, to an 'increasingly internal, psychological process' where the mourner was no longer 'integrated into a social network of grief'.[60] By 1939, the massive death toll of the Great War, the devastating impact of the influenza epidemic of 1919, and the increasing secularisation of society, had resulted in 'fewer displays of grief and mourning' for the dead. Death was 'unwelcome and the extended periods of mourning were not continued'.[61]

For those who waited desperately for news, the homefront was barren and void, a volatile and contingent place, where their emotional lives remained in a state of flux. Absence was replaced by an obsession with a vociferous desire for detail about the serving soldier. This was a way in which parents could absorb themselves in the presence of the soldier and defy the possibility of death. As in the First World War, the war drew together a community of those awaiting death, seeking to share emotional trauma, as well as sustaining a continuity of the memory of their sons with others.[62] Mrs Roberta Miller wrote to the family of Wilfred Burrows, who had perished in action in 1943, in desperate need of information about her son Col:

Each and every day we have clung to the hope we may receive news of Col, until it is now in the thirteenth week and still the silence ... we received a most beautiful letter from a Mrs Keddie, who used to entertain our boys after church every Sunday evening, and she very thoughtfully enclosed your home address ... I do hope I hear from you, as we seem to be known to one another, although we haven't met ... Wilf and Col had an understanding if either failed to return they would look after one another's personal belongings to be sent home, so now we will have to rely on the Air Force, as I know of no other boy other than the crew and Wilf, who was intimate with him ...

She had located the families of men on the crew. 'I am very friendly with another one of the boy's mothers, [that of] Don Charlwood, – perhaps Wilf has spoken of him in your letters, and his letters home are the only connection I have left now of the news of the twenty boys who trained in Canada.' She had been most active in contacting other relatives: 'I have written to Col's pilot's wife, Mrs Morphett in W.A and she is still hoping like us all. Keith Bond from NSW was the air-gunner in Col's crew and we have contacted his people too ... As you will see, I have followed the boys' doings closely.'[63]

The absence of news created a tenuousness, where the waiting was intolerable. Ann Quinn wrote in desperation:

I and the wives of Noel's crew have been so anxious for news. We have been trying to find out details from any and every source available and consequently the stories were many and varied. To get the true story is a relief even though it still leaves everything in the air. I shall continue to hope for their safe return though it will be a long wait.[64]

One mother described the news through absence as 'the fearful shock one is dealt by the shattering news of the loss of one's son in air operations ... Like so many mothers all the world over, I can now only wait, & hope & pray.'[65]

Others wrote to their sons in vain in the hope of contacting them. 'You may never get this letter,' wrote the mother of Sergeant-Pilot Leonard Williams, with high hopes in 1942, 'but I feel that I must write ... if only a few lines. If you are in the land of the living son you will know you have been posted as missing and I'm sure you have felt that we have been very near you this week ... I'm just hoping you know son we love you so and have missed you much.'[66] His father wrote similarly: 'Just wherever you are you are still our Son, and the week that has passed since we received the telegram ... has only made the Bond between us the stronger. You are more than ever now the subject of many very fervent Prayers.' Crissie Prettejohn expressed this desperation to the Chaplain E. Webber: 'It means so much to a widowed Mother, to hear news of her boys [I have two in the Forces] especially when they are thousands of miles from home. Even if the news is sad, I think everything should be told [to] the Mothers.'[67] Another woman wrote: 'These are indeed terrible days for those who have menfolk at the front. A friend of mine, till lately, had heard nothing of one of her twin sons, who was taken prisoner at Singapore; and the other twin and his father are in the forces here. She has taken a war job which takes up all the morning, to "keep her mind off things".'[68]

The longing created by absence was expressed by one mother. 'We have been listening in to the Boys over there talking on the wireless', wrote one mother, and 'I wish you could talk to us one night it would be great to hear your voice [on] air.' Her letters become conveyers of domestic detail and daily events of the homefront: 'if you were here dear things would be swell. We miss you dreadfully Dearest. Home is not the same since you went away ... give our kindest regards to all your friends and tell them we still think of them and pray that it won't be long before you are all home again'.[69] These letters recorded the attempts to create a presence out of absence – 'we are always talking about you and what you would do or say if you were here' – and the counting of time and days – 'you have been away three months this Friday, and it seems like three years. We miss you terribly.'

Even when death was likely, relatives were sustained by the possibility that their men might have survived, as hope could temper the uncertainty of waiting. One wife wrote to Chaplain Trathen thanking him for details of the accident which apparently had killed her husband. 'In spite of all you know to be true', she wrote, 'I still find it hard to give up hope completely ... praying for miracles.'[70] Marjorie Bailey expressed similar sentiments. A mother of three children, aged between five and three months, Bailey wrote, 'my heart is just frozen it's nearly twelve months since we have seen him'.

> Strange to say I have every hope and believe he is alive somewhere, even a prisoner. I hope so anyway. I have just been praying and hoping in God that Jack may turn up somewhere, I have also had some masses said for him and that is all I can do . . . we are all still hoping and praying that it won't be long before we hear some news of him . . .[71]

A small fragment of hope sustained many parents. One mother wrote asking Chaplain Trathen,

> do you think the crew had gone with him or would there be any possible hope for them to bail out & perhaps be taken prisoner, only seeing that we have not been notified only to say that Geoff was missing I wondered if we can go on hoping, my daughter is just living on her hopes . . .[72]

Another wrote, 'We are all hoping to hear some news of him soon, as so many of the boys are turning out of the bush, and we must go on hoping and praying for a safe return.'[73] Desperate questions were asked of incidents in which their sons had been involved. Ben Drakes asked the chaplain:

> Do you think the crew – or even one of the crew – could have parachuted from the bomber before it crashed and perhaps have got to shore on enemy territory – the bomber going further on, on its own for some time? And how did it become known that it came to within 50 miles of the home base – were they in contact by wireless on the return journey?[74]

As others have noted, it was the Second World War that enshrined the figure of the prisoner of war in collective memory.[75] By 1942, over 22 000 Australians were prisoners of the Japanese. If we include those captured in North Africa, Greece and Crete, 30 000 Australians were being held. These numbers were significant in a small sized population. As a result, most Australians knew a prisoner of war, or the relatives of one. As Hank Nelson observes: 'Most of the relatives of the men and fifty-nine women captured by the Japanese heard no definite word during the first year, and even by September 1943 there were still some 5000 Australians who were thought to have been captured, but whose names had appeared on no lists, and who had sent no letters and made no broadcasts.'[76] That is not to say that relatives had no impression from which to formulate a sense of the fate of their men. Reports filtered through of atrocities. In 1944, news was reaching the homes of Australians of the death of 2000 of the

10 000 Australian troops in Burma and Thailand. Numbers proved to be higher, of course, with 2800 dead and 13 000 Australians having worked on the railway. But during the war, 'anxiety in every home connected to the prisoners was high'.[77]

During this period, the relatives of prisoners of war emerged as a distinctive group whose lives became inextricably tied to wartime news. Following the surrender of Singapore in February 1942, the families of prisoners of war endured four years of uncertainty. The anticipation of loss was a form of bereavement: it shared the characteristics of actual loss, like shock, denial and sadness. When death did eventually come for those Australians taken prisoner by the Japanese – in all 7777, or just over one-third, died in captivity[78] – another process of mourning was set in train.[79] Networks were established through the efforts of the Red Cross, the media and the government which provided relatives with a community of support. In January 1942, relatives formed the Prisoners of War Relatives Association in Sydney, and in June a Melbourne branch was formed.[80] The AIF Women's Association also offered a support network for relatives of prisoners of war. Friends and relatives would gather at monthly meetings where they would read letters aloud from prisoners of war. In September 1942 this practice was outlawed, because it was felt that 'too much circulating of good news about prisoners of war had a bad effect on the morale of our troops and civilian population'. The gatherings would nevertheless continue, 'for people whose sons were prisoners together were able to meet and to talk about them and thus comfort each other'.[81] In replicating the relationships experienced by their husbands and sons, relatives felt they would be closer to their men.

News was erratic and unreliable. During the course of the war, the press in particular was an important source of information about prisoners. In June 1942, the first mail service was introduced where relatives could send letters – of one sheet only – once a month, although it took about a year for such letters to reach prisoners.[82] By the following month, a parcel service was in operation.[83] Those who sent messages drew strength from these services as they provided hope that they would not have to accept the news of death.

As in the First World War, information became imperative. The *Argus* ran a War Prisoners' Next of Kin column in 1942, and in 1944 provided a space entitled 'Messages to POW' where readers would air their grievances.[84] In 1943, after the Japanese authorities stipulated that relatives could send only twenty-five words and that these had to be typewritten, the Melbourne *Sun* offered a typing service.[85]

This public expression of grief, and an assertion of the rights of relatives of prisoners to know more, assisted in the process of articulating a politics of grief. As the possibility of death heightened with each month that the prisoners were held in captivity, the demands of relatives became more insistent. In 1944, one woman wrote with great indignation at the apparent neglect by governments of their predicament. As in Europe, wives of prisoners of war endured hardship and loneliness.[86] 'The women-folk of prisoners of war', she argued, 'had borne the hardest burdens.' These women through 'long weeks, months, years they have waited, some in hope, but too many in an agony of suspense for news of the men they love, who may be dead, missing, prisoners in some dreaded camp'. It was now time to demand a better service from the government:

We must insist on a better system of communication, fairer distribution of the right to send messages ... It is time for women concerned, and those whose sympathy is with them ... to demonstrate in no uncertain manner. Let the Government cease sheltering behind the ineptitude of minor officials ... otherwise, let the women act.[87]

By 1945, the relatives of prisoners were demanding privileges. Sydney Smith, the secretary of the New South Wales branch of the Australian Prisoners of War Relatives Association, wrote to the Prime Minister John Curtin, requesting a priority permit for travelling interstate. 'My Association finds itself at a great disadvantage', he wrote,

because we do not possess any Priority Permit for the purpose of travelling by rail or plane between the various States. It is often very necessary for me ... to attend meetings ... regarding matters pertaining to Australian Prisoners of War ... [but] am often unable to make the trip because I do not possess a Priority Permit.[88]

Many of the condolence letters which soldiers wrote to their comrades' families were filled with details about the atrocities soldiers endured in Japanese camps. These tales of endurance and survival were to shape family narratives as it was through such details that a continuity and cohesion in family memories was established. Warrant Officer David Smith died in 1943 while a prisoner of war. The condolence letters detail his condition before death. One chaplain reported that he had died 'from the effects of malnutrition and malaria ... died very quickly'.[89] Another case in the camps was described in terms to ease the pain. Noel Kettlewell, a captain in the British Army, wrote to the mother of Flying Officer Vernon Smith in 1945, outlining the circumstances of his death. 'On the whole', he wrote, 'the officers in the Kuching camps were not seriously ill treated and a very few suffered from physical violence. Malnutrition was the major hardship and the main cause of your husband's death.'[90] Army officials could not always provide adequate information in relation to prisoners of war. Harold Copelin's death (he died while a prisoner in Sandakan) drew the following response from an official to his father: the 'Japanese Government ... failed to comply with the terms of the Geneva Convention, one of which provides for the prompt interchange of information regarding Prisoners of War'.[91] The fact that Japan had not been a signatory to the Geneva Convention meant that the usual rules in the POW camps did not apply. The Japanese contempt for the prisoners heightened the traumatic impact of losing a relative in these camps.[92]

Others advertised for information regarding the death of their sons or husbands. Private Lewis Wynn died in 1943 during internment as a prisoner of war. His mother placed an advertisement in the *Sun* requesting information. At this stage, the full extent of conditions in camp life was unknown. One Captain Mills replied:

after acute stages of cholera have been overcome the patient is free of all symptoms but is extremely exhausted, and that is the stage recovery depends on good conditions, good food rather than any special treatment ... we did not have good conditions nor good food and his severe illness proved too much ... he passed away quickly in that quiet part of that dreadful area.[93]

Those who replied to her request were certainly cautious and sensitive of the impact such news may have on relatives. ''Tis not my intention at this stage to reopen such a wound,' one correspondent replied, '[but] the information I have related, irrespective of what the military may have said, is sincere and without any doubt the entire truth ... so many parents have been given so many different tales'.[94] The details of camp life and conditions remained crucial in shaping family histories. One soldier wrote to a mother, claiming that the circumstances of her son's death were never as she may have thought:

After the action was over, a number of our surviving were, to the everlasting disgrace of the Japanese beasts, put to death. It was not until the war was over, nearly four years later, that this was discovered. I would like you to believe, as I do, that your son was one of those who met his death in action. You will realise that this is just as possible as that he was one of those unfortunate prisoners who was killed later by Japanese murderers.[95]

As in the First World War, the absence of a body and, in some cases, the lack of information of how their men perished, especially in the camps, made it difficult for families to allow for the closure of death, for its finality.[96] Among relatives of prisoners of war, anticipating death created another form of bereavement and loss. The impact of these processes is especially stark in the experience of mothers and widows, the subject of the following chapters.

7   Grieving Mothers

> 'Tis hard not to fret for our dear ones and we wonder why we are picked out for such sorrow. I often go to see Mrs Cole ... He was her only child. We have made friends with one another, through our maternal sorrow and try to help one another ...[1]

Lieutenant George Gill was killed while serving in the 2/48th Battalion in 1942. Gill's mother was shattered when she received the telegram which announced his death. Her initial outcry was a response of shock and raw emotion. She wrote to her daughter describing her anguish:

> I was alone at the time and almost dressed to go into town. The cable came and as usual I hunted for my glasses, asking myself 'is it joy or sorrow', decided it was joy ... Can you imagine the shock? We regret and inform you etc ... I've had just one line of callers and so far about 50 letters and many telegrams ... Everybody tells me how brave I am – Ede Mitchell expected to find me prostrated. I told her a brave son must have a brave mother; but darling more than half my waking hours I can't believe it ... I'm heart broken and the dreadful 'never again' is more than I can bear. I feel that half my world has gone. I shouldn't say it I know, but no son could have been loved more. No need to tell you my feelings. I fear you are broken hearted too, and we are so helpless, can do nothing ... Everybody [has been] most kind, *but* nothing can bring him back. My tears are very close but Julie [her daughter] sits before me and sees my every move and I dare not. Alone, in my bed I can do as I feel and cry my heart out for him. Isn't it all so sad?[2]

She reflected on how her son's future had been so traumatically eclipsed:

> Marjorie Fulcher has been very close to me. She has loved him for years and feels his loss very keenly ... all my boy deserved ... He told me he loved her and would ask her to marry him on his return. His photos came only a few days before we heard, and he smiles in them and looks so happy. I can't believe he has gone.

The routine of daily life provided the mechanisms for coping:

> The first few nights Julie and I were alone and we sat before the fire with folded hands and were almost dumb. I'm not looking very far ahead, just living from day

to day. Tis Saturday afternoon and no callers. I think most friends and acquaintances have been. Just imagine it, my rising and doing things as usual, breakfasts . . . clean fire place, wash up, beds and rushing to be presentable before callers come. Perhaps the necessary things saved my life. No. I'm not wearing black. Julie objected and we both think our dear one wouldn't wish it . . . don't worry for me – I too am a soldier.[3]

As the days proceeded, she began to imagine a life without her son, preferring to be left alone to experience her grief:

My heart is breaking at my loss – You know how I loved him, but darling I won't go under. Your mother is made of sterner stuff than that. Through my sorrow I'm proud of my boy. Thank God for the beautiful 27 years of his life. I must send a copy of a letter received yesterday. I wept but it was a lovely letter . . . I'm feeling very keenly for you dear. You are no doubt sorrowing both for me and for your brother – but we can do nothing – just weep and try to see the silver lining. There must be one somewhere . . . I've not been out anywhere and somehow have no wish to go . . . I'd naturally like to have someone of my own round me . . .[4]

She took comfort in the public accolades her son received. 'One hears of such wonderfully nice things said of Boy. All men both returned and abroad speak of him with the highest praise. One man recently speaking at Legacy Club meeting mentioned Boy as all that was fair and just and one of the best soldiers in his Battalion.'[5] Her pain was not all grief. 'Of course I weep tears, but often they are tears of pride and love, as well as our loss.'

The desolation experienced by mothers like Mrs Gill has not figured in histories of the Second World War. Our understanding of how Australian women lived through the war has been shaped largely through the experiences of young single women. The stories of mothers of deceased sons, and of widows, do not fit easily into the narratives of liberated munitions workers or tales of new sexual pleasures which have come to symbolise women's experience during the war. In making the public sphere of paid work and entertainment a priority, historians have replicated the hierarchy which has concentrated on women's public activity at the expense of their private, domestic experience.

If women's emotions have extended into consideration, they have been those of passion, desire and sexual adventure. Marilyn Lake's pathbreaking work has suggested ways in which the war shaped a new femininity. Women's pursuit of romance and sexual pleasure has become the prism through which women's history on the homefront has been written.[6] Other scholars have followed this lead, noting how women's lives were transformed through their encounter with heterosexual romance, sexual adventure and lesbianism.[7] But for other women, it was not sexual pleasure which gave the war its defining expression, but loss and grief; their femininity was not one of pleasure and glamour but of sacrifice and mourning.[8]

These moments of anguish were never to leave grieving mothers, but publicly, their individual grief was dissipated into a body of statistics. It is through global figures that the magnitude of war is conveyed. The statistics – 6 million Jews killed, 20 million Soviet casualties, over 3 million Russian prisoners of war killed in Germany – are often quoted.[9] But, as others have asked, 'what does statistical exactitude mean, where the orders of magnitude are so astronomic?'[10] Does this numerical containment distance the grief of war, its ghastliness and grotesqueness, so that it is managed and easy to digest? In the transformation of a private individual memory to a public, collective one, it is the specificity of individual grief which is lost. Once the memory of war becomes generic, a mother's sacrifice becomes invisible.

Through an examination of *individual* grief we can see how mothers' experience was acknowledged and valued in the private realm, even if in public it is not seen as *the* primary sacrifice. Mothers did not attain the same sacrificial status as they did during the course of the First World War, possibly because conscription was not a contentious issue. Unlike the bitterness of the earlier war, Australians were prepared to accept a system whereby, until 1942, men were conscripted locally while volunteers served abroad. But from January 1943, Australian men were called upon for compulsory military training.[11] As Australia's shores were threatened with attack, the need for overseas conscription was accepted by those, like Prime Minister Curtin, who had earlier been critical of it. Here, unlike the earlier war, there was no public exhortation to mothers to give their sons. Their grief, however, was as profound and, as others have argued, the rupturing of the maternal relationship could have devastating effects on both mother and child.[12]

Mythologies of war were shaped within what Maurice Halbwach refers to as 'domestic memory', as families began to write their own narratives and traditions.[13] For an understanding of this, it is necessary to look at how the homefront and the battlefront were separated in Australia, and how a community of mourners was brought together in particular ways.

Individual Grief

Grief is an individual journey. One experience of mourning and loss can be charted in the diary of Una Falkiner. Falkiner, a leading light of the upper classes in the Riverina district in New South Wales, was married to the wealthy pastoralist Otway Falkiner.[14] She was his second wife – his first having died young – and she cared for his three children before bearing two of her own, a daughter and a son.[15] In January 1922, Falkiner experienced the death of her daughter at twenty months, after a three-month illness. She became protective of her son and shocked herself at the thought of the possibility of his premature death.[16]

Twenty years later, her worst fears were confirmed as she relived the trauma of losing a child. In September 1942, Falkiner's son, John, died in a plane accident while in combat. The air force casualties were high in a war which was fought as much in the air as on the ground. The official casualty figures for the air force recorded that there were 10 000 men killed in action in a total number of 34 000 Australian deaths. About 12 per cent of the total of Australia's war deaths occurred in bomber command alone.[17] Falkiner's son was included in these statistics, a death she perceived in terms of the obliteration of light: 'Life has stopped for me today! and hence forth I shall go through my time left with the blinds down. The sun and radiance have ceased to sparkle ... The day seemed 100 years I felt 100 but I know He is safe in his father's House. Safe, safe, at last!'[18] It was with this mixture of heightened euphoric pride, a religious sense of purpose, and yet bitter disappointment that she received the news of her son's death:

All night, all night! and in the day time too, I always pray that our gallant son still be safe and in His father's keeping and I know when he goes up over, John's hand is in God's and he will be guided by His divine wisdom ... It is wonderful for him! and to be in the glory unspeakable ... But one cannot not help being so disappointed, bitterly, that he could not have been left here to be an inspiration to those he met, in his path of life – He stood like a rock for good! and all that was beautiful.

Falkiner's journey through grief was charted through nostalgia and sentimentality, the paradox being that, in making his name 'shine' with glory, her own world was eclipsed:

He was passionately fond of children and was so looking forward to his home and happiness and when he would have time to write, which he did so charmingly, and would have done so brilliantly and his wit was as keen as a knife, I mean quick! and always to the point and amusing not to hurt ever! ... and he did the most brilliant shooting ever done at the University ... When John was a little boy he always said he would make his name to shine! and he Has! ... The sun and radiance have ceased to sparkle ...[19]

The first Christmas spent without John was recorded as 'All radiance flown from life!'[20] After a year-long anniversary of his death, 'it seems an aeon since our darling was called home ... But I know how glorious and happy he will be in loveliness & light.'[21] The shades of darkness and light mirror the contrasts of nostalgia and regret, pride and sorrow which carried Falkiner through grief.

Anniversaries reactivated the mourning process and were celebrated with private rituals.[22] 'Sunday! The first Sunday on earth for 24 years without my John Alexander! "Mother mine!" and "Darling" were his names for me!' A year after his death she wrote, 'Otway and I both feel ill & broken hearted this evening.' Mother's Day held a special place in her memory: 'I will never forget the last Mother's Day our darling spent on earth, he sent me that very beautiful box of chocolates ... all kinds of sweets chosen by ... John A. Falkiner in London for his Mother to arrive on Mother's Day.' After four years, the recollection had not faded: 'This is the day four years ago our darling John was called to his reward. We grieve for his footsteps not coming & going with ours but we rejoice that he is where he is in all happiness, serving his God.'

A retreat into nostalgia and sentimentality – into a world without loss – protected her from the pangs of despair, in the ever-present interplay between absence and presence. John's death rekindled idealised family memories, which became a part of the process of denial. In one entry she wrote, 'Otway just reminded me of John and Nurse Wilson ... a Scotch girl who was splendid and loved him. "It is your birthday John and you can be naughty today if you want to!" [she said] ... "Nursie", said John, 'Can I *have* that naughty day another day?" Six years old, he was.' On another occasion, she asked her son, 'John dear, How are you going to keep your trousers up without braces and a belt?' to which he replied, 'I'll keep them up by will power, like Dad does!' On the last outing she recalled,

I pictured again the scene, when my angel boy left for Canada ... [we] were bobbing about in our little launch below his ship, the Monterey, & how we sailed down ... right to the bridge, beside his big ship which gained momentum ... how [he] stood with his little knot of friends, waving, two newspapers in his hands, his arms stretched out then over his head! So distinctive so I did the same on the launch – the last time to see him – our adored.

In another reflection, 'He loved the great out doors in all its phases & painted a beautiful sunset when he was six years old.' A call from Geelong Grammar where he had been educated rekindled another memory: 'Really he was good at all sports ... Always, always I think of him.' The task of distributing clothes revived the pain. 'I went over my darling John's beautiful suits & ties, & distributed them where I think he would have liked them to go.' His remaining possessions seemed few and somehow diminished: 'Our darling John's personal belongings have arrived in Australia & are being sent to us, the list seems so meagre.'

It is in these narratives that family mythologies were made where the loss of life at such an early age inspired the elevation of it through sacrifice and honour:

> we that are left on this beautiful earth to be bereft of the delight of our dear ones & the flower of my life ... who gave his ... life so manfully 24 years he has been our joy! ... everyone who met him fell to his simplicity & charm & wit ... we know the sterling worth of his boyish wish to be in arms ...

If the bomber had been under her son's instructions, Falkiner believed it would have been saved: 'flying under John's brains, would have saved it'. Another friend pointed to the idealisation of death at a young age. 'I am glad that you can think of him as alive', wrote Mary McLarty; 'John will never know the burden of age or illness or loss. His short life was perfect.' This fantasy of a perfect life provided protection, a way of coping with premature death, as a new 'family' had to be constituted without her son.

Falkiner sought comfort from others whose lives had been blighted by death. Mothers who had lost sons shared their experiences and offered their condolences. One correspondent wrote:

> Allow me as one Mother to another [who] understands what you are suffering at present, you loved John dearly and so did I love my own darling John dearly ... Oh! Mrs. Falkiner though written or spoken words do little to heal the constant heartache which separation from our loved ones brings was – still – to know that the loving thoughts of others are with us in a time of loss such as your own and mine does help considerably. I sincerely trust that you will be sustained and strengthened in your great sorrow.

This sort of support was comforting, but not enough to sustain her: 'I still feel I will wake up presently from a nightmare.' But her own sorrow made her alert to the pain of others: 'Poor Newman Family!' she wrote when she read the news of the death of Sergeant-Pilot Arthur John Newman. 'Their eldest son Bill gone. I had hoped he was a prisoner.' Strength came from other soldiers who had known John. In March 1944, Falkiner packed a picnic basket for Bob Appleton,

> John's bomber & 2nd pilot, who is holidaying at a Cottage in Palm Beach, with his wife & little daughter. He is such a dear boy & loved our John with a love that they had often faced death together & joy. He was so proud that John had got his promotion just the day before he was taken.

Above all Falkiner took refuge in religious explanations. As a committed spiritualist, she attempted to make contact with her son. In June 1944 she wrote,

Never did I expect to hear my darling son John speak again till I went to Heaven but there he was! ... The lady lecturer said everyone loved him. So! smiling & bright & the work he had chosen was stupendous & he was doing magnificently. John said himself that ... words fail to say how delighted he was that I had opened the door ... It was too amazing and marvellous! 'I am doing my best', He kept saying & I longed to know what his best was.

The spiritual dimension of this experience was never far away, as it served as a defence against her loss:

I was lying in bed, full of thoughts in the early hours this morning – when – out of the surrounding darkness my beautiful boy's face appeared. It gathered momentum and grew and smiled so brightly at me, like one of the suns of the morning! and was gone. So that is how my John wants us to remember him and to know he is radiantly happy.

Finally, she spoke to him directly. 'After lunch', she recorded in September 1948, 'I had the most wonderful talk with my John ... through Mrs Templeton. John was able to speak himself this time for the first time! Wonderful! After telling me Lovely things, he said, "Would it interest you to know that I have risen lately?" '[23]

While the influence of spiritualism has been identified among mourners of the First World War,[24] there has been little research undertaken on those who had lost family members during the Second.[25] Leading organisations like the Spiritualist Association of Great Britain, formed in 1872, continued to operate, but there was no discernible increase in membership or activity during the war years. The 'spirit guides' may have lost some of their credibility when they emphatically assured their hearers that there would be no war.[26] Falkiner was not alone in attempting to reach deceased soldiers. The association in Britain recorded one episode during the war whereby one of their guides 'received spirit communications from dead airmen through the hand of a non-professional medium'. In 1943, four soldiers who had been killed 'became regular communicators at a special ... circle arranged by the famous medium'. The parents of the soldiers were invited to attend.[27] There was a proliferation of mainly British autobiographical accounts and manuals during this time, which Falkiner could have read.[28] At a time when the 'spectre of death' loomed large over a society, a philosophy gained currency which claimed that communication with the dead was possible through 'the mediumship of certain people, who inherit well developed psychic faculties'.[29] Others wrote of their existential experiences; in July 1944 Mrs A. J. Harrison shared an experience relating to her son:

Suddenly on that night I heard someone beside me trying to speak but I knew they were in the water choking and that it was a man. I jumped up in a fright and ran into my husband's room thinking it was him, but he was asleep ... A few days later we received a telegram to say he [her son] was missing ... but I think he was trying hard to convey some message to me, probably to look after his wife and child. He was very dear to me.[30]

In the private reflections she recorded in her diary, Falkiner's memories of grief and loss were fragmentary, as she rekindled and rewrote past memories and created fantasies of the future. Her reflections were framed by nostalgia and sentimentality in family mythologies, and by private rituals. Recording details of solitary reflection in a diary was one way in which women channelled their grief and dealt with death. Another way was through the letters they exchanged with chaplains, soldiers and other mothers, which drew them further into a circle of mourners.

Familial Grief

Charles Williams died in Germany on 16 May 1943, one week before he was to marry Gwen Parfitt. In November 1943, Hedwige Williams wrote of her feelings and those of her daughter Sheila, in finally hearing that her son had died after some uncertainty:

it is now six months since we first heard the bad news, and as it has turned out would have been better if it had been final. Hope deferred makes the heart sick. This news was just too much for Sheila ... Sheila took the news about Charles very hard. They were the closest pals and had many good times together.[31]

Through a series of fragmentary memories, there is a summation of a life – what Halbwach calls 'gripping abbreviation'[32] – in a few remembered scenes and episodes: 'A friend of mine was talking about the time Charles played tournament tennis in Torrens Creek with Sheila barracking for him. "Good shot little boy". "Play up". "Well played little boy". He won too. All these memories [wind] in and out.'[33] Williams fantasises about those activities she had shared with her son, memories she would rewrite in light of death and commemorate: 'When I returned home and used to sit sewing Charlie was never far away,'[34] she recalled. It was positive images that sustained her:

Much sadness disappears through the passing years, and we have to be thankful for the times when our loved ones were with us. I am so glad to hear the Aussies are the favourites ... It is a consolation to me to know Charlie had a wonderful time during the last months and that he learnt to love England. It used to worry me when he used to write how he hated the dreadful cold and was longing for sunny Australia.[35]

Reconstructing a particular persona of her son through the fragmentary collections of family myths, as a way of keeping him alive, was an important part of the grieving process:

I know he could never be scared or afraid. It was just not in him. He never used to lose his presence of mind in any experience ... Whenever anything wanted mending or done there was a call for Charlie. No matter what it was he could always find a way to do it and if he made up his mind to do a thing, no matter how difficult he would do it and do it well. He had such clever hands. Charlie is the only one of the family who took after me in colouring, stature and disposition. I am sure you must miss him terribly and so do I ... As you say memories are built up on such tiny things and when all is gone become mountains.[36]

There developed a close relationship between Charlie's sister and his fiancée. In 1943, Sheila Williams wrote to Gwen about 'the other girl Charlie was engaged to':

She has consoled herself very quickly – I believe is married by now – can't say I care very much anyhow ... I'm quite convinced that during that period when Charlie wasn't hearing from her she was playing around elsewhere – probably with a yank ... She couldn't stick to one job for very long so it's quite possible that she couldn't stick to one man either.

Sheila felt she could be intimate and started to share details. 'Charlie told me that you and I are very alike', she wrote, 'but I'm the taller. I'm 5ft. 4½ inches in stocking feet. Doug, my other brother, is a six footer and since he has been in the Army carries about 13 or 14 stone with it. We are both brunettes. Charlie is the only blonde in the family.' She offered sympathy and support, understanding and appreciation for Gwen's support of Charlie:

It must have been grand for him to have had your love and companionship all the time he was on operations. Men are such lonely souls when they are away from home and family ... I have lost my friends one by one – boys with whom I have grown up and gone to dances with etc – My greatest pal went about 18 months ago on his first operation. Just 'missing' after a raid on Essen. I expect you've also received the further report we had 'Now believed to have lost his life on the night of May 16'.[37]

The family endured a difficult loss. Sheila wrote that her mother had 'taken things very well, considering she had the double blow to bear – but it is a terrific strain. We lost Dad a few days after we heard the news about Charlie. He was in hospital and we knew he couldn't live very much longer so he was spared having to hear of his son.'[38]

After the safety of nostalgia came a wave of hatred and angst. Hedwige Williams wrote of the rage and anger she felt: 'Somehow in the back of my mind I feel they made a safe landing but were shot owing to the dire destruction they caused and the thought just makes my blood boil. How I cheered to hear Dusseldorf got another pounding.'[39] Elusive memories were all that were retained and remembered: 'If after the war and funds allow and I am still well I hope to make the trip to his grave and if possible remove his dear remains from that hated German soil. How I wish I could meet and talk to some of the lads who are doing such gallant tasks.' Her memories were mixed with pride, but this was not her ruling emotional response. 'Of course I am proud to be the mother of one of them, but that does not lessen my grief which after all no one knows much about. As you yourself know we cannot help feeling sick about it, but that will not make us lose hope.' The shared grief as well as resentment is a powerful motif in her writings:

> When I think that our lad might have been alive and well but for the twisted Nazi mind, who cannot see beyond 'Reprisal' it makes our hatred very bitter and unforgiving. We and so many thousands of others have every reason for a bitter hatred ... I always feel where I hear of the number of bombers that failed to return that someone's dearest has gone and more sorrowing hearts, and I never cease to think of them in my prayers.

Collective Grief: Chaplains

Mothers and fathers turned again to the army chaplain for news of the final moments of their sons' lives. During the course of the Second World War, about 750 chaplains served in the Australian Army, with fifteen of them killed and thirty-seven taken as prisoners of war.[40] Chaplains were expected to be the 'confidant and adviser of the individual officer and man', and it was observed that a closer relationship exists than usually develops between an officer and another soldier.[41] Matters of an intimate nature were to be dealt with by the chaplain. Some soldiers certainly utilised the opportunity. Chaplain J. C. Salter recalled that a man 'would ask the Padre to pray with him just as naturally as he would ask the orderly for medicine or treatment'.[42] Chaplains were to be found in the most oppressive and brutal locations – including the prison camps along the Burma–Thailand railway and in Changi – preaching to the soldiers, trying to sustain a high morale, and 'at times paying the price of ministry with their lives'.[43]

One chaplain, Eric Webber, received many letters from parents whose sons had been injured or who had died during the war. Agnes M. Booth lost her son in February 1944, and wrote in subdued, idealised acceptance rather than celebration of heroism: 'He was the most wonderful son a mother ever had. So strong and cheery, and brave always. I have a large case of silver cups Tony won while a pupil at Scots College. He represented Scots at all schools [and] always successfully. He was so strong.' Booth wrote seeking more detail of his death:

If you get time at all please be kind and tell me of his suffering and passing, and if possible what the illness was and where he is buried ... My heart is breaking – I adored him. Only time and prayer will heal the awful wound. Once more thank you for your beautiful letter and hoping for further news ...[44]

Similar themes of an idealised life, with the desire to know more, characterised another letter from a Mrs Doggeth, who wrote of her son George:

He was a good lad lived a good life and looked after himself and hated drink. It is terrible to think he is struck down in his ... manhood. That is war and I realise many parents are going through far more than ourselves ... Any letters you may have opened could now be destroyed as they will be of little help to George ...[45]

Chaplain Trathen also attracted a range of letters from those who wanted details of their sons' fates. Ruby Goodisson echoed a desperation and an anguish as she insisted on procuring explicit details of her son's death:

Would you kindly write me *all* the details of his last hours after the crash. Exactly what his serious injuries were, do not try to spare me the sorrow of it all. *Please*, I want to know everything ... I always like to be told the truth about everything in life, no matter how it hurts, and not left wondering and to grope in the dark. No mother has ever been given a better son ... Thankyou for everything ... call and see us ...[46]

In contrast to the public silence on a 'mother's sacrifice', it was an issue discussed in private commemorations. Chaplain Fred McKay wrote to Mrs Laver, the mother of Leonard Laver, who died in 1943 in an aerial battle over Sicily, that 'Len's mother remains much in the continuing thoughts of everybody in the Squadron for Len was really part of the original family of fellows who made the first traditions. I have met countless lads who are just thrilled to know that I know you.'[47] When Flight Lieutenant William Newton died in October 1943, one respondent wrote to his mother claiming: 'Will you excuse me writing in this vein, but I did want to tell the mother of a truly noble son – that the hearts of all present at the ceremony today were with you during the citation and on your receipt of that v.c.'[48]

Friends wrote to the chaplain when mothers were far too distressed to address their grief. Jean Bonner wrote on behalf of one grieving mother who had lost her only son, Stan. 'His mother has taken the news very badly', wrote Bonner:

has refused to see anyone, and is under the care of the Dr. Stan was her only son, and has meant everything to her as she lost her husband when Stan was 2 years old. She is very anxious to know just what happened to him, for all the news they have had so far is that they crashed at landing, and naturally she is anxious to know more ... She would very much appreciate a letter from you ...[49]

In death, some turned to religion in the hope of renewal. Captain Stuart Graham had been converted to religious explanations through his experience. He wrote:

I hoped against hope that I would never have to write this letter and I don't know where to begin, so if I hurt you through my clumsiness please understand and forgive me. Before the war I was a bit of a cynic ... but since then I have seen a lot of brave men die, and sometimes I've cursed and thought there is no God. I don't any more – I believe in Him earnestly, and I know you do, and I know Ray is with Him now ... I believe Ray lives now in a better world than this mad-house waiting for us.[50]

'Believe with me', wrote Florence Bayliss on the death of her son, 'that the very best I could have planned for Cliff, all that I would have given him, abundantly and with such great love, is not as beautiful as that ... given him by a Love greater than mine.'[51] Although Michael McKernan may be accurate in his assessment of the chaplains that the 'times were against them and their leaders too often proved incapable of understanding the spirit of the Australian in times of hardship',[52] letters by mothers suggest many of their sons were appreciative of their efforts and that they too were comforted by them.

Mothers to Mothers

While chaplains and spiritualist explanations comforted some, the most sustaining networks were those between mothers which shaped a dialogue of grief and mutual support where memories were kept alive.

Discussing the specific pain of maternal loss was an important part of this process for it elevated it to a privileged status. 'Although a stranger I would like to write and offer you my sympathy ... A mother's heart goes out to you in your sad loss. We too lost our only son in the last war; so just know how you must feel. I am enclosing 2 little poems. I am a lover of verse and find solace in it.'[53] A relative wrote to one mother who had lost her son: 'Only a mother can know the heartaches of parting with their sons through war, but I suppose time will heal your bruised heart.'[54]

Mothers drew solace from their collective understanding of grief. Rosa Taylor wrote in December 1941 to a mother who had lost her son, that 'hope you will understand from this brief note as from one mother to another, that my thoughts are with you and for you. It is useless to say bear up I know – I couldn't do it *my*self. There's not much use in living is there? The ones we love and live for are just being sacrificed.'[55] It was considered to be a particular form of loss. Lois Atock was told, after the death of her only child Ken, that it 'hurts the mothers more than anybody and only a mother knows so dear cheer up and be the same lovable Lois as always'.[56] The dilemma confronting mothers and the predicament they bore was articulated by the following letter to a grieving mother:

I have always thought that you were very much to be admired in that you let him go, when you could so easily have kept him with you for a year or two longer. Nobody would have thought any less of you if you had kept him back for a little. But I can understand how proud you were that he wanted to go, and how you would have thought less of yourself in keeping him. You can be as proud of yourself as you are of Ken.[57]

Mrs Ada Hough of South Australia experienced the double trauma of losing her husband during the First World War and her only son, Pilot Officer William Hough, in the Second. The mother of a soldier who was in the same plane as her son, Mrs Shipton, wrote in empathy and support.

In June 1946, Shipton explained that her son Sergeant A. G. Shipton had been the engineer on board the *L. J. Sterling 940* which had crashed. They were bonded, she said, by their communal grief:

We like you, waited and waited these many months, until at last, I wrote to the Mayor of Vierzon [in France] last June, and asked him if he could find out what happened to the crew. I received a letter from him stating that the bodies were so badly charred they could not identify them. Shortly afterwards, I had another letter and photo of the cemetery where our dear ones are buried ... Since then I had a letter and two more photos of the graves, and they asked me to let the next of the crews' families know.[58]

She reassured Mrs Hough that she was making an effort to respect their graves:

I have a lady friend in Paris, who is staying in England in May and I gave her sufficient money to put flowers on all the crews' graves. I hope this will prove a comfort to you, as it has done to my husband and myself. Although it cannot bring them back, it is nice to feel even in another land they are not forgotten.[59]

Grieving Mothers

Shipton wrote again to Mrs Hough in October 1946, expressing her deepest sympathy. 'I am sorry to hear of your double sorrow in losing your dear husband and your son as well', she wrote:

I hope you will be given a double share of strength to carry on, although we wonder if it is worthwhile, don't we? I have enclosed you a small photograph of the cemetery where our darlings are at rest ... You can keep it. I can't tell you which grave is theirs – but I do know it is one of them.[60]

She had enclosed an account of the monument set in place by the mayor of Vierzon to commemorate the death of the airmen. Shipton had been in touch with the mothers of the men in the accident: 'I have written a letter from [sic] Mrs. Dutton, also Mrs. Fielder, Mr. Walker, and Mrs. Henry (all the crews' parents)'. An intimate bond of friendship formed through their shared grief: 'I would like to thank you for your kindness in sending me some fruit etc. We are very short of food here nearly everything is rationed and on points, we queue for our food for hours, sometimes, but still we still rub along.'[61] Hough corresponded with a Frenchman who maintained the grave. J. Cazale wrote in October 1951:

I know very well that a mother could never forget, but with the passing of years, the pain shall weigh less upon you in the knowledge that the tomb of your dear son shall be well cared for ... the tomb of your dear Bill will blossom in chrysanthemums and there shall also be some late roses; we still have many flowers in our garden ... do not worry about the tomb of your child, I regard it as if it belonged to me.

These efforts were made to keep the memories of their sons alive, as Shipton wrote to Hough in 1946: 'I wonder why it should all have to be and really, how quickly the world seems to have forgotten their sacrifice.'[62] It was not so much that the memories of sacrifice would be forgotten, but that, in dealing with grief, those who carried these memories would in years to follow replace the detail of the events with nostalgia and sentimentality – idealisations which displaced their loss.

Soldiers and Mothers

As in the First World War, soldiers also initiated correspondence. The guilt of surviving an incident when others died is suggested in these letters. The pain where friendships are broken prematurely was well summarised by one soldier who lost his best friend:

I scarcely know how to start, yet there is so much I should like to say. To merely express sympathy is not nearly enough, for me, Tas was as a dear brother ... his passing has meant that there is a irreplaceable gap in my life ... The surge of events and memories of past days are clouded with callous whims and strange fancies of war, but through it all are friendships which will never be broken and live forever ... hope I am not disturbing too many sorrows in your memory of Tas ... the Tas I knew will never be forgotten.[63]

Another exchange related similar themes. In March 1945, at the age of twenty-three, Russell Stark was shot down with three other crew members in Germany. There had been 15 000 Australians involved in the air war against Germany and Italy. In this theatre, about 6600 men in the Royal Australian Air Force (RAAF) died in action, or an astounding 20 per cent of all Australian war deaths in all services and campaigns.[64] Stark's mother, Mrs M. E. Stark, wrote to one of the survivors of the accident, J. R. Dixon, and he replied in September 1945. 'First let me thank you for writing ... it was a very pleasant surprise for me.' He offered his condolences:

let me say how sorry I am for you, Mrs. Bairnsfather, Mrs. Lovett and Mrs. Gilbert, also for Rousel's girlfriend of whom he thought and spoke so much of. We all thought the world of Russ especially as he was the youngest member of the crew, he was the best friend and Pilot anybody could wish for, the whole squadron was deeply shocked and surprised when they heard of loss of our crew.

Dixon went on to describe the series of events which had caused Stark's death. After bombing an oil refinery in Hamburg, he writes,

I was temporarily blinded by my own gunfire when something hit my turret and set it on fire ... a few seconds later Russ gave orders to jump out immediately. I tried to get out and had a bit of a fight to do it as my turret was now well alight, Russ kept control of the plane to give us a chance to get out ... I saw our plane hit the ground in flames, Russ and Ralph must have died at once.

Dixon emphasised her son's self-sacrifice in saving the lives of others:

I honestly believe Russ could have saved his life at the risk of the others, but as you and I know Russ thought of his crew first. He gave his life to try and save others, three other mothers gave their sons in the cause of Freedom so we can only hope that Russ, Ralph, Gus and Paddy lie peacefully at rest once again.[65]

The local paper, the *Glenelg Guardian*, stressed these heroic aspects, and expressed the hope that Stark's 'steadfast courage at the end will forever shed a radiance in the hearts of his people, who, with so many others, are mourning the loss of a son who gave his life for the Empire'.[66] Dixon told Mrs Stark how he had been taken as a prisoner of war and offered to 'send you [my] Diary that I have made of those days in Germany, you can let me know later'. He encouraged her to reply to his home address.

It is unclear whether Stark's mother took up the offer. Other soldiers and their families certainly wished to consolidate this bond. Jack Slee, a friend of Keith Manttan, a pilot who died in 1943, was appreciative of the correspondence he developed with Manttan's mother. 'May I take this opportunity', he wrote, 'to say how grand it was of you to write to me, when your heart and hand were so heavy ... My parents will only be too glad for [your other son] to come and stay with them. They have entertained many of them. It is almost an obsession with them.'[67] Loss inspired a desire for intimacy. Tom Selby wrote, as many others did to make contact of this sort:

You have probably never heard of me but I hope my writing to you won't displease you and make you sad. I am always afraid these letters have the wrong effect. In any case I have asked my mother to call on you ... I think you'll like my mother – she has had 5 of the family in the army – my sister is out now.[68]

Parents certainly valued the letters from friends of their sons, which prompted the most heartfelt and intimate details.

Norm Mellett wrote in deepest appreciation to the mother of his best friend, George Gill, who was killed:

I have not had the pleasure of your acquaintance, but [I] did know and admire your son, to such an extent, that I feel this constitutes a Mutual Bond ... I started this war as a very new recruit and any success ... has been due to Tas' leadership and friendship when soldiering was a new and hard business ... I always found it hard to remember that this was also his first war ... I say without hesitation, that your son was the finest officer I've met ... Someday when this ghastly business is over, I hope we may meet if only to fill in for each other those gaps in Tas' life of which we are both ignorant.

Gill's mother noted, 'Isn't it a nice letter?'[69]

Mothers took great solace in receiving letters from friends of their sons, and men were adopted as surrogate sons. 'Because you are one of Cliff's friends,' wrote Florence Bayliss, the mother of William Clifford Bayliss, who died in June 1943,

I want you to know that this home, our home, that I made for Cliff, is ever open to you, and I want you to come here, if ever you have an opportunity, and share in the hospitality that we both would have extended to you. All that you can tell me of Cliff I want to hear, everything, whatever it is – his talks with you, his work, his funny ways and sayings ... Whenever you have time to spare and can see me please let me know and say just when and where you would like to meet me.[70]

There were positive outcomes, for with

the taking of something infinitely precious I was given a sustaining power, a strength, an ever lasting and ever present companionship... You, Alan, Ian, Alex and Ken, are my very precious links with Cliff. Wherever I am there will always be a very, warm welcome given to each of all of you – and all my help if ever you need it.

Memories

What was retrieved and remembered in personal loss, in both material and emotional terms, was telling.

The possessions of soldiers were treasured in retaining memories of the deceased and were important in the gradual process of accepting death. Sheila Allan lost her father in a POW camp. The mementos he left behind were deemed to be of considerable value. One soldier could see the value of a soldier's possessions. 'Your father had incidentally left in my case for the benefit of the hut', wrote K. A. Blacker in June 1945, 'a surveyor's tape to which he attached great sentimental value: this I am handing over to the camp trustee and he will doubtless forward it to your mother in due course.'[71] Another soldier reiterated this suggestion that 'you apply to get your representative for *all* of his belongings this side to be handed over to you, say you want them, otherwise you might not get them'.[72] From the hospital came another possession. 'I am sending you his wallet, with the money I had in my charge', explained J. Moran.[73] A widow noted with concern that 'I myself would have given much to have had one or two of my husband's personal possessions back, but they were all lost with him when he was killed in the landing in Sicily.'[74] Another widow expressed her gratitude to one soldier who had kept her husband's possessions:

I also want to thank you for saving some of our things and they will be treasured by me as they will be the only things I'll have of our house. I do think it was very wonderful of you to keep them hidden from those Japanese all those years and at such a risk... I am having a photo taken from a small one I had of my husband in... uniform, and as soon as it is finished I will [send] you one.[75]

Stages of grief can also be suggested in dreams. Joy Bowral wrote to her mother in May 1945 describing the shift of her brother's memory from one of sorrow to pleasure.[76] 'Today', she confessed, 'I feel contented somehow and quiet inside for the first time since that awful day we lost our darling.' She was used to dreaming about Ray, but

I've never once seen him in my sleep since he died, and it has been as though he'd gone right away – as though I'd closed a lovely book called 'My brother' and couldn't ever read it again. Well, last night I saw him – but not as he was last time we met. As he was when he was 16. It was so real – I even saw in every detail, that grey suit he used to wear. I don't know what the dream was about – I only know I woke up crying my heart out, but feeling very near to him. If I write any more about it, I'll cry again – but it was wonderful Mum; and I know that he hasn't gone away – he's only waiting for us all, in all his beautiful youth.

The dream restored a different memory of her brother, one which was of another time and place:

Don't think that he is the Ray I saw last night. I remember in one part of it, I asked him to dance with me, and he said 'OK. If you don't mind me just walking', and as we danced I held him tightly, and he was shorter than me – he was the kid brother of a few years ago. Not the man who was so tired. I've only ever been able to think of him as a tired, tall Young Digger – but now I've recaptured again *our* Ray. Don't cry Mum darling, please. I'm trying not to. I hope I haven't made you sad, Mum and Dad – but I had to tell you . . .[77]

In death, mythologies are made, and memories of things that otherwise would have been forgotten or discarded are amplified, recorded and remembered. Religion, nostalgia, sentimentality, denial and the imaginary of what was – these were the mechanisms by which relatives structured their grief during the war. These are the psychological mementos which are never lost. Finding the language to express such anguish was difficult, for it meant accepting and establishing new family dynamics and mourning the loss of past relationships which had previously cemented 'the family'. In some cases, this was a traumatic shift. Joyce Browning wrote to one mother who had lost her son, trying to reassure her that a 'better time will come, but it won't give back husbands to wives who have lost them, or sons to their mothers. My dear, when I heard of your tragedy, I felt I would like to write, tho' words seem so useless just at present.'[78]

Unlike mothers, war widows were determined that their anguish be acknowledged in public remembrances and not be lost in an understanding of sacrifice which marginalised their own.

8   A War Widow's Mourning

> His passing came as a heavy blow to us as we were all expecting to see his dear face any day ... He was counting the hours waiting to come home to us. It is hard to understand why one so good and loveable as Allan should be taken but we dare not question God's will as he sees all and his will and doings is flawless ... [I have] fond memories of the husband I loved so well to help me in this saddest time of my life ...

On New Year's Day 1942, Mrs Josephine Johnson, the widow of Corporal John Johnson, wrote to Private Charlie Fraser, a member of her deceased husband's battalion. Johnson had died a year earlier, in Tobruk, at the age of thirty-nine. 'You, no doubt are wondering who is writing to you', she wrote self-consciously after such a period of time had elapsed, 'but as John always referred to you as my pal Charlie I feel it is quite right addressing my letter that way.' She thanked him for the companionship he offered her husband, and knew that he and his fellow soldiers would understand her predicament, for they would 'know how great my loss is. I will never get over it. It is purely and simply hell trying to carry on without him but I must do it and with a smile too, as I promised him I would.'[2] The moment of death not only remained with her, but also marked the memory of the couple's eight children. Their family of six sons and two daughters ranged in age from fourteen years to five months at the time of Johnson's death. Forty years later, Don Johnson recalled: 'I was lighting the dining room fire at Walwa when Edna Osmand came in the front door with Mum and as I held the match Mum told me that Dad had been killed. Every time I light a fire I recall that moment and feel bad because it reminds me of Dad's death.'[3] His brother, Jack, remembered that he was told of

> Dad's death at Northcote late that evening. There was a knock on the door answered by Auntie Rose. There was some mumbling then she came in and said: 'That was a policeman – your Dad has been hurt very badly.' She was crying and then said: 'He has been killed.' It wasn't a very good time for me I must say from then on.[4]

Another son, Barry, recalls that, as he was washing potatoes,

> Mum called me and told me Dad was dead. I was devastated... First we went to Uncle Morris who was told, and he cried. He came with us to Gran's... Uncle Morris told her and she was so devastated – poor Gran. It was terrible with Grandma crying out, calling for her baby. Gran cried so much – she never got over it.[5]

This familial pain was accentuated when the war ended. On that day, when there were 'big bright union flags, red Australian ensigns of all sizes ... balloons and laughing happy people, calling out their joy',[6] Len Johnson remembered that

> For one brief moment I was happy until I realised that this national joy was not for us. It seemed... that while the war continued [Dad] was still a part of our family... Now suddenly, the war was finished [and] the careful fabric of our family life... disintegrated into one blow. I couldn't bear it. I walked out of school and went home... Mum had pushed a small tattered paper ensign into a crack between bricks beside the front door. I could see that she was trying her hardest to celebrate with all the rest but I knew it was just a brave display... For the first time in my life I felt an adult emotion – I was really sad, not for me but for Mum. I ran home thinking someone should be with her, saying in my head: 'Poor Mum, it's over and Dad is never coming home to her.'[7]

The legacy of the war for the children, as well as for their mother, was in the grinding poverty many of them endured in a family without a male breadwinner. Len Johnson recalled that when the family lost their father they became dependent on the welfare system, which began the cycle of economic hardship: 'For the remainder of Mum's life there were to be no luxuries, no accumulation of assets, no days without fear of shortage of money... For her children there was to be no father, no male direction, or physical support, no carefree child's life, no freedom from humiliation.' They struggled endlessly against 'a callous and uncaring society which generally failed us, against an arrogant bureaucracy which at every turn humiliated us, and against a remote government which kept us just below the poverty line'.[8] After his father's death, 'the whole system took away our economic future and left us with only emotion'.[9]

A lingering sense of neglect remained with the families. In her autobiography, Josie Arnold, one of Josie Johnson's children, recalled how they carried their humiliation:

> My mother instilled in us a sense of righteous grievance which I know to be common to war widows and their children: that the country owed us something for the loss of our fathers and that there was unforgivable tardiness in that recognition, much less the repayment, of this debt... We would not forget but it

seemed to me very early in life that we would be the only ones to remember ... The Australian community quickly forgot the easy war promises and felt resentment at the 'special' treatment war widows received.[10]

Community of Support

Initially, communities rallied to protect those who had become vulnerable. Widows, like mothers, found comfort and solace in the active networks which were formed with other widows and soldiers. Driver Neil Mackenzie wrote to Josie Johnson, trying to comfort her through his own sense of loss:

I can safely say here & now how proud we were to know & to work with such a chap as your husband was & his place will be hard to fill & as for my-self Mrs Johnson I lost a good mate when he went ... Now Mrs Johnson as you have already written to my wife & she was really glad to get a letter from you & appreciated it very much ... don't take your husband's death too hard ... but I know Johnno would not want you to grieve & make yourself miserable ...[11]

Johnson and other wives had formed a close community of support, reciprocating information, while their husbands were serving. Mackenzie's wife Dulcie describes the networks that were formed:

Well yesterday I was just ready to go out & I thought I would have a look & see if there was any mail for me, & believe me I was quite prepared not to see any, Lo and behold there was 6 letters all Air Mail too ... thank you very much indeed for sending me the Border Mail which I also received ... it was so good of you to send it to me ... Concerning your 7 soldier wives having an afternoon by turn at each other's place it must be very nice, although I'm not there in person allow me to be present in spirit & thought. Thanks for the advice to keep my chin up I'll certainly do my best ... Remember me to the group of wives & give them my best wishes ...[12]

When death came, the condolences arrived like a tidal wave of compassion, elevating Johnson's deed to heroic status and offering a widow with eight young children emotional comfort in her time of utter desolation. 'Well Josie you & the children have my deepest sympathy in your great loneliness', wrote cousin Mary Wall. 'John thought it was his duty to go & fight the Demon Hitler & his mad gang, he did his duty well ... I cannot realise that he has left us, the dear, kindly, good natured even tempered old Soul, he never harmed anyone in thought or deed & had a good word for all.'[13] Others shared their stories of loss, finding comfort in understanding death as God's work. 'Dear Josie, your lovely Johnnie was so good in every way to have to fight so God knew a way & the best way so. God called him away & now there is just one thing left for you & us all & that is to be brave like Johnnie.'[14] Another wrote that it 'is often a comfort to us to know that others care, and I assure you we all do care and will remember too'.[15]

But it became clear that the extent of this support was limited, and these heroic accolades alone could not sustain the family in dealing with their duress. Len Johnson articulated the bitterness many years later:

> The local people always called us Johnnie Johnson's kids. They spoke of him as the great man of Walwa who gave his life for his country, his glorious death and noble sacrifice never to be forgotten. They all said a debt was owed. Promises were made. Families would be cared for. It was the nation's sacred obligation ... but we could only use it to disguise our tears. We couldn't eat the words or heaped praise; they never bought a second school uniform, a new pair of boots, a football or a holiday for Mum who suffered most.[16]

A feeling of neglect and abandonment characterises Johnson's testimony fifty years later, an anger which remained with many widows and their families after the war. For some, being a war widow would be their central identity for the rest of their lives. Sustaining this intimate continuity with the past gave them an avenue through which to fully and publicly express their anger at a time when they felt that their sacrifices were being marginalised in the remembrance of war. It gave some women legitimate access to a place within public discussion.

Channelling Grief

Historians have not asked questions about war widows' emotional experience. We know of it only through the history of repatriation. We are aware of the pensions they received; the conditions of these pensions; the attitude of governments towards them; the campaigns they launched to have their demands met. In other words, we have come to know the war widow through her relationship to the state.[17] This relationship is the focus of the only full-length study of war widows in Australia, by Mavis Thorpe Clark, which is an organisational history of the War Widows Guild.[18] *No Mean Destiny* is also a biographical study of the guild's founder, Jessie Vasey, who in many respects has come to personify the trials of war widows after the war (Chapter 6). Beyond Australia, where the full extent of human suffering of the Second World War defied comprehension, mourning for war victims, it has been argued, was fraught with denial and defensiveness.[19] It is puzzling that research on war widows – particularly in Germany and Britain – has not included emotional concerns, but continues to be shaped by questions of repatriation and remuneration.[20] Within these discussions the intense anger, resentment and pain have been extinguished from the record. A consideration of these emotions leads us to reflect on the ways in which war widows channelled their grief.

Following the Second World War, there were about 10 000 war widows in Australia. The average age of these women was about twenty-six, and most of them had one child and little financial support. Although the war widow's pension was 50s and 12s 6d for each child,[21] it trailed behind the basic wage.[22] Earlier, the widows of the First World War had received a basic pension rate of 42s a week and were given 10s for the first child, 7s 6d for the second and 5s each for the others. They were entitled to few other benefits, although after 1924, war widows and their dependents could claim medical treatment and obtain supplies.[23] Nevertheless, for many of these women, after both First and Second World Wars the loss of a breadwinner ushered in a period of financial stringency.

Sorrow, Pride and Pensions

It was this lack of support that inspired Jessie Vasey to take up the plight of widows following the Second World War. Vasey was exceptional as a woman of private means whose life-long endeavour was to promote the war widow's cause. But there were many others who followed her in this quest. They may not have done so for the same reasons, nor did they necessarily share a similar history. Widowhood came to women in many different ways and at different times. Their experience of it changed over time and varied in relation to class and age. But for all the unique and individual experiences in each of their stories, the collective relationship to past loss and their resentment helped to shape a collective and individual identity which sustained them.

Vasey's loss was a particularly public one (Chapter 6). In 1945, the Prime Minister, John Curtin, described the death of General George Vasey as a 'shocking blow to Australia'.[24] He offered 'deepest sympathy' to the families of the men who perished in the aircraft accident, but believed that it would be 'some consolation to relatives to know that their loved ones were lost in the service of their country when setting out to confront the enemy. The whole nation would join them in their proud sorrow.'[25]

'Proud sorrow' was an appropriate description of what Jessie Vasey internalised as she was forced to continue her life without her husband. Her pride in her husband's achievements may have allayed some of her initial pain, but it could not diminish the anguish of her grief. In 1946 she was clear about the purpose of the newly formed War Widows Guild, which was open to 'every widow of the 1939–1945 war'.[26] The aim of the organisation, she claimed, was not only to benefit war widows materially, but to keep alive the memories of lost ones. 'It is no mean destiny', she claimed, 'to be called upon to go on for a man who has laid down his life.' Retaining this relationship to past glories was *their* responsibility. These words 'were the right words to use to the wives of fighting men, the women who had been left to carry on the fight alone'.[27] Vasey believed that the guild would provide some direction – 'in grief and bewilderment we must grope for some meaning to life' – but they were also 'not to be a drag on the victory for which our men laid down their lives'. During the war, she asserted, war women shouldered heavy burdens, but 'the war widow may never lay hers down'.

These widows became a testimony to remembrance. To resist being forgotten, war widows organised several protests. In July 1947, 2000 war widows from throughout Victoria met at the Melbourne Town Hall. Vasey claimed at the meeting that the men who had died on service had expected that their widows 'would be decently treated if they were killed, but she was afraid Australia had failed them'. It was not the war widows who were being paid, but 'the country was paying the dead soldier the price of his life'.[28] For Vasey, this payment was not a remuneration, but a symbol of the price society paid for its war dead. Widows did not want to be humiliated by being made to feel like 'pensioners'. Vasey insisted that the guild was 'trying to help needy war widows who were too proud to ask'.[29]

Others disagreed with their campaign. In August 1947, Mrs C. A. Vaughan of the War-Bereaved Dependent Parents Association, wrote to the *Argus* suggesting that it was a 'grave error' for Jessie Vasey not to seek the support of widowed mothers and dependent mothers of men killed in action. Such mothers, she claimed, were in a 'lower category than widows and de facto widows'.[30] In response, Mrs W. Riggall, the honorary secretary of the War Widows Guild, claimed that the guild had 'never refused any support that has been offered to us to fight this battle for compensation for our husbands' lives . . .'.[31]

Others argued that a distinction should be made between widows with and without children. One correspondent noted that 'Quite a number of war widows are without children and are in the bloom of their life', and for them, 'the pension they receive is adequate, more especially as the finer spirits among them would desire to work for and help the country that their husbands died the same'.[32] Vasey thought this view outrageous. The suggestion that the pensions of childless war widows 'would have to be reduced to enable widows with children to receive more was contemptible'. Vasey asserted that 'childless widows had every right to compensation for their husbands' lives'.[33] As widows were compelled to work, and thus were 'prevented from giving their children the attention they needed, the greater number of delinquents were children of deceased servicemen'. Further, it was unjust that men who were classed as 'permanently and totally disabled' be given more pension than the dependents of those who died.³⁴

Guild members responded to this call. Mrs G. H. Brock, the treasurer of the Melbourne branch, claimed that there was an underlying assumption that if those who received 'anything approaching compensation for the loss of their husbands in the country's service they instantly would become selfish and idle'. While it was true that 'being occupied brings more contentment than idleness ... no citizen should begrudge the full compensation due to a woman whose husband gave his life for their safety'.³⁵ Aboriginal women waited longer for their compensation. Until 1959 Aborigines were largely denied social security on the basis that they were not citizens of Australia. In the immediate postwar period, for instance, Aborigines in Western Australia, Queensland and the Northern Territory were 'denied the right to vote, the right to move freely, and the right to work'.³⁶ Despite the complexity which plagued the administration of social security payments, Aboriginal widows of non-Aboriginal and Aboriginal soldiers were eligible for payments, although this was only allowed if their marriage was a registered one.³⁷

Despite feeling so often under siege, the widows did attain support from other groups.³⁸ In 1947, the RSL organised a state-wide campaign in South Australia to 'stir the entire community into action on behalf of war widows'. Plans had been made, it was reported, 'for incessant protests to reach the Federal government until it was left with no alternative but to improve conditions for war widows'. A sub-committee was formed to arrange public protest meetings in every town in the state.³⁹ The RSL also stressed that 'by their sacrifice these women deserve special treatment'.⁴⁰ The RSL claimed that soon 'there would be no recognition at all of public gratitude to the war widow for the gift of her husband in service of country', and it was a disturbing thought that the margin between the invalid pension and the war widow had narrowed. Those who lost their breadwinners in war should be better regarded, argued the RSL.⁴¹ There were also reports of the War Widows Guild establishing a nursery for children of war widows aged between two and a half and five years with the financial assistance of the Red Cross.⁴² The *Argus* attempted to raise money for the guild when it was first formed, advertising its achievements and aspirations. The guild was presented as a welcoming warm community of women, whose weaving and expertise in textiles was perceived to be a money-making venture. Patriotic organisations, army groups, women's groups and individuals donated to assist the guild to become established. By July 1946 (after almost six months), the *Argus* had raised £2878 9s 9d, with a cheque for £500 from the Country Women's Association.⁴³ It was suggested by the AIF Women's Holiday House Association that a scholarship be funded for children of war widows or for war orphans. 'As the war was left further behind', noted the president of the association, 'widows and orphans were becoming more important than the families of the men who had returned, and who should by now have settled into their places in the community.'[44]

Legacy initially offered support to war widows, although considerable tension developed between the guild and Legacy. The guild's members were widows of men who had died on active service; Legacy was concerned with the wives and children of ex-servicemen who died after the war. Members of the guild did not want to be given direction by men. The other source of conflict was financial. The guild argued for a pension equal to the basic wage, while the RSL and other groups were prepared to settle on an increase of ten shillings per week.[45]

Vasey used the compensation argument to justify an increase in payments. 'We are told', she claimed in June 1947, 'that we are able to work to supplement our meagre pensions, but it is not generally realised that most widows are still breaking their hearts permanently through shock and grief.' The pension, she claimed, was not a gift, but 'something that should be only a reasonable workers' compensation for loss of life'.[46]

Widows' sense that they were being ill treated was accentuated when they came under surveillance for leading 'irregular lives'. Vasey stated that she would check reports that the Repatriation Commission had stopped the pensions of fifteen war widows.[47] There were other accusations in regard to the morality of war widows. At a conference of the Australian Legion of Ex-Servicemen, Lady Stanton Hicks claimed that 'the only chance a widow has of remarrying is to ask a man into her home. Although this is dangerous, she is too frightened to be seen outside with him.' She reported that investigators, 'working in pairs', had been known to 'pull out drawers searching for evidence of immorality'. The conference 'expressed its disgust at these investigations', and would ask the 'Federal Government to stop this miscarriage of British justice'.[48] The response by the government was to deny such accusations, as it claimed that the Repatriation Commission 'was not at present investigating any allegations, and any inquiries that had been made were unauthorised and these would be investigated'.[49]

One of the major concerns regarding the families of war widows was the syndrome of what was referred to as 'broken families'. In June 1956, Vasey addressed the New South Wales branch of the War Widows Guild claiming that it was unfair that women were forced to be breadwinners as well as mothers. She claimed we 'must struggle against an idea that a woman can always manage somehow'.[50] War widows, Vasey asserted, suffered particular physical and mental stresses, and she called on the government to establish guidance clinics 'where harassed war widows could get expert advice about their own and their children's problems'. Because most war widows had to work, they could not be proper mothers, and their 'children suffered maladjustment because of the loss of their father'.[51] Vasey argued that women needed a co-operative effort for rearing their children, and this was more easily managed in flats.

The question of fatherless children arose again, as it had during the First World War, but there was also a concern with the impact war had on the nature of family relationships.[52] Vasey attended two conferences, in 1957 and 1958, which discussed the question of the 'problems of fatherless families'. In November 1957 Vasey reported on a conference on fatherless families, held in Rome, where it was said that mothers should not try to 'assume father's responsibilities'. It was agreed at the conference that there had been a 'lack of appreciation of the full extent of the burdens of fatherless families', and 'the level of the family's income should be that which they enjoyed in the father's lifetime'.[53] There were serious material repercussions for families without a breadwinner. Thelma Courtman lost her husband in July 1943. She wrote to Chaplain Trathen of the difficulty ahead with the children and her loss:

It is hard to write this letter, every time I think of my darling Husband I break down. 3 weeks today since Dan was taken from me & children. He left 2 young children, may God watch over them, they are only babies, the eldest was only 2 years last week baby only 10 months ... I feel so lonely I keep waiting for a letter from Dan and knowing I will never receive one again from him. His poor Darling children keep saying Daddy. They will never know who their father was. It is so hard for their sake.[54]

After the death of their father, Josie Johnson distributed her eight children among friends and relatives. She had decided to move from the small town of Walwa to Melbourne, and attempted to secure a Housing Commission house, because her income was low and the pension did not cover the cost of renting a private home.[55] Len Johnson recalled the difficulty of separation: 'I missed [Mum] and the closeness of family at that moment. I was unhappy because we were all separated and I missed the other children. We had been brought up by Mum to stay together ... This day I felt bad from loneliness and fear, and missed every-one.'[56] 'Everything about us', noted Josie Arnold, 'spoke of poverty and fatherlessness.'[57]

Working for the War Widows Guild eased the pain of widowhood for women like Vasey as she committed herself to the war widow's cause. 'To a war widow', she insisted, 'every day is an Anzac day ... we must show the general public that we remember, otherwise how can we expect them to do so'.[58] There was for Vasey the commonality of grief which drew war widows together. 'It is only the women who have faced the problems and the terrors of that long walk in the shadows', she insisted in October 1945, 'who can understand what the other widow must face and know how to give her a helping hand.'[59]

A community of widows was brought together through the War Widows Guild. In the early 1950s, accommodation was advertised in the guild's newsletter, with war widows offering to share with other widows. In 1952, Mrs Haase of the Melbourne suburb of Moorabbin 'would be ... glad to have a war widow share her house with her – preferably a middle aged business woman – non-drinker, non-smoker'. Mrs D. Dixon would also be 'glad to hear of a middle aged widow who would like to accompany her on occasional trips to Daylesford, where she and her sons go for holidays'.[60] Later that year another woman wrote that she was a 'widow living at Nhill [who] would like to share her home with a war widow [to] share the housework and living expenses'.

Widows jealously defended their status and excluded those who forfeited it by remarriage. A dispute over the loan of badges highlighted this point. Nancy Scott, the daughter of a soldier who died in Borneo, remembers how her mother 'wore her widow's badge on a visit to a shop to buy some sheets at a time when coupons still had to be produced to purchase them'.[61] The life membership badges were on loan to members of the War Widows Guild and were returnable on remarriage, but they clearly became a difficult item to retrieve. 'You will realise and feel as we do', it was reported in the guild circular, 'that it would be most unfortunate if any of our badges got into the hands of non-war widows and were worn merely as ornaments ... should any of you be contemplating re-marriage, make a point of returning your badge before the wedding'.[62] Relinquishing a former identity and inventing another was fraught with difficulty for some women.

Others did not wish to sever any ties with the War Widows Guild, in the event of remarriage. To accommodate these women an auxiliary was formed in 1950 for all members of the guild who had remarried, 'to permit them to continue to work for the Guild and attend meetings'.[63] The war widow's badge became a symbol of a sustaining identity. In New South Wales, the guild members were convinced that the badges would be returned. In 1954, they agreed that 'if we can watch our badges and persuade our people that they are on loan I think that the great bulk of them will be returned on remarriage or death'. It was suggested that the badges be inscribed with the wording 'property of War Widows' Guild'.[64]

Vasey believed war widows needed to find new interests and a new circle through the War Widows Guild. 'If we grouped ourselves together ... [and] found new interests and told our friends about them, ways and means would soon be found to foster and encourage those interests.'[65] The practice of a craft was seen as a salvation by members of the guild, while psychoanalysts such as Melanie Klein see it as a productive expression of mourning.⁶⁶ 'Weaving and such the world over', Vasey claimed, 'have done a great deal to bring healing to broken lives, and for us, on our meagre pensions, these hobbies have the great advantage of bringing pleasure and profits and friends.'⁶⁷ Their bonding was stipulated in the motto of their news sheet:

> We all belong to each other,
> We all need each other ...
> Sacrificing for our common good,
> That we are finding our true life.⁶⁸

It was within the safety of their own circle that Vasey believed they would find refuge from the broader community's patronising treatment of them. The whole trend, observed Vasey, was 'to make her feel a social outcast'. She despised references to the war widow as a 'pensioner' and potentially a criminal, threatened with fines for misstatements.⁶⁹ The slur of 'charity' was offensive and unnecessary, and they did not intend to become financially dependent. Such a dependency, which 'is so easily created by "handouts", destroyed self respect and self reliance, "qualities" we must preserve if our children are to be worthy of their fathers'.⁷⁰ The pride and self-esteem attached to being a war widow in the early 1950s, she believed, was degraded by low payment. Despite a concern that the 'nation can never repay its heroes', there was little done to help the plight of the war widow. Countering accusations of dependency was extremely important for Vasey, who, coming from a middle-class background, was insulted by the idea of charity. 'There is nothing charitable', she maintained, 'about a country paying the widows of men who lost their lives defending it.'⁷¹ In the complex intersection of class and gendered identities, Vasey perceived herself in emotional terms as an *outcast*, marginal and adrift.

In this respect, the War Widows Guild served a particular purpose. A dominant theme in its literature was the exclusiveness of the war widow's experience. As we have seen, only other war widows, it was claimed, would be able to understand and sympathise with the emotional plight of what they experienced. They were at pains to stress their distinctive identity. In preparation for the Royal Tour of 1954, Vasey expressed a hope that the war widow would be given privileges. 'I don't think it is advisable for war widows who are real war widows to surrender any of their prerogatives on these occasions as it is only due to our hard fought battle for these prerogatives that we have got anywhere at all in seeing that reasonable treatment is accorded [to] war widows.'⁷² Arrangements had been made to organise civilian widows, remarried widows, mothers, cousins, aunts who had as many privileges as the war widow herself. 'I hope that by the time the Royal Tour takes place all these [injustices] will be corrected.'[73] The third annual conference of the guild during August 1949 reinforced this collective identity. 'The spirit of the conference' was 'remarkable for the happiness felt by all at being together and the strength it gave us all to have other women's support, interest and understanding'.[74] The anger and resentment at being neglected were pronounced; that they were slighted, neglected and disappointed became a pivotal part of war widows' argument for increased remuneration and subsidies by the state. They were not prepared to accept a marginalised position; war widows were determined to have their voices heard, and to challenge assumptions that they would mourn passively. They refused to become what Jean Elshtain has termed 'The Beautiful Soul', the 'frugal, self sacrificing ... delicate woman', representing home and hearth.[75]

The War Widows Guild was not merely an organisation which provided women with information and services. It served to sustain, reinforce and define their identity as war widows.[76] The women's mourning provided an opportunity to continuously 're-experience their loss',[77] but it also provided a means through which to empower themselves. They were, they insisted, not 'ordinary' widows: the war elevated their loss and gave it a particular legitimacy and meaning.

Crucially, however, their war widow status gave them an avenue through which to express their anger fully and publicly. A sentiment which was not an acceptable part of the 1950s model of femininity was projected towards the authorities, ostensibly because of their lack of remuneration and recognition but also as an expression of their mourning. The identity of a war widow allowed them – in Klein's terms – to 'rebuild with anguish the inner world, which is felt to be in danger of deteriorating and collapsing'.[78]

Public Mourning

The second arena where war widows felt aggrieved and which allowed them to release their anger was in the ritual of public mourning. This became a contentious issue and the source of much dispute in relation to Anzac Day. In the 1953–54 annual report of the War Widows Guild, Vasey noted that a matter 'of concern' to the guild was that the Melbourne ceremony for Anzac Day 1953, 'from the war widow's point of view', met with 'almost universal disapproval'. The widows were offended by being placed 'well to the side on rough forms and opposite a trodden piece of turf in which they were asked to thrust little wooden crosses'. This behaviour was 'cruel and thoughtless'. War widows felt that the honour supposedly paid to their husbands' memories was 'farcical when the widows of those same men were so pointedly ignored'.[79]

The widows' resentment of their neglect reached a crisis in the furore which arose over the Anzac Day ceremony in 1954. The War Widows Guild decided that it would no longer 'take part officially in the Anzac Day Service under the present arrangements'. The anger elicited by the perceived slight was fierce and forceful. 'For years now', wrote Vasey, 'widows have been telling us of the pain they felt, *not because they themselves were snubbed* – after all, they are used to it – but because the general disregard of the war widows and widowed mothers made them feel the sacrifices of our own beloved husbands and sons were thereby being ignored.'[80] The guild organised its own service on Remembrance Day in 1954, thus giving the widows – in their terms – a 'feeling of a shared rather than an isolated burden'.[81]

The Queen's visit in the same year made their perceived marginalisation particularly poignant. The peripheral space allocated to them at the Shrine of Remembrance in Melbourne was a source of frustration for some of the widows who had gathered. Mrs N. R. Hall claimed that 'war widows have only memories left – But to be so treated was an insult to those memories'.[82] According to Mrs G. L. Thomas, 'our reserve looked good [on paper], but the high granite wall in front and the slope behind made it very poor. Then, on top of this, we were pushed back further. It just took everything away from us.'[83]

Vasey was horrified to report that at the Shrine dedication, most war widows and mothers were 'pushed behind walls away from their allotted place', so they could not hear or see the service. Other people had told her of their shame in 'occupying a position in front of the war widows'. 'If it had not been such a sacred occasion,' Vasey warned, 'we would have taken the seats by force.'[84] The lack of recognition which accentuated her loss fuelled her anger. Vasey's personal hurt was most evident. 'There were', she insisted, 'two groups of widows on the day: those who had a distant view of the ceremony and could hear a little of it and so felt they had taken part ... and those heartbroken widows and mothers who were pushed round to the east steps and could neither hear nor see'.[85]

War widows had few avenues available to them to express their anger. Raymond Evans has noted that herein lies one explanation for the violent behaviour in public by some women who had lost men during the First World War. As a 'process of repression and projection', he argues, the 'sublimation of grief carried the potential for impacting more profoundly on women than on men, accustomed as the former normally were to displaying their emotions openly and fulsomely'.[86] The homefront conflicts, which exacerbated the pressures widows were forced to contain during the First World War, were absent in the Second because there was much less social strife. Nonetheless there remained few outlets for such expression and release.

Maintaining Memories

Besides the war widows' emphasis on their identity and their demand for a place in public mourning, a third dimension of grief and loss emerges: the ways in which many of these women kept alive memories of their husbands. Jessie Vasey did this by upholding the image of her husband as a gallant soldier. She adopted her husband's language and his vision; she evoked his spirit and the imagery of battle when she spoke on behalf of the War Widows Guild. Such immortalisation suggests she had not established boundaries between herself and her husband; she was unable to comprehend the 'reality of separateness'.[87] The existence of the lost object which is 'psychically prolonged' recalls Freud's distinctions between mourning and melancholia, where the mourner succeeds in departing, while the melancholic returns to 'the traumatic event in dreams, fantasies and other substitute forms'.[88] But, as Eric Santner argues, it is more accurate to 'speak of a continuum or a layering ... of mourning in any specific experience of loss'.[89] It is often through nostalgia – a desire 'for the time and not for the thing to be recovered'[90] – that can, as many have argued, mark a 'sort of half-way house between melancholia and mourning'.[91] Others have conceptualised this through regret, sustained by 'nostalgia's desire that things might be different'.[92]

The nature of Jessie Vasey's relationship to past events, and her identity as *Mrs Vasey*, was defined by a range of complex intersecting processes.[93] A mere two years after her loss, in 1947, Vasey insisted that the war widow 'is the person for whom there can be no post war normality'.[94] But during the ensuing years, the War Widows Guild became an institution which attempted to establish a degree of normality for women whose lives had been dislocated by war.

In utilising the language of war, Vasey also encroached on the exclusive knowledge of soldiers, which also allowed her to attain a degree of autonomy. By upholding the memory of her husband, she revisited a 'lost time'[95] to retrieve a sense of herself, and, within the context of the 1950s, this identification helped her to obtain a voice, a degree of power in the public realm.

Following her husband's death, Vasey received hundreds of letters from friends offering their condolences. Sustaining a link with the past through nostalgia – which it has been suggested is a 'feminine' form of melancholia[96] – became an important way of protecting against loss.

Doris McCutcheon perhaps was typical in helping Vasey sustain her husband's memory. She was moved to comment on the 'wonderful tributes [that] are being paid to his qualities as a soldier and a man, and we all know how the men loved him and would have followed him anywhere'. 'How proud', she says, 'you will always be of his great contribution to his country in the time of your great need. We believe that his influence will still be with those who have to carry on, so that things may be accomplished.'[97] Annette Sage of the Australian Army Nursing Service wrote that she would 'trust you will be comforted by the knowledge that his grand service is known to so many who will treasure that memory for many many years to come'.[98] It was expected that General Vasey's glory would sustain Mrs Vasey through her period of grief. G. H. Knox observed that she should have 'tremendous pride in his outstanding career which may do something to lessen your own grief'.[99] In death was a mixture of glory and pain: 'mixed with your sadness your heart must be filled with pride for your husband who was such an outstanding man and loved by all', wrote Doris Disher.[100] Frank Berryman noted that at 'the height of a brilliant career he has been taken and may the knowledge of his successful service and outstanding record help to temper your grief'.[101] Rene Graham perhaps most succinctly stated how Mrs Vasey's own identity was inextricably part of her husband's. 'You have the comfort of knowing that all through your married life', she wrote, 'you did all in your power to help him.'[102]

It was common for war widows to define themselves in relation to their husbands in their demand for proper remuneration. 'Our women', Vasey insisted in 1947, 'don't want to be objects of charity, pity and patronage ... the most dangerous of all forms of social service is benevolence from above ... we want to give these women hope to make them proud of being war widows, and not ashamed'.[103] At the first annual meeting of the New South Wales branch of the War Widows Guild in September 1947, the members were animated 'by the spirit that inspired your husbands, you are striving to be more reliant'.[104] The evocation of their husbands' spirit of self-reliance and independence was as common as their insistence that they were carrying on their husbands' patriotic work. These metaphors and images became an important part of Vasey's public repertoire. Our 'men died for this wonderful land', she declared in 1952, and 'we must carry on our own rich heritage of pride and country and bonds of Empire, and we must fight with all our strength every insidious attempt by any subversive section of the community to undermine this pride'.[105] Vasey urged women to remember that our 'husbands fought against hopeless odds and overcame them; we can do the same for ... [from] their sacrifice will come our strength'.[106]

This perspective certainly helped to legitimise their claims. At various points, the press drew on the tragedy of the war widows' plight. In October 1945, the Melbourne *Herald* reported that the loss suffered by war widows has no parallel. No one will deny that the death of a civilian causes sorrow and distress in some homes; but the war widow's loss arises from the stark tragedy of war ... their wives had every right to look forward to many years of happiness and companionship after five or six years of sacrifice and separation.[107]

Vasey retained her connection with her husband's image, but it should be remembered that it was difficult to resist any other identity apart from that of Mrs Vasey, even if she desired it. Widows whose husbands were of more junior rank were not under the same public scrutiny as the wife of a general. George Vasey was one of the army's most illustrious commanders, whose memory the army would never obliterate. In 1957, the Royal Australian Infantry requested a 'little item that belonged to the late General. It matters not how small or modest it may be. This we would ... display in our Mess.' In a comment which would have heartened Jessie Vasey, twelve years after her husband's death the letter mentioned 'how fresh his memory remains with us'. Such memories were most important for her. When Brigadier John Field sent Mrs Vasey a photograph, she wrote, it is 'little things like this which make me feel that some of his own personality still lingers with the men who knew him'.

Other reminders came from biographers. From one author came the request for a discussion about General Vasey because he was a 'unique personality', and wanted to speak about her husband 'as only you knew him'. These requests continued for many years. In 1960, H. J. Manning wrote to Mrs Vasey informing her that he was giving a radio talk about 'the services of your husband ... I only hope I can do justice to the subject, and will certainly send you a copy of a script.' Clive Morton, who was writing a biography of Evelyn Owen, the inventor of the 'well known sub-machine gun', wrote to Vasey requesting whether 'your late husband, may have mentioned the Owen to you by conversation or correspondence, and in some way recorded his opinion of it'. Mrs Vasey replied apologetically that 'terrible responsibilities were on my husband's shoulders and during the war my contact with him was not very great. I am sorry to say that I have no recollection at all of any opinion expressed by him concerning the Owen gun.' Another inquiry came from Cleve H. Carney, for 'an original specimen of your late husband's signature. For some years I have been compiling a collection of autographs of people of high reputation and outstanding achievement.' The collection included some 130 generals of both world wars and he would be 'very grateful if I could ... add General Vasey's signature to this collection'.

There is no doubt that Vasey willingly adopted the persona of her husband. Helping war widows, initially his vision, became her central quest and she was fond of recalling that it was her husband who spoke of them to her. He had alerted her to the 'sad patient faces' of the widows of the First World War and he reminded her that we, as a community, 'had been so heedless of the price they had paid for our survival'.

There were other ways in which the presence of General Vasey loomed among the shadows. After one of her public speaking engagements in 1949, Sir Stanton Hicks wrote to Vasey observing that 'seemingly our beloved leader George Vasey, has come back and spoken'.[108] She encouraged the comparisons. In the last letter General Vasey wrote to his wife, she confessed to a journalist in October 1947, he said that 'war has its moments for men, but nothing beyond stoical endurance for the woman who must wait at home'. She had then taken up his cause, using, as was noted in the report, 'her husband's favourite soldier's adjectives'. The journalist noted that she had the 'charm of manner and forthrightness of expression that endeared her husband to tens of thousands of Diggers of the AIF'.[109] In 1947, it was reported that she called the granting of a pension increase as a 'small step', and used 'soldierly language'. Although Mrs Vasey modelled her public style on both the presence and absence of her husband, we should also remember that the media could deal with women in public life only by masculinising them. Mrs Vasey, the 'fighting wife of a fighting soldier', reported the *Daily Telegraph*, was an 'unusual woman', because she 'speaks her mind as frankly as a man, without being masculine'.[110] It was in this space where Vasey did not separate herself from her husband's identity that she gained a voice in the public arena.

Through the War Widows Guild, Vasey touched the lives of many women. 'It was with profound admiration', wrote Edith McLeod in November 1945, 'that I read and re-read the stirring appeal which came from you ... I heartily congratulate you ... and I feel sure your proposed effort to [form] the Guild will be welcomed by hundreds of war widows.'[111] For Vasey, war widows were a part of the 'unanchored people – people with only a place on the fringes of society'.[112] This metaphor suggests dislocation and fragmentation; it was these gaps and rifts which enabled Vasey and other women to negotiate their wartime grief and shape a sense of themselves which was both productive and sustaining.

Conclusion

Judith Butler draws a connection between grief, its public acknowledgement, and political activism, arguing that if 'the grief remains unspeakable, the rage over the loss can redouble by virtue of remaining unavowed'. She observes that 'collective institutions for grieving are thus crucial to survival, to reassembling community, to rearticulating kinship, to reweaving sustaining relations'.[1]

In this book I have explored the experience of loss in war where mothers, widows, fathers and limbless soldiers attempted to articulate a public language of grief to claim a legitimacy for their private loss. In mourning their loss, they attempted to sustain the memory of *their* sacrifice. This study suggests that this mourning process was a productive one, as grief became politicised. During the postwar years, mothers, fathers, widows and limbless soldiers channelled their grief through protest, as a way of redefining notions of sacrifice. They organised public meetings, formed associations, distributed newsletters, and lobbied politicians, demanding a privileged recognition of their grief and a revered place in public memory.

In the Australian context this process was given particular expression by the separation of the homefront and the battlefront. This brought mourners together in intimate ways, where their sense of loss and absence was shaped by the *anticipation* of bereavement. The bodies of Australian soldiers remained in Europe and they were buried there. For the bereaved, this encouraged an obsession with the details of death and with the grave site. Without the ritual of a funeral and a dead body, it was difficult for some to imagine that the soldier whom they had last seen alive was now deceased. Relatives of both wars were desperate to obtain all the details they could about their deceased sons and husbands. In doing so, some absorbed themselves in the presence of the soldier and resisted the possibility of death. These circumstances forged particular relationships between soldiers and mothers and between mothers; in the mourning process the mother developed both a detachment from, and a continuity with, her deceased son. Soldiers who were absorbed with grief took care to capture the details of death for relatives. Their letters were often written from the weight of guilt but, in writing about death, they eulogised the military persona they themselves were shedding.

When the soldiers returned, women became marginalised within public memory. The sacrifice of men abroad, serving in glory with other nations, was evoked as the only 'sacrifice'. By the 1930s, the identity of the sacrificial mother had been conflated with the generic category of 'woman', thus denying mothers' entry into the public memory of war through their maternal sacrifice. These repressions would later be projected as anger and resentment. Remuneration in the form of the war widow's pension – considered 'blood money' – seemed both inadequate and inappropriate as a way of compensating for widows' loss.

The division of the homefront from the battlefront accentuated this ideal. It fuelled the Anzac mythology which glorified and elevated soldiers' heroism. In the stark separation of the two fronts, the myth-making associated with the battlefields overshadowed the grief of others at home. Paradoxically, while the distance from the battlefields of Europe may have lessened the impact of war on the population, without the rituals and rites of mourning, the process of separating from the deceased was often protracted. When this boundary was dissolved in February 1942, with the Japanese attack on Darwin on the northern coast of Australia, the privilege of being removed from the frontline was momentarily lost. But this was not a sustained invasion and the Japanese attack was repelled. After the British could no longer be relied upon to come to Australia's aid, Prime Minister John Curtin made a plea to America to come to its assistance. With the end of Australia's dependent relationship on Britain came a lament and sense of loss at its passing.

My concern in this book has been to explore intimate, personal and individual forms of grief not centred on public sites of mourning, like monuments and memorials. While the expression of loss may have been freer and looser during the Second World War than the First, in both wars, the individual journey into nostalgia – a time without loss – through family narratives was a path forward for those dealing with loss. Family history provided continuity and connectedness with the deceased, as new family dynamics had to be forged, and the loss of past relationships had to be mourned.

It is difficult to make conclusions about how the nature of death in wartime – through disease, in captivity, or through frontline combat – affected mourners. The vociferous desire for detail of how death occurred characterised the response by relatives, but the sites of death also connected strangers to each other. Relatives of prisoners of war, for instance, felt bonded. As for the prisoners of war themselves, the captivity experience drew the relatives into a common grief, and it inspired them to organise as a particularly grief-stricken group. Similarly, battles drew together relatives whose sons had perished together in frontline combat.

In forging these bonds, fathers could often join in the mateship and camaraderie of male organisations, while widows' and mothers' organisations were not given such legitimacy. Fathers achieved an exalted masculinity vicariously through their sons, as they displaced their own desire to be heroes onto them. Women, on the other hand, were expected to live by a morality appropriate to those deemed responsible for perpetuating a sacrificial memory; war widows had to justify their claims and prove their moral worth as welfare recipients. Resentment between war widows was fuelled as those women who had lost their men felt they would be forever blighted by the war. Poor remuneration politicised some widows who lobbied politicians for an increase in their pensions. Immediately after both wars, widows insisted that their anguish not be lost in understandings of sacrifice which marginalised their own.

Black Australians attempted to attain legitimacy for the loss they endured through violent displacement and dispossession, but their memories of their wars could not be a part of these structures of white supremacy. During the inter-war years, they protested against the denial and neglect of their dispossession, but the memories of the battles they had waged were not a source of white commemoration, as Aboriginal land was handed to returned servicemen. Although pensions for war widows provided some recognition of the contribution of Aboriginal soldiers during and after the Second World War, the loss and grief of Aboriginal communities remained in the shadow of white appropriation.

The two world wars transformed the ways in which white Australians mourned their dead. Because such huge numbers of men had perished in war, there were no longer the elaborate public processions for the dead. The impact on communities like Australia was to make mourning a simpler practice and a more private matter. In individual terms, in these stories we can see how a different sense of self was shaped through the experience of grief induced by war. New identities as war widow, father or mother of a deceased soldier, allowed the bereaved to begin imagining an alternative life without the dead, which was a necessary part of their journey towards healing and closure.

Notes

INTRODUCTION

1 Sigmund Freud, 'Thoughts for the Times on War and Death' (1915), in *Civilisation, Society and Religion: Group Psychology, Civilisation and Its Discontents and Other Works*, London, Penguin, 1985, p. 61.
2 ibid., p. 65.
3 Adrian Gregory, *The Silence of Memory: Armistice Day, 1919–1946*, Oxford, Berg Publishers, 1994, p. 20.
4 George Hagman, 'Mourning: A Review and Reconsideration', *International Journal of Psychoanalysis*, no. 76, 1995, pp. 916–17.
5 For the process, see Robert Gaines, 'Detachment and Continuity: The Two Tasks of Mourning', in *Contemporary Psychoanalysis*, vol. 33, no. 4, 1997, pp. 549–71.
6 Douglas Crisp, 'Mourning and Militancy', *October*, no. 51, 1989, pp. 3–7.
7 See in particular, Jay Winter, *Sites of Memory, Sites of Mourning: The Great War in European Cultural History*, Cambridge, Cambridge University Press, 1995; Joanna Bourke, *Dismembering the Male: Men's Bodies, Britain and the Great War*, London, Reaktion Books, 1996; Eric Leed, *No Man's Land: Combat and Identity in World War I*, Cambridge, Cambridge University Press, 1979; Klaus Theweleit, *Male Fantasies, Volume 1: Women, Floods, Bodies, History*, Minneapolis, University of Minnesota, 1987.
8 Pat Jalland, *Death in the Victorian Family*, Oxford, Oxford University Press, 1997; and David Cannadine, 'War and Death, Grief and Mourning in Modern Britain', in Joachim Whaley (ed.), *Mirrors of Mortality: Studies in the Social History of Death*, London, Europa Publications, 1981, pp. 187–242; Winter, *Sites of Memory, Sites of Mourning*.
9 Eric Santner, 'History Beyond the Pleasure Principle: Some Thoughts on the Representation of "Trauma"', in Saul Friedlander (ed.), *Probing the Limits of Representation: Nazism and the 'Final Solution'*, Massachusetts, Harvard University Press, 1992, p. 145.
10 See Winter, *Sites of Memory, Sites of Mourning*, pp. 119, 127–33, 223.
11 George Mosse, *Fallen Soldiers: Reshaping Memory of the World Wars*, New York, Oxford University Press, 1990, p. 6.
12 The literature on these fields is now vast. For more recent references, see Winter, *Sites of Memory, Sites of Mourning*; Mosse, *Fallen Soldiers*; Thomas Laqueur, 'Memory and Naming in the Great War', in John Gillis (ed.), *Commemorations: The Politics of National Identity*, Princeton, Princeton University Press, 1994, pp. 150–67; Lyn Spillman, *Nation and*

Notes to page 2 165

Commemoration: Creating National Identities in the United States and Australia, New York, Cambridge University Press, 1997; Daniel Sherman, 'Mourning and Masculinity in France After World War One', *Gender and History*, vol. 8, no. 1, 1996, pp. 82–107; Pierre Nora, *Realms of Memory and Rethinking the French Past*, New York, Columbia University Press, 1996; Paula Hamilton and Kate-Darian Smith (eds), *Memory and History in Twentieth-Century Australia*, Melbourne, Oxford University Press, 1994; K. S. Inglis and Jock Phillips, 'War Memorials in Australia and New Zealand: A Comparative Survey', in John Rickard and Peter Spearritt (eds), 'Packaging the Past: Past Histories', *Australian Historical Studies*, vol. 24, no. 6, 1991; K. S. Inglis, 'Entombing Unknown Soldiers: From London and Paris to Bagdad', *History and Memory*, vol. 5, no. 2, 1993, pp. 7–31; Ken Inglis, 'Men, Women and War Memorials: Anzac Australia', in Jill K. Conway, Susan C. Bourque and Joan W. Scott (eds), *Learning About Women: Gender, Politics and Power*, Ann Arbor, University of Michigan Press, 1989, pp. 35–59; Raphael Samuel, *Theatres of Memory, Volume 1: Past and Present in Contemporary Culture*, London, Verso, 1994; James Young (ed.), *The Art of Memory: Holocaust Memorials in History*, New York, Prestel Verlag, 1994; Geoffrey Hartman (ed.), *Holocaust Remembrance: The Shapes of Memory*, Oxford, Basil Blackwell, 1994; Raphael Samuel and Paul Thompson (eds), *The Myths We Live By*, London, Routledge, 1990; Catherine Speck, 'Women's War Memorials and Citizenship', *Australian Feminist Studies*, vol. 11, no. 23, 1996, pp. 129–45; Susanne Brandt, 'The Memory Makers: Museums and Exhibitions of the First World War', *History and Memory*, vol. 6, no. 1, 1994, pp. 95–122.

13 See Stephen Garton, *The Cost of War: Australians Return*, Melbourne, Oxford University Press, 1996, pp. 103–8.
14 Winter, *Sites of Memory, Sites of Mourning*, p. 5.
15 For the literature on welfare, see Clem Lloyd and Jacqui Rees, *The Last Shilling: A History of Repatriation in Australia*, Melbourne, Melbourne University Press, 1994; Garton, *The Cost of War*; Lorraine Wheeler, 'War, Women and Welfare', in Richard Kennedy (ed.), *Australian Welfare: Historical Sociology*, Melbourne, Macmillan, 1989, pp. 172–93; Jill Roe, 'The End is Where We Start From: Women and Welfare since 1901', in Cora Baldock and Bettina Cass (eds), *Women, Social Welfare and the State*, Sydney, Allen & Unwin, 1983, pp. 1–19.
16 See Nancy Chodorow, 'Gender as a Personal and Cultural Construction', *Signs*, vol. 20, no. 1, 1995, p. 517; Teresa Brennan, 'An Impasse in Psychoanalysis and Feminism', in Sneja Gunew (ed.), *A Reader in Feminist Knowledge*, London, Routledge, 1990, pp. 114–38; Patricia Elliot, 'Politics, Identity and Social Change: Contested Grounds in Psychoanalytic Feminism', *Hypatia: A Journal of Feminist Philosophy*, vol. 10, no. 2, 1995, pp. 41–55; Wendy Wheeler, 'After Grief? What Kind of Selves?', *New Formations*, no. 25, 1995, p. 94; Esther Faye, 'Psychoanalysis and the Barred Subject of Feminist History', *Australian Feminist Studies*, no. 22, 1995, pp. 77–97.
17 Sally Alexander, *Becoming a Woman and Other Essays in 19th and 20th Century Feminist History*, London, Virago, 1984; Lynne Hunt, 'Psychoanalysis, the Self and Historical Interpretation', *Common Knowledge*, vol. 6, no. 2, 1997, pp. 10–19; Lyndal Roper, *Oedipus and the Devil: Witchcraft, Sexuality and*

Religion in Early Modern Europe, London, Routledge, 1994; John Rickard, *A Family Romance*, Melbourne, Melbourne University Press, 1996.
18 Santner, 'History beyond the Pleasure Principle', p. 6.
19 Sigmund Freud, 'Mourning and Melancholia' (1917), in *On Metapsychology: The Theory of Psychoanalysis*, Volume 11, Penguin Freud Library, London, Penguin, 1991, pp. 251–68.
20 See Kathleen Woodward, 'Freud and Barthes: Theorizing Mourning, Sustaining Grief', *Discourse*, vol. 13, no. 1, 1990–91, pp. 93–6; Eric Santner, *Stranded Objects: Mourning, Memory and Film in Postwar Germany*, Ithaca, Cornell University Press, 1990, p. 3.
21 Jane Flax, *Disputed Subjects: Essays on Psychoanalysis, Politics and Philosophy*, New York, Routledge, 1993, pp. 94–6.
22 Wendy Wheeler, 'After Grief? What Kind of Selves?', p. 79.
23 For an engagement along these lines, see, George Hagman, 'Mourning: A Review and Reconsideration', *International Journal of Psychoanalysis*, no. 76, 1995, pp. 909–25; George Hagman, 'The Role of the "Other" in Mourning', *Psychoanalytic Quarterly*, LXV, 1996, pp. 327–52; Mardi J. Horowitz, 'A Model of Mourning: Change in Schemes of Self and Other', *Journal of the American Psychoanalytic Association*, vol. 38, no. 2, 1990, pp. 297–324.
24 Melanie Klein, 'Mourning and Its Relation to Manic Depressive States' (1940), in Melanie Klein, *Love, Guilt and Repatriation and Other Works, 1921–1945*, London, Virago, 1988, p. 360; Judith Butler, 'Melancholy Gender: Refused Identification', in Judith Butler, *The Psychic Life of Power: Theories of Subjection*, Stanford, Stanford University Press, 1997, pp. 147–8.
25 For a discussion of displacement and projection, see Rosalind Minsky, *Psychoanalysis and Gender: An Introductory Reader*, London, Routledge, 1996, pp. 28–30; Graham Dawson, *Soldier Heroes: British Adventure, Empire and the Imagining of Masculinities*, London, Routledge, 1994, pp. 27–33.
26 For a recent discussion on memory and history, see Alon Confino, 'Collective Memory and Cultural History: Problems of Method', and Susan A. Crane, 'Writing the Individual Back into Collective Memory', *American Historical Review*, vol. 102, no. 5, 1997, pp. 1386–1403 and 1372–85, respectively.
27 Julia Kristeva, *Black Sun: Depression and Melancholia*, trans. Leon S. Roudiez, New York, Columbia University Press, 1985, p. 60.
28 See Paul Antze and Michael Lambeck (eds), *Tense Past: Cultural Essays in Trauma and Memory*, London, Routledge, 1996, pp. xv–xxi.
29 Mary Ann Doane, *'Femmes Fatales': Feminism, Film Theory, Psychoanalysis*, New York, Routledge, 1991, p. 90.
30 Michel de Certeau, *Heterologies: Discourse on the Other*, trans. Brian Massumi, University of Minnesota Press, Minneapolis, 1986, p. 4; For a discussion of the relationship between the historian and psychoanalyst, see Karl Figlio, 'Historical Imagination/Psychoanalytic Imagination', *History Workshop Journal*, no. 45, 1998, pp. 199–221.
31 For Australian studies, see Hamilton and Darian-Smith (eds), *Memory and History in Twentieth-Century Australia*; Chilla Bulbeck, 'Aborigines, Memorials and the History of the Frontier', in Rickard and Spearritt (eds), *Packaging the Past*, pp. 168–78; Tom Griffiths, *Hunters and Collectors: The Antiquarian Imagination in Australia*, Melbourne, Cambridge University Press, 1996; and

Chris Healy, *From the Ruins of Colonialism: History as Social Memory*, Melbourne, Cambridge University Press, 1996.
32 Garton, *The Cost of War*; Alistair Thomson, *Anzac Memories: Living with the Legend*, Melbourne, Oxford University Press, 1994.
33 Raelene Frances and Bruce Scates, *Women and the Great War*, Melbourne, Cambridge University Press, 1992; Michael McKernan, *Padre: Australian Chaplains in Gallipoli and France*, Sydney, Allen & Unwin, 1986; Inglis, 'Entombing Unknown Soldiers'. See also Jacqueline Manuel, ' "We are the women who mourn our dead": Australian Civilian Women's Poetic Responses to the First World War', *Journal of the Australian War Memorial*, no. 29, 1996.
34 Raymond Evans, ' "All the Passion of Our Womanhood": Margaret Thorp and the Battle of the Brisbane School of Arts', in Joy Damousi and Marilyn Lake (eds), *Gender and War: Australians at War in the Twentieth Century*, Melbourne, Cambridge University Press, 1995, p. 248.
35 See for instance, John R. Gillis (ed.), *Commemorations: The Politics of National Identity*, Princeton, Princeton University Press, 1994.
36 Beverley Raphael, *The Anatomy of Bereavement*, New York, Basic Books, 1983, p. 57.
37 Winter, *Sites of Memory, Sites of Mourning*, pp. 29–53; Jalland, *Death in the Victorian Family*, p. 375.
38 Modris Eksteins, *Rites of Spring: The Great War and the Birth of the Modern Age*, Boston, Houghton, 1989, pp. 254–6.
39 For the need to consider individual responses, see George Hagman, 'Mourning: A Review and a Reconsideration'; and mourning as a social process, see Hagman, 'The Role of the "Other" in Mourning'.
40 The most comprehensive study remains the work by Graeme M. Griffin and Des Tobin, *In the Midst of Life: Australian Responses to Death*, Melbourne, Melbourne University Press, 1982/1997. See also Marian Aveling, 'Death and the Family in Nineteenth-Century Western Australia', Patricia Grimshaw et al. (eds), *Families in Colonial Australia*, Sydney, Allen & Unwin, 1985, pp. 32–41; Leonie B. Liveris, *The Dismal Trader: The Undertaker Business in Perth, 1860–1939*, Perth, Park Printing, 1991; Kerreen Reiger and Margaret James, 'Hatches, Matches and Dispatches', in Verity Burgmann and Jenny Lee (eds), *A People's History of Australia*, Melbourne, McPhee Gribble/Penguin, 1988, pp. 14–17; 'Old Age and Death', in Graeme Davison, J. W. McCarty and Ailsa McLeary (eds), *Australians 1888*, Sydney, Fairfax, Syme and Weldon, 1987, p. 323; K. S. Inglis, 'Passing Away', in Bill Gammage and Peter Spearritt (eds), *Australians 1938*, Sydney, Fairfax, Syme and Weldon, 1987, pp. 234–458; Kathy Charmaz, Glennys Howarth and Allan Kellehear (eds), *The Unknown Country: Death in Australia, Britain and the USA*, London, Macmillan, 1997; Grace Karskens, 'Death Was in His Face: Dying, Burial and Remembrance in Early Sydney', *Labour History*, no. 74, 1998, pp. 21–37.
41 See Peter Read, *Returning to Nothing: The Meaning of Lost Places*, Melbourne, Cambridge University Press, 1996.
42 Winter, *Sites of Memory, Sites of Mourning*, pp. 78–116; Daniel Sherman, 'Mourning and Masculinity in France After World War One', pp. 82–107.
43 Daniel J. Sherman, 'Bodies and Names: The Emergence of Commemoration in Interwar France', *American Historical Review*, vol. 103, no. 2, 1998, pp. 443–66.
44 Winter, *Sites of Memory, Sites of Mourning*, pp. 29–53.

45 For this process, see Raphael, *The Anatomy of Bereavement*, p. 50.
46 Humphrey Morris, 'Narrative Representation, Narrative Enactment, and the Psychoanalytic Construction of History', *International Journal of Psychoanalysis*, no. 74, 1993, p. 38.
47 Gertrude Stein, *Wars I Have Seen*, London, Batsford, 1945, p. 2.

1 THEATRES OF GRIEF, THEATRES OF LOSS

1 'The New Communion', (July 1917) by H. B. Higgins, Folder 1, H. B. Higgins Papers, MS 2525, National Library of Australia (hereafter NLA).
2 See Paul Fussell, *The Great War and Modern Memory*, Oxford, Oxford University Press, 1975, pp. 191–230.
3 E. W. D. Laing, 22 November 1917, 1 DRL/0023, Australian War Memorial (hereafter AWM). (Quotations from manuscript letters are verbatim except for the correction of obvious errors of spelling and punctuation.)
4 The difficult process of relinquishing these bonds is described in Raphael, *The Anatomy of Bereavement*, pp. 43–4.
5 For the impact of the war on rituals of death see, for instance, Jalland, *Death in the Victorian Family*, pp. 358–80.
6 Karskens, 'Death Was in His Face', p. 36.
7 ibid.
8 'Old Age and Death', in Davison, McCarty and McLeary (eds), *Australians 1888*, p. 340.
9 ibid.
10 Peter C. Jupp, 'Why Was England the First Country to Popularise Cremation?', in Charmaz, Howarth and Kellehear (eds), *The Unknown Country*, p. 146.
11 Raphael, *The Anatomy of Bereavement*, pp. 29–30.
12 ibid., p. 57; Kathy Charmaz, 'Grief and Loss of Self', in Charmaz, Howarth and Kellehear (eds), *The Unknown Country*, pp. 232–4.
13 Raphael, *The Anatomy of Bereavement*, p. 57.
14 For a discussion on the cultural and historical practice of letter-writing, see 'Men/Women of Letters', Special Issue, *Yale French Studies*, no. 71, 1986; Linda S. Bergmann, 'The Contemporary Letter as Literature: Issues of Self-Reflexivity, Audience and Closure', *Women's Studies Quarterly*, nos. 3 and 4, 1989, pp. 128–39; Trev Lynne Broughton and Linda Anderson (eds), *Women's Lives/Women's Times: New Essays on Auto/Biography*, New York, State University of New York Press, 1997.
15 The process is considered theoretically in Dawson, *Soldier Heroes*, pp. 19–26.
16 Fussell, *The Great War*, p. 170.
17 This is in contrast to Fussell's argument that soldiers wrote letters which were generic. See ibid., pp. 181–2.
18 See Rose Lucas, 'The Gendered Battlefield: Sex and Death in *Gallipoli*', in Damousi and Lake (eds), *Gender and War*, p. 156; Bourke, *Dismembering the Male*, pp. 124–70.
19 Lieut. John A. Archibald, 11th Battalion, 1 October 1917, 1DRL/0023, AWM.
20 Sgt Livingstone to Mrs Chapman, 17 October 1917, 1DRL/0198, AWM.
21 J. K. Forsyth to Mrs Derham, 1 June 1916, Letters to 'APD', 7/1/1c, Alfred Derham Papers, University of Melbourne Archives.
22 ibid.

23 Frank Lind to Mrs Derham, 14 January 1915, 7/1/1c, Derham Papers.
24 Pte W. H. Wallace to Mr Naylor, 7 April 1917, George Naylor Papers, MS 10024, La Trobe Library, State Library of Victoria (hereafter SLV).
25 'Alex' to Mr & the Misses Hislop, 19 August 1916, Allan Hislop Papers, MS 10989, MSB349, La Trobe Library, SLV.
26 Capt. R. F. French to Mrs Anderson, 29 August 1916, 2DRL/0165, AWM.
27 C. S. D. Adamson, 11 September 1918, 2DRL/0726, AWM.
28 This aspect is often overlooked in war narratives. The most recent example is Samuel Hynes, *The Soldiers' Tale: Bearing Witness to Modern War*, New York, Allen Lane/The Penguin Press, 1977, who argues, 'Nobody, however young, returns from war still a boy, and in that sense, at least, war does make men' (p. 5).
29 Will Brydie to Mr Briggen, 11 March 1918, E. H. Briggen Papers, MS 10170, MSB507, SLV.
30 William T. Goodman to Mrs Hislop, 20 October 1916, Hislop Papers.
31 Goodman to Mrs Hislop, 19 February 1917, ibid.
32 ibid.
33 ibid., 21 October 1917.
34 Capt. Norman W. Sunder to Mr Allan, 25 September 1917, 1DRL/0023, AWM.
35 Thomas W. Laqueur, 'Names, Bodies, and the Anxiety of Erasure', in Theodore R. Schatzki and Wolfgang Natter (eds), *The Social and Political Body*, New York, Guilford Press, 1996, p. 126.
36 Moriaty, Australian Red Cross, Kent, to Mr Chapman, 6 May 1917, 1DRL/0198, AWM.
37 F. McInerney to Dear Earnie, 13 July 1917, 1DRL/0081, AWM.
38 ibid.
39 Lieut. John A. Archibald to Mr Allan, 1 October 1917, 1DRL/0023, AWM.
40 Fussell, *The Great War and Modern Memory*, p. 161; Martyn Lyons and Lucy Taska, *Australian Readers Remember*, Melbourne, Oxford University Press, 1992, p. 58.
41 Fussell, *The Great War and Modern Memory*, p. 175.
42 J. E. Norman Osborne to Mr Briggen, 16 March 1918, Briggen Papers.
43 Capt. R. M. Anderson to Mr Briggen, 11 March 1918, ibid.
44 Roy Youdale to Mrs Martin, 14 June 1918, 1DRL/0485, AWM.
45 Maj. B Coy to R. A. McDonald, 24 November 1916, PR86/197, AWM.
46 Mayor of Brisbane to Mrs Annie Hislop, 27 November 1916, Hislop Papers.
47 A. H. Peake to Madam, 26 December 1918, Duncan Family Papers, 1916–19, PRG544, Mortlock Library, State Library of South Australia (hereafter SLSA).
48 Shire Secretary to Mrs Leahy, 23 November 1917, PRG938/2, Claude Leahy Papers, Mortlock Library, SLSA.
49 Lieut. John Archibald, 11th Battalion, 1 October 1917, 1DRL/0023, AWM.
50 Michael McKernan, *Padre: Australian Chaplains in Gallipoli and France*, Sydney, Allen & Unwin, 1986, pp. xi–xii.
51 ibid., p. xiii; Michael McKernan, *Australian Churches at War: Attitudes of the Major Churches, 1914-1918*, Canberra, Australian War Memorial, 1980, p. 53.
52 'Royal Australian Army Chaplains Department', in Peter Dennis et al. (eds), *The Oxford Companion to Australian Military History*, Melbourne, Oxford University Press, 1995, p. 512.

53 Raphael, *The Anatomy of Bereavement*, p. 35.
54 Liveris, *The Dismal Trader*, p. 148.
55 Raphael, *The Anatomy of Bereavement*, p. 35.
56 Chaplain A. E. Lapthorne to Mrs Leahy, 14 January 1914, PRG938/2, AWM.
57 Alex MacDonald to Mrs Albert, 31 January 1917, PR86/197, AWM.
58 F. W. Rolland to Mrs Albert, 2 November 1916, PR86/197, AWM.
59 Alan Wilkinson, *The Church of England and the First World War*, London, SPCK, 1978, p. 244.
60 Chaplain W. K. Douglas, 12th Battalion, 26 September 1917, 1DRL/0023, AWM.
61 C. Bullock, Catholic Chaplain, n.d., 1DRL/0056, AWM.
62 ibid.
63 David Hunter to Mrs Chapman, 5 June 1917, PR86/389, AWM.
64 William Moore, Statement, n.d., 1DRL/0640, AWM.
65 Rev. Eric Thornton to Mrs Higgins, 14 January 1929, Series 1, item 603e, Higgins Papers, MS 1057, NLA.
66 Michael McKernan, *The Australian People and the Great War*, Melbourne, Nelson, 1980, pp. 25–6.
67 ibid.
68 Reginald Pound, *The Lost Generation*, London, Constable, 1964, p. 118.
69 John Williams, *The Home Front: Britain, France and Germany, 1914–1918*, London, Constable, 1972, p. 126.
70 Winter, *Sites of Memory, Sites of Mourning*, pp. 29–53.
71 For immigrant letters, see David Fitzpatrick, *Oceans of Consolation: Personal Accounts of Irish Migration to Australia*, Melbourne, Melbourne University Press, 1995, pp. 23, 479.
72 Ruth to Alfred, 8 December 1914, Letters from Sister Ruth, 1914–1916, 7/2/1/5, Derham Papers, University of Melbourne Archives.
73 Frankie to Alfred, 14 May 1916, ibid.
74 *Official Year Book of the Commonwealth of Australia*, no. 8, 1915, p. 697; no. 9, 1916, p. 699; no. 10, 1917, p. 737; no. 11, 1918, p. 719.
75 ibid., no. 12, 1919, pp. 722–3.
76 ibid., no. 13, 1920, p. 1066.
77 Bourke, *Dismembering the Male*, pp. 21–2.
78 See Fussell, *The Great War and Modern Memory*, for an extensive discussion of the uniform postcard, pp. 185–7.
79 Frankie to Alfred, 6 November 1914, 7/2/1/6, Derham Papers.
80 Frankie to Derham, 5 November 1915, ibid.
81 Marianne Wiggins, *John Dollar*, London, Penguin, 1989, pp. 13–14.
82 Other communities bonded in relation to the dead. See Winter, *Sites of Memory, Sites of Mourning*, pp. 30–50.
83 H. M. Blann-Ashton to Mrs Brooks, 24 July 1918, 2DRL/0726, AWM.
84 Lyons and Taska, *Australian Readers Remember*, p. 72.
85 R. B. Walker, *The Newspaper Press in New South Wales, 1803–1920*, Sydney, University of Sydney Press, 1976, p. 250.
86 M. Barrett to Mrs Derham, 16 May 1915, Letters to Derham Parents Support at being Wounded, 7/1/1a&b, Derham Papers.
87 Isabelle M. Walker to Mrs Derham, 23 May 1915, ibid.
88 Ruby Fony? 'Monday', ibid.

89 Cassie Vial, 'Friday', ibid.
90 Mary Gibson to Mrs Derham, 15 May 1915, ibid.
91 Jane? to Mrs Derham, 19 May 1915, ibid.
92 Ruth Falkingham to Mr and Mrs Derham, 16 May 1915, ibid.
93 Myrtle Forrester, 'Friday', ibid.
94 For collective identities see Sigmund Freud, 'Group Psychology and the Analysis of the Ego' (1921), in Sigmund Freud, *Civilisation, Society and Religion*, pp. 98–106; Daniel Pick, 'Freud's Group Psychology and the History of the Crowd', *History Workshop Journal*, no. 40, 1995, pp. 50–3.
95 Ruth Falkingham to Mr and Mrs Derham, 6 May 1915, 7/1/1a&b, Derham Papers.
96 D. G. Cullen to Mr Derham, 15 May 1915, ibid.
97 Annie Samuel to Mrs Derham, 15 May 1915, ibid.
98 M. Barrett to Mrs Derham, 16 May 1915, ibid.
99 Ethel Clarke to Mrs Derham, 25 May 1915, ibid.
100 Elsie Barker to 'My dear friend', 14 May 1915, ibid.
101 Gracie Derham to Alfred, n.d., Letters from Other Australian Relatives, 7/3/3, ibid.
102 Forsyth to Mrs Derham 1 June 1916, 7/1/1c, ibid.
103 Raphael, *The Anatomy of Bereavement*, p. 50.
104 Mother to Alfred, 7 December 1914, 7/2/1/1, Derham Papers.
105 ibid.
106 ibid., 8 November 1915.
107 Ruth Derham to Alfred, 15 October 1916, Letters from Sister Ruth, 1914–1916, Derham Papers, 7/2/1/5, ibid.
108 Enid to Alfred, 6 December 1914, Letters from Sister Enid, 7/2/1/4, ibid.
109 Frankie to Derham, 12 September 1916, 7/2/1/6, ibid.
110 ibid., 14 May 1916.
111 ibid., 10 September 1916.
112 ibid., 12 September 1916.
113 ibid., 19 September 1916.
114 This was also evident in the case of immigrant letters. See Fitzpatrick, *Oceans of Consolation*, p. 478.
115 Frankie to Derham, 15 October 1916, 7/2/1/6, Derham Papers.
116 ibid.

2 THE SACRIFICIAL MOTHER

1 Edward H. Segden to Mrs Stirling, 26 April 1915, Malcolm Stirling Papers, MS 10739, Box 957/1, La Trobe Library, SLV.
2 *Argus*, 9 January 1919, p. 4.
3 George Pearce (1870-1952) was defence minister in five governments from 1910 to 1921. *Australian Dictionary of Biography*, Volume 11: 1891–1939, Melbourne, Melbourne University Press, 1988, pp. 177–82.
4 *Argus*, 8 January 1919, p. 6.
5 Stuart Macintyre, *The Oxford History of Australia, Volume 4: 1901–1942*, Melbourne, Oxford University Press, pp. 177–9.
6 Garton, *The Cost of War*, p. 77.

7 For a discussion of loss, identity and melancholia, see Judith Butler, 'Melancholy Gender: Refused Identification', in Judith Butler, *The Psychic Life of Power: Theories of Subjection*, Stanford, Stanford University Press, 1997, p. 138.
8 Richard White, 'War and Australian Society', in M. McKernan and M. Browne (eds), *Australia: Two Centuries of War and Peace*, Sydney, Allen & Unwin/Australian War Memorial, 1988, p. 418.
9 ibid.
10 Edward H. Segden to Mrs Stirling, 26 April 1915, Stirling Papers.
11 'Sid' to Mother, 16 January 1915, Charles Murrell Papers, MS 11202, MSB638, La Trobe Library, SLV.
12 Mother to George, 'Sunday Evening', n.d., MS 10229–1, MSB193, George Cameron Doig Papers, La Trobe Library, SLV.
13 Mother to George, n.d., ibid.
14 Murrell, 'From the Trenches', 22 November 1915, Murrell Papers.
15 Mother to Alfred, 22 October 1914, 7/2/1/1, Derham Papers.
16 Mervyn Higgins to Mother, 8 November 1915, Series 2, item 2976, Higgins Papers.
17 Mother to Alfred, 21 August 1916, 7/2/1/1, Derham Papers.
18 ibid.
19 *Our Empire: The Official Organ of the Sailors' and Soldiers' Fathers Association of Victoria* (hereafter *Our Empire*), vol. 1, no. 4, 19 August 1918, p. 2.
20 Bill Gammage, *The Broken Years: Australian Soldiers in the Great War*, Ringwood, Vic., Penguin, 1975, pp. 7, 18–19.
21 ibid.
22 ibid, p. 21.
23 See Raymond Evans, *Loyalty and Disloyalty: Social Conflict on the Queensland Homefront, 1914–18,* Sydney, Allen & Unwin, 1987; Marilyn Lake, *A Divided Society: Tasmania During World War I*, Melbourne, Melbourne University Press, 1975.
24 *Argus*, 24 May 1916, p. 12.
25 ibid., 12 July 1916, p. 12.
26 *Australian Worker*, 12 October 1916, p. 6.
27 Judith Smart, 'Eva Hughes: Militant Conservative', in Marilyn Lake and Farley Kelly (eds), *Double Time: Women in Victoria – 150 Years*, Ringwood, Vic., Penguin, 1985, pp. 180–9.
28 ibid., p. 186.
29 *Argus*, 20 September 1916, p. 12.
30 ibid.
31 G. Keirt Piehler, 'The War Dead and the Gold Star: American Commemoration of the First World War', in John R. Gillis (ed.), *Commemorations: The Politics of National Identity*, Princeton, Princeton University Press, 1994, p. 170.
32 *Argus*, 27 September 1916, p. 16.
33 ibid., 2 August 1916, p. 12.
34 ibid.
35 ibid., 31 May 1916, p. 2.
36 ibid., 6 September 1916, p. 12.
37 ibid., 13 September 1916, p. 10.

38 See *Daily Telegraph*, 3 January 1917, p. 10; 20 March 1917, p. 8; 26 June 1917, p. 8; 8 October 1917, p. 5.
39 Sheila Adams, 'Women, Death and *In Memoriam* Notices in a Local British Newspaper', in Charmaz, Howarth and Kellehear (eds), *The Unknown Country*, pp. 98–112.
40 *Argus* 22 September 1916, p. 1.
41 ibid., 26 September 1916, p. 1.
42 *Daily Telegraph*, 6 June 1917, p. 6.
43 *Argus*, 29 September 1916, p. 1.
44 Mother to Alfred, n.d., 'Tues. Even', Letters from Mother Ellen Derham and Father Thos Derham, 1914–27, 7/2/1/1, Derham Papers.
45 Mother to Alfred, 22 October 1914, ibid.
46 ibid., 8 November 1915.
47 ibid.
48 ibid., 22 December 1915.
49 *Daily Telegraph*, 26 April 1918, p. 5.
50 ibid., 21 July 1919, p. 14.
51 ibid., 12 November 1920, p. 5.
52 ibid., 26 April 1920, p. 6.
53 *Sydney Morning Herald*, 26 April 1921, p. 8.
54 *Daily Telegraph*, 26 April 1924, p. 8.
55 ibid., 27 April 1925, p. 5.
56 ibid., 26 April 1927, p. 8.
57 *Sydney Morning Herald*, 26 April 1930, p. 13.
58 ibid., 27 April 1931, p. 10.
59 *Daily Telegraph*, 25 April 1931, p. 6.
60 ibid., 26 April 1932, p. 8.
61 ibid., 25 April 1933, p. 5.
62 Mary Louise Roberts, *Civilisation Without Sexes: Reconstructing Gender in Post-War France, 1917–1927*, Chicago, University of Chicago Press, 1994, p. 10.
63 *Argus*, 26 April 1938, p. 2.
64 *Age*, 27 April 1938.
65 ibid.
66 ibid.
67 *Argus* 30 April 1938, p. 6.
68 ibid., 4 May 1938, p. 10.
69 ibid., 7 May 1938, p. 6.
70 ibid., 10 May 1938, p. 10.
71 ibid., 26 April 1938, p. 10.
72 Jill Roe, 'Chivalry and Social Policy in the Antipodes', *Historical Studies*, vol. 22, no. 88, 1987; Marilyn Lake, 'The Independence of Women and the Brotherhood of Man: Debates in the Labor Movement over Equal Pay and Motherhood Endowment in the 1920s', *Labour History*, no. 63, 1992, pp. 16–17. See also Helen Pringle, 'The Making of an Australian Civic Identity: The Bodies of Men and the Memory of War', in Geoffrey Stokes (ed.), *The Politics of Identity in Australia*, Melbourne, Cambridge University Press, 1997, p. 102.
73 Kerreen Reiger, *The Disenchantment of the Home: Modernising the Australian Family, 1880–1940*, Melbourne, Oxford University Press, 1985, pp. 128–52.

74 Marilyn Lake, 'Feminism and the Gendered Politics of Antiracism, Australia, 1927–1957: From Maternal Protectionism to Leftist Assimilationism', *Australian Historical Studies*, vol. 29, no. 10, 1998, pp. 91–108.
75 For a detailed account of this, see Andrew Markus, *Governing Savages*, Sydney, Allen & Unwin, 1990.
76 T. W. Kewley, *Social Security in Australia; Social Security and Health Benefits from 1900 to the Present*, Sydney, Sydney University Press, 1965, pp. 103–4.
77 ibid., p. 115.
78 Garton, *The Cost of War*, p. 78.
79 Lloyd and Rees, *The Last Shilling*, pp. 23–4.
80 Garton, *The Cost of War*, pp. 79–82.
81 Gammage, *The Broken Years*, p. 10.
82 ibid., p. 239.
83 *Official Year Book of the Commonwealth of Australia*, no. 11, 1918, p. 1179.
84 ibid., no. 13, 1920, p. 1111.
85 *Argus*, 12 October 1921, p. 15.
86 Application for Assistance, 26 July 1918, Box 14, Folder 3, MS 2864, Anzac Fellowship of Women (hereafter AFW) Papers, NLA.
87 Application for Assistance, 3 December 1917, ibid.
88 Application for Assistance, 4 July 1918, ibid.
89 Application for Assistance, 17 June 1918, ibid.
90 Application for Assistance, 16 July 1918, ibid.
91 Application for Assistance, 7 December 1917, ibid.
92 Application for Assistance, 20 August 1917, ibid.
93 *Australian Dictionary of Biography*, Volume 7, p. 294.
94 *Daily Telegraph*, 9 April 1920, p. 5.
95 Raymond Evans, '"All the Passion of Our Womanhood": Margaret Thorp and the Battle of the Brisbane School of Arts', in Damousi and Lake (eds), *Gender and War*, p. 241.
96 See Garton, *The Cost of War*, p. 54.
97 *Argus*, 10 October 1928, p. 21.
98 *Daily Telegraph*, 23 November 1920, p. 3.
99 *Age*, 31 January 1919, p. 6.
100 ibid.
101 ibid., 13 January 1925, p. 6.
102 ibid., 2 November 1926, p. 13.
103 Series no: A458; item no: M382/2, Australian Archives (hereafter, AA) Canberra.
104 *Sydney Morning Herald*, 14 November 1928, p. 9.
105 ibid.
106 T. W. Kewley, *Social Security in Australia*, p. 144.
107 *Sydney Morning Herald*, 16 October 1928, p. 9.
108 ibid.
109 *Argus*, 21 August 1926, p. 29.
110 Isabel Williams to Mrs Derham, 'Sunday', 7/1/1a&b, Derham Papers.
111 Annie Robinson, 4/1915, ibid.
112 Adam Phillips, *On Flirtation*, London, Faber and Faber, 1994.

3 A FATHER'S LOSS

1. *Our Empire*, 18 July 1919, p. 17.
2. 'Australian Imperial Force', in Dennis et al. (eds), *The Oxford Companion to Australian Military History*, pp. 69–72.
3. *Our Empire*, vol. 3, no. 12, 18 April 1921, p. 17.
4. Garton, *The Cost of War*, p. 203.
5. For various aspects of these see, Kerreen Reiger, *The Disenchantment of the Home;* Michael Gilding, *The Making and Breaking of the Australian Family*, Sydney, Allen & Unwin, 1991; Jan Kociumbas, *Australian Childhood: A History*, Sydney, Allen & Unwin, 1997; Ralph La Rossa, *The Modernisation of Fatherhood: A Social and Political History*, Chicago, University of Chicago Press, 1997.
6. See Mark Lyons, *Legacy: The First Fifty Years*, Melbourne, Lothian, 1978, pp. 1–35.
7. ibid., pp. 25–32.
8. ibid., p. 23.
9. Roe, 'Chivalry and Social Policy in the Antipodes', pp. 400–1; Garton, *The Cost of War*, p. 203.
10. G. L. Kristianson, *The Politics of Patriotism: The Pressure Group Activities of the Returned Servicemen's League*, Canberra, ANU Press, 1966, p. 9.
11. Stefan Collini, *Public Moralists: Political Thought and Intellectual Life in Britain, 1850–1930*, Oxford, Clarendon Press, 1991, p. 100.
12. ibid., p. 116.
13. Allen Warren, 'Popular Manliness: Baden-Powell, Scouting and the Development of Manly Character', in J. A. Mangan and James Walvin (eds), *Manliness and Morality: Middle Class Masculinity in Britain and America, 1800–1940*, Manchester, Manchester University Press, 1987, p. 201.
14. John MacKenzie, 'The Imperial Pioneer and Hunter and the British Masculine Stereotype in the late Victorian and Edwardian Times', in Mangan and Walvin (eds), *Manliness and Morality*, pp. 188–9.
15. John Tosh, 'What Should Historians Do with Masculinity? Reflections on Nineteenth-Century Britain', *History Workshop Journal*, no. 38, 1994, pp. 186, 196.
16. Jalland, *Death in the Victorian Family*, pp. 250–3.
17. Cannadine, 'War and Death, Grief and Mourning in Modern Britain', p. 213.
18. Jalland, *Death in the Victorian Family*, p. 380.
19. Freud, 'Thoughts for the Times on War and Death', p. 61.
20. Peter C. Jupp, 'Why Was England the First Country to Popularise Cremation?', in Charmaz, Howarth and Kellehear (eds), *The Unknown Country*, p. 145.
21. Cannadine, 'War and Death, Grief and Mourning in Modern Britain', p. 215.
22. J. N. I. Dawes and L. L. Robson, *Citizen to Soldier: Australia Before the Great War: Recollections of Members of the First AIF*, Melbourne, Melbourne University Press, 1977, p. 105.
23. Edward Bechevaise to his uncle, MS 10153, MSB177, La Trobe Library of Victoria, SLV.
24. Dawes and Robson, *Citizen to Soldier*, p. 129.
25. 'Dad' to 'Gib', 13 June 1915, Gilbert McDonald Papers, PRG795/2, Mortlock Library, SLSA.

26 H. Mawson to 'dear Old Tom', 12 July 1918, 2DRL/0726, AWM.
27 J. R. MacDonald to Colonel Martin, 14 September 1918, 1DRL/0431, AWM.
28 Lieut. A. Archibald to Rev. Allan, 1 October 1917, 1DRL/0023, AWM.
29 F. McInerney to Dear Earnie, 13 July 1918, 1DRL/0081, AWM.
30 John Rickard, *H. B. Higgins: The Rebel as Judge*, Sydney, Allen & Unwin, 1984, p. 228.
31 ibid., p. 230.
32 H. B. Higgins, 'The Shadows on the Slope' (New Year 1917), Higgins Papers.
33 Hagman, 'The Role of the "Other" in Mourning', pp. 327–9.
34 Daniel Pick, 'Freud's Group Psychology and the History of the Crowd', *History Workshop Journal*, no. 40, 1995, p. 52.
35 Graeme M. Griffin and Des Tobin, *In the Midst of Life: The Australian Response to Death*, Melbourne, Melbourne University Press, 1997, p. 34.
36 *Our Empire*, vol. 2, no. 12, 19 April 1920, p. 13.
37 Hector MacDonald to 'Dear Derham', 15 May 1915, 7/1/1/a&b, Derham Papers.
38 Dawes and Robson, *Citizen to Soldier*, p. 147.
39 Hagman, 'The Role of the "Other" in Mourning', p. 334.
40 For analysis of individual release through groups, see Freud, 'Group Psychology and the Analysis of the Ego', in Sigmund Freud, *Civilisation, Society and Religion*, p. 101.
41 *Our Empire*, vol. 1, no. 1, May 1918, p. 1.
42 See ibid., vol. 3, no. 2, 18 June 1920, p. 6; vol. 3, no. 1, 18 May 1920, pp. 5–6.
43 ibid., vol. 3, no. 3, 19 July 1920, p. 7.
44 ibid., vol. 1, no. 4, 19 August 1918, p. 7.
45 ibid., vol. 1, no. 2, 18 June 1918, p. 16.
46 ibid., vol. 1, no. 4, 19 August 1918, p. 16.
47 *Argus*, 26 February 1926, p. 16.
48 ibid., 19 March 1937, p. 11.
49 ibid., 12 March 1926, p. 9.
50 ibid., 11 April 1929, p. 4.
51 ibid., 6 May 1927, p. 6.
52 I. Turner, '1914–1918', in F. Crowley (ed.), *A New History of Australia*, Melbourne, Heinemann, 1974, p. 351; Heather Radi, '1920–1929', ibid., p. 366.
53 H. B. Higgins, 'Eleventh of November 1928', Folder 2, Higgins Papers.
54 Griffin and Tobin, *In the Midst of Life*, p. 30; Hagman, 'Mourning: A Review and Reconsideration', p. 3.
55 *Daily Telegraph*, 25 February 1920, p. 7.
56 *Our Empire*, vol. 1, no. 2, 18 June 1918, p. 7.
57 ibid., vol. 1, no. 3, 18 July 1918, p. 14.
58 ibid., vol. 3, no. 3, 19 August 1920, p. 5.
59 ibid., vol. 3, no. 11, 18 March 1921, p. 4.
60 ibid., vol. 1, no. 8, 18 December 1918, p. 10.
61 ibid., vol. 2, no. 11, 18 March 1920, p. 3.
62 ibid., vol. 1, no. 6, 18 October 1918, p. 6.
63 ibid., vol. 1, no. 10, 18 February 1919, p. 12.
64 ibid., vol. 1, no. 1, May 1918, p. 1.

65 ibid., vol. 1, no. 6, 18 October 1918, p. 1.
66 ibid., vol. 3, no. 2, 18 June 1920, p. 2.
67 ibid., vol. 1, no. 10, 18 February 1919, p. 2.
68 Heather Goodall, *Invasion to Embassy: Land in Aboriginal Politics in New South Wales, 1770-1972*, Sydney, Allen & Unwin/Black Books, pp. 124, 136–7.
69 ibid.
70 *Our Empire*, vol. 2, no. 10, 18 February 1920, p. 2.
71 ibid., 18 May 1921, p. 5.
72 ibid., p. 4.
73 ibid.
74 ibid., 18 March 1921, p. 2.
75 ibid., 19 January 1920, p. 13.
76 Winter, *Sites of Memory, Sites of Mourning*.
77 Jalland, *Death in the Victorian Family*, p. 374.
78 Hagman, 'The Role of the "Other" in Mourning', p. 309.
79 For this tendency, see H. John Field, *Toward a Programme of Imperial Life: The British Empire at the Turn of the Century*, New Haven, Greenwood Press, 1982, p. 233.
80 John Roberts, Diary 1918, 13 September 1918, Box 265/4, MS 8183, La Trobe Library, SLV.
81 Horowitz, 'A Model of Mourning', p. 307.
82 Roberts, Diary, 14, 15, 17 September, 13, 15 October 1918.
83 Higgins to Frankfurter, 27 December 1918, Folder 1, Higgins Papers.
84 Roberts, Diary, 10, 11 October, 31, 20 December 1918.
85 Griffin and Tobin, *In the Midst of Life*, p. 30.
86 Roberts, Diary, 5 December 1918; 10, 13 October 1918; 6 March 1921; 30 March, 17 July, 18 August 1919; 20 September, 4 October 1918; 7 February 1919; 17 January 1920; 23 August, 16 December 1918.
87 Hagman, 'The Role of the "Other" in Mourning', pp. 329–30.
88 Roberts, Diary, 9 January, 18 March, 1 April, 1 September, 28 August 1919; 29 January, 30 September 1920; 4 February 1919; 20 September 1918; 28, 18 August 1919; 6 March 1920; 17, 27, 30 September, 4, 19 October, 10 December 1918; 6 January, 1 September 1919.
89 John Byng-Hall interviewed by Paul Thompson, 'The Power of Family Myths', in Samuel and Thompson (eds), *The Myths We Live By*, p. 216.
90 Roberts, Diary, 13, 28, 30, 14 September, 21 October, 30 September, 2, 3 November, 2 December 1918; 1 March, 1 September, 13 March 1919; 23 July, 13 September 1920; 27 September 1918.
91 *Our Empire*, vol. 2, no. 12, 19 April 1920, p. 13.
92 ibid., vol. 2, no. 10, 18 February 1920, p. 2.

4 THE WAR WIDOW AND THE COST OF MEMORY

1 Victor Ryan, State War Council to Board of Trustees, 28 August 1917, Series A2479, Item no. 17/67, Australian Archives (hereafter AA), Melbourne.
2 Frankie to Derham, 11 August, Letters to Alfred Derham from Frances Anderson, 1914–1916, 7/2/1/6, Derham Papers.
3 Macintyre, *The Oxford History of Australia*, p. 158.
4 Frankie to Derham, 25 November 1914, 7/2/1/6, Derham Papers.

5 ibid., 5 November 1915.
6 ibid., 12 September 1916.
7 ibid., 10 September 1916.
8 See, for instance, Tamasin Day-Lewis (ed.), *Last Letters Home*, London, Macmillan, 1995; David Nott (ed.), *Somewhere in France: The Collection of Letters of Lewis Windermere Nott: The Somme, January–December 1916*, Sydney, HarperCollins, 1996.
9 Patricia Grimshaw, Marilyn Lake, Anne McGrath and Marion Quartly, *Creating a Nation: 1788–1990*, Ringwood, Vic., Penguin, 1994, p. 211; Kay Saunders and Raymond Evans (eds), *Gender Relations in Australia: Domination and Negotiation*, Sydney, Harcourt, Brace and Jovanovich, 1992; Michael Gilding, *The Making and Breaking of the Australian Family*; Kerreen Reiger, *The Disenchantment of the Home*.
10 Frankie to Derham, 10 September 1916, 7/2/1/6, Derham Papers.
11 ibid., 12 September 1916.
12 ibid., 19 September 1916.
13 Susan Kingsley Kent, *Making Peace: The Reconstruction of Gender in Inter-War Britain*, Princeton, Princeton University Press, 1993, p. 97.
14 Judith Allen, *Sex and Secrets: Crimes Involving Australian Women Since 1880*, Melbourne, Oxford University Press, 1990, pp. 130–56; Marilyn Lake, *The Limits of Hope: Soldier Settlement in Victoria, 1915–1938*, Melbourne, Oxford University Press, 1987, pp. 29–30; White, 'War and Australian Society', pp. 414–15; Garton, *The Cost of War*, p. 28.
15 Quoted in Kent, *Making Peace*, p. 102. See Allen, *Sex and Secrets*, Garton, *The Cost of War*, pp. 143–75, For the German case, see Karl Theweleit, *Male Fantasies, Volume 1: Women, Floods, Bodies, History*; and for the British, see Bourke, *Dismembering the Male*.
16 J. I. Roe, 'Mary Booth', *Australian Dictionary of Biography*, Volume 7, 1891–1939, p. 346.
17 Circular from Mary Booth, 14 April 1917, Box 14, Folder 1, AFW Papers.
18 Pamphlet, 3 June 1921, Box 14, Folder 7, ibid.
19 Soldiers' Club Diary, 20 June 1919, Box 16, ibid.
20 ibid., 28 January 1918.
21 ibid., 18 September 1919.
22 ibid., 1 November 1919.
23 Soldiers' Club Pamphlet, 3 June 1921, Box 14, Folder 7, ibid.
24 Allen, *Sex and Secrets*, pp. 130–2.
25 White, 'War and Australian Society', p. 413.
26 Wheeler, 'War, Women and Welfare', p. 180.
27 Quoted in Lloyd and Rees, *The Last Shilling*, p. 19.
28 *Argus*, 4 June 1923, p. 8.
29 Roe, 'The End is Where We Start From', p. 11.
30 Stephen Garton, *Out of Luck: Poor Australians and Social Welfare, 1788–1988*, Sydney, Allen & Unwin, 1990, p. 113.
31 Mavis Thorpe Clark, *No Mean Destiny: The Story of the War Widows' Guild of Australia, 1945–85*, Melbourne, Hyland House, 1985, p. 4.
32 See also Rosemary Pringle and Sophie Watson, 'Fathers, Brothers, Mates: The Fraternal State in Australia', in Sophie Watson (ed.), *Playing the State:*

Australian Feminist Interventions, London, Verso, 1993, p. 230; Garton, *The Cost of War*, p. 86.
33 For a history of these developments, see Russell McGregor, *Imagined Destinies: Aboriginal Australians and the Doomed Race Theory, 1880–1939*, Melbourne, Melbourne University Press, 1997; John Chesterman and Brian Galligan, *Citizens Without Rights: Aborigines and Australian Citizenship*, Melbourne, Cambridge University Press, 1997; Alastair Davidson, *From Subject to Citizen: Australian Citizenship in the Twentieth Century*, Melbourne, Cambridge University Press, 1997.
34 Lyons, *Legacy*, pp. 90–1.
35 Roe, *Beyond Belief*, p. 8.
36 *Official Year Book of the Commonwealth of Australia*, no. 13, 1920, p. 1111.
37 Garton, *Out of Luck*, pp. 52–3; Jean Aitken-Swan, *Widows in Australia: A Survey*, Sydney, Council of Social Service of New South Wales, 1962, p. 1.
38 Roe, *Beyond Belief*, p. 11; Garton, *The Cost of War*, p. 100.
39 Garton, *Out of Luck*, p. 124.
40 Progress Report of the Select Committee on Widows' Pensions and Child Endowment, Votes and Proceedings of the Legislative Assembly, 1936, *Victorian Parliamentary Papers*, p. 4.
41 Acting Solicitor-General, Re: Widows of Soldiers who Die after Discharge, 21 September 1918, Series A2481, Item no. A18/5872, AA, Melbourne.
42 ibid.
43 Surgeon-General, Director, General Medical Services, to Commandant, 3rd Military District, 23 June 1914, Series A2023, Item no. 110/1/70, AA, Melbourne.
44 Mary Emma Skinner to the Secretary, Military Board, Defence Department, 23 June 1914, ibid.
45 Grimshaw et al., *Creating a Nation*, p. 223.
46 *Argus*, 25 January 1923, p. 9.
47 Marilyn Lake, 'Mission Impossible: How Men Gave Birth to the Australian Nation: Nationalism, Gender and Other Seminal Acts', *Gender and History*, vol. 4, no. 3, 1992, pp. 305–22.
48 Frank Cain, *The Origins of Political Surveillance in Australia*, Sydney, Angus & Robertson, 1983, p. 188.
49 E. Sylvia Pankhurst, *The Home Front: A Mirror to Life in England During the First World War*, London, Cressett, 1932, reprinted in Jere Clemens (ed.), *The First World War*, London, Macmillan, 1972, p. 242.
50 See Marjo Buitelaar, 'Widows' Worlds: Representations and Realities', in Jan Bremmer and Lourens van der Bosch (eds), *Between Poverty and the Pyre: Moments in the History of Widowhood*, London, Routledge, 1995, pp. 1–18.
51 See Shurlee Swain with Renate Howe, *Single Mothers and Their Children: Disposal, Punishment and Survival in Australia*, Melbourne, Cambridge University Press, 1995.
52 Buitelaar, 'Widows' Worlds: Representations and Realities', pp. 8–9; Aitken-Swan, *Widows in Australia*, p. 2.
53 Georges Duby and Michelle Perrot (eds), *A History of Women in the West, V: Towards a Cultural Identity in the Twentieth Century*, London, Belknap Press, 1994, p. 53.

54 Colin Dyer, *Population and Society in Twentieth-Century France*, London, Hodder and Stoughton, 1978, p. 43.
55 Jay Winter, *The Great War and the British People*, London, Macmillan, 1987, p. 274.
56 Richard Bessel, *Germany after the First World War*, Oxford, Clarendon Press, 1993, p. 275.
57 Francesca Lagorio, 'Italian Widows of the First World War', in Frans Coetzee and Marilyn Shevin-Coetzee (eds), *Authority, Identity and the Social History of the Great War*, Oxford, Berghan Books, 1995, p. 177.
58 ibid., p. 53.
59 ibid. See Karin Hausen, 'The German Nation's Obligations to the Heroes' Widows of World War I', in Margaret Higgonet, Jane Jenson, Sonya Michel and Margaret Wietz (eds), *Behind the Lines: Gender and the Two World Wars*, New Haven, Yale University Press, 1987; Robert Weldon Whalen, *Bitter Wounds: German Victims of the Great War, 1914–1939*, Ithaca, Cornell University Press, 1984, pp. 69–81.
60 Susan Pedersen, *Family, Dependence and the Origins of the Welfare State, Britain and France, 1914–1945*, Cambridge, Cambridge University Press, 1993, pp. 12–17.
61 Bessel, *Germany after the First World War*, pp. 222–6; Pankhurst, *The Home Front*, pp. 18–30.
62 Coetzee, and Shevin-Coetzee (eds), *Authority, Identity and the Social History of the Great War*, p. 177.
63 Query re Benefits Available to Widow of Deserter, Deputy Comptroller L. E. Tilney to Comptroller, Department of Repatriation, 29 March 1919, Decision of the Commission, 26 June 1919, Series A2487, Item no. 1919/4134, AA, Canberra.
64 Defence Act 1903/27 Sec. 57: Member of the Military Forces killed on duty: Provision for Widow and Family out of Consolidated Revenue Fund: whether an illegitimate child should be provided for, Series A432/86, Item no. 1932/1616, AA, Canberra.
65 Wheeler, 'War, Women and Welfare', p. 187; Garton, *The Cost of War*, p. 93.
66 Lloyd and Rees, *The Last Shilling*, p. 272.
67 Widows' Pensions Bill, Second Reading, *NSW Parliamentary Debates*, Sessions 1925–26, Legislative Assembly, 1926, p. 2766.
68 ibid.
69 Progress Report on Widows' Pensions and Child Endowment, p. 5.
70 South Australian Police, 26 May 1926, Series B741/3, Item no. V/2588, AA, Melbourne.
71 Deputy Commissioner, Adelaide, memorandum to Commonwealth Investigation Branch, 11 May 1926, ibid.
72 ibid.
73 Repatriation Commission to Director of Commonwealth Investigation Branch, 26 June 1926, ibid., Item no. V/2721.
74 Report of Sen. Const. Elliot, Ballarat Police Station, 8 July 1926, ibid.
75 Summary of Particulars for Application for Assistance, Series A2487, Item no. 19/2483, AA, Canberra.
76 Report from the Victorian Police, 9 July 1926, Series B741/3, Item no. V/2792, AA, Melbourne.

77 Report from Const. G. Geddes, 13 July 1926, ibid.
78 ibid., Item no. V/1940.
79 Report from Sgt Hill, Dandenong Police, 21 November 1925, ibid.
80 Deputy Commissioner to Commonwealth Investigation Branch, 29 June 1926, ibid.
81 Garton, *The Cost of War*, pp. 85–7.
82 Payment of Funeral Expenses to Widow of Ex-Serviceman, Series A2487, Item no. 1919/9472, AA, Canberra.
83 Series B741/B, Item no. V2741, AA, Melbourne.
84 Director, Attorney-General's Dept, to the Deputy Commissioner of Repatriation, 13 July 1926, ibid.
85 Complaint by widow of soldier about lack of benefits, Lydia Young to Senator Millen, 14 November 1918, Series A2487, Item no. 1919/7500, AA, Canberra.
86 ibid.
87 Lydia Young to Department of Repatriation, 24 February 1919, ibid.
88 See Janet Sayers, *The Man Who Never Was: Freudian Tales*, London, Chatto and Windus, 1995, pp. 181–2.
89 Lloyd and Rees, *The Last Shilling*, p. 22.
90 *Argus*, 2 October 1920, p. 22.
91 Maud Whittle to Senator Pearce, 15 November 1916, Series A2023, Item no. 272/8/51, AA, Melbourne.
92 27 November 1916: The Secretary to the Treasury, ibid.
93 Mrs O. Reynolds to Mr Hughes, 12 February 1920, Series A2487, Item no. 1920/5297, AA, Canberra.
94 Temporary Employment, Public Service, Employment of War Widows, Nellie Strutt to Mr Johnson, MLA Marrickville, 19 June 1919, Series A2, Item no. 1919/2673, AA, Canberra.
95 ibid.
96 Ministry of Pensions, *Instructions on the Training of Widows*, British Government, 1918, p. 2.
97 Petition to Prime Minister Bruce from Sailors' and Soldiers' War Widows Association, n.d., Series A458, Item no. M382/2, AA, Canberra.
98 Complaints re pensions and allowances paid to widows of servicemen, Racheal Allison and Lily Challenger to Senator Millen, 13 March 1919, Series A2487, Item no. 1920/4304, AA, Canberra.
99 Lily Challenger et al. to Senator Millen, 9 February 1920, ibid.
100 Town Clerk to Sir Granville Ryrne, 11 February 1920, ibid.
101 ibid.
102 *Australian Dictionary of Biography*, Volume 7, pp. 345–6.
103 Pamphlet, The Anzac Fellowship of Women, Constitution, Box 14, Folder 7, AFW Papers.
104 Director, Investigation Branch, to Deputy Commissioner of Repatriation, 6 May 1925, Series B741/3, Item no. V/1178, AA, Canberra.
105 Report of Sen. Const. Simpson, Orbost, 30 April 1925, ibid.
106 Request for Assistance, Widow of Imperial Soldier, Series A2487, Item no. 1919/7806, AA, Canberra.
107 Representation by R. Richard for assistance for widow of deceased ex-serviceman, Mrs M. E. Gapper, Series A2487, Item no. 1919/11, AA, Canberra.

108 Lyons, *Legacy*, p. 16.
109 The Centre for Soldiers' Wives and Mothers, Minute Book, AFW Papers.
110 Alice Thomas, Hon. Secretary, Housewives Association (Victorian Division), to A. S. Rogers, Federal Parliament House, 3 June 1921, Housewives Association on Increasing War Widows' Pension, Series A2487, Item no. 1921/9855, AA, Canberra.
111 South Australia Clothing for Widows and Children, Series A2479, Item no. 17/803, AA, Canberra.
112 *Age*, 15 November 1928, p. 12.
113 *Argus* 4 June 1923, p. 8.
114 *Daily Telegraph*, 27 September 1920, p. 3.
115 White, 'War and Australian Society', pp. 413–14.
116 Re Assistance to War Widow Mrs M. S. Corkett, Series A2487, Item no. 1921/1801, AA, Canberra.

5 RETURNED LIMBLESS SOLDIERS: IDENTITY THROUGH LOSS

1 Jane Bettless to her Sister, 4 May 1919, Jane Bettless Letters 1919–1922, D7094(L), Mortlock Library, SLSA.
2 Lance-Corp. A. Hislop to Mother, 1 September 1916, Hislop Papers.
3 For a discussion of 'the grotesque', see Geoffrey Galt Harpham, *On the Grotesque: Strategies of Contradiction in Art and Literature*, Princeton, Princeton University Press, 1982, p. 3.
4 Modris Eksteins, *Rites of Spring: The Great War and the Birth of the Modern Age*, Boston, Houghton, 1989, p. 256.
5 For a discussion of 'renaming' injury, see Elaine Scarry, *The Body in Pain: The Making and Unmaking of the World*, New York, Oxford University Press, 1985, pp. 61–72.
6 *Limbless Soldier*, vol. 1, no. 10, December 1925, p. 30.
7 For these perspectives, see Joanna Bourke, 'The Battle of the Limbs: Amputation, Artificial Limbs and the Great War in Australia', *Australian Historical Studies*, vol. 29, no. 110, 1998, pp. 49–67; Bourke, *Dismembering the Male*, pp. 31–75; Seth Koven, 'Remembering and Dismemberment: Crippled Children, Wounded Soldiers, and the Great War in Great Britain', *American Historical Review*, vol. 99, no. 4, 1994, pp. 167–202.
8 This was common in other countries. See Gregory, *The Silence of Memory*, p. 53.
9 Lake, *Limits of Hope*, pp. 101–42.
10 *Medical Journal of Australia*, 16 March 1918, p. 217.
11 Sir William MacEwen, 'On the Limbless', *The Inter-Allied Conference on the After Care of Disabled Men, Second Annual Meeting, 20–25 May 1918*, London, 1918, pp. 373–4.
12 Wheeler, 'War, Women and Welfare', p. 172; Garton, *The Cost of War*, p. 85.
13 Eksteins, *The Rites of Spring*, pp. 256–8.
14 C. H. Stevens, *Limbless Soldiers' Association of Victoria: 1921–1971*, Melbourne, Limbless Soldiers' Association of Victoria, 1971, p. 6.
15 *Argus*, 22 September 1921, p. 8.
16 ibid., 23 September 1926, p. 20. According to the *Argus* (15 November 1923, p. 4), there were 4000 limbless soldiers in Australia in 1923.

17 *Argus*, 8 August 1922, p. 5.
18 Stevens, *Limbless Soldiers' Association*, p. 10.
19 *Argus*, 10 December 1924, p. 23.
20 Other soldiers were more reluctant to wear badges. See Garton, *The Cost of War*, p. 11.
21 *Argus*, 28 September 1922, p. 8.
22 ibid., 23 February 1922, p. 8.
23 *Our Empire*, vol. 2, no. 10, 18 February 1920, p. 1.
24 Garton, *The Cost of War*, p. 11.
25 Stevens, *Limbless Soldiers' Association*, p. 14.
26 *Limbless Soldier*, vol. 9, no. 2, December 1935, pp. 5–6.
27 ibid., vol. 6, no. 3, March 1933, p. 9.
28 ibid., vol. 6, no. 6, June 1933, p. 3.
29 ibid., vol. 10, no. 4, June 1937, p. 10.
30 Anthony Giddens, *The Consequences of Modernity*, Stanford, Stanford University Press, 1990, ch. 1. For the Australian context, see Kosmas Tsokhas, 'Modernity, Sexuality and National Identity: Norman Lindsay's Aesthetics', *Australian Historical Studies*, vol. 27 no. 107, 1996, pp. 219–41.
31 *Argus*, 14 April 1926, p. 26.
32 See Rita Felski, *The Gender of Modernity*, Cambridge, Harvard University Press, 1995, pp. 2–4.
33 *Argus*, 8 January 1916, p. 5.
34 ibid., 8 August 1922, p. 5.
35 W. Fitzpatrick, *The Repatriation of the Soldier*, Melbourne, Victorian State War Council, 1916, p. 30.
36 *Argus*, 17 September 1926, p. 11; 18 December 1925, p. 10; 11 December 1931, p. 11; 8 August 1923, p. 9; 29 September 1927, p. 14; 12 November 1924, p. 17; 15 April 1925, p. 9; 23 August 1927, p. 15 (see also 17 August 1920, p. 19); 27 July 1926, p. 18; 14 March 1924, p. 16; 18 September 1920, p. 27; 20 December 1928, p. 5; 22 September 1920, p. 19; 5 July 1922, p. 9.
37 *Limbless Soldier*, 16 September 1924, p. 29.
38 *Argus*, 20 December 1921, p. 8.
39 ibid., 8 July 1922, p. 22.
40 *Limbless Soldier,* vol. 9, no. 2, December 1935, p. 10.
41 *Argus*, 29 December 1920, p. 6; 25 February 1922, p. 24; 26 October 1921, p. 5; 20 July 1921, p. 9; 29 June 1921, p. 8; 8 November 1921, p. 7.
42 Garton, *The Cost of War*, p. 94.
43 *Argus*, 5 April 1922, p. 14; 26 October 1926, p. 5; 20 July 1927, p. 19; 18 May 1922, p. 8; 20 July 1922, p. 8; 30 June 1922, p. 14; 1 November 1921, p. 5.
44 See Grant McBurnie, 'Angela Booth: The Importance of Being Well Bred', in Lake and Kelly (eds), *Double Time: Women in Victoria – 150 Years*, pp. 312–21; Ann Curthoys, 'Eugenics, Feminism and Birth Control: The Case of Marion Piddington', *Hecate*, vol. 15, no. 1, 1989, pp. 73–87; Michael Roe, *Nine Australian Progressives: Vitalism in Bourgeois Social Thought, 1890–1960*, St Lucia, University of Queensland Press, 1984.
45 Davidson, *From Subject to Citizen*, pp. 193–204; McGregor, *Imagined Destinies*.
46 *Limbless Soldier*, vol. 1, no. 5, 16 September 1924, p. 18.
47 ibid, p. 22.

48 ibid., vol. 6, no. 2, December 1932, p. 2.
49 ibid., vol. 1, no. 10, December 1925, p. 27.
50 ibid., vol. 1, no. 18, December 1927, p. 28.
51 *Argus*, 26 April 1927, p. 11.
52 ibid., 9 July 1924, p. 20.
53 ibid., 26 March 1926, p. 5; 1 June 1926, p. 20.
54 Gregory, *The Silence of Memory*, p. 120.
55 *Limbless Soldier*, vol. 9, no. 2, December 1935, p. 23. See Gregory, *The Silence of Memory*, p. 123.
56 *Argus*, 9 December 1926, p. 13.
57 *Limbless Soldier*, vol. 9, no. 2, December 1935, p. 18.
58 *Argus*, 1 June 1921, p. 9.
59 Lake, *The Limits of Hope*, p. 64.
60 Similar developments took place in Britain. See Gregory, *The Silence of Memory*, p. 54.
61 *Argus*, 21 March 1922, p. 4.
62 ibid., 15 November 1923, p. 4.
63 Garton, *The Cost of War*, p. 91.
64 *Argus*, 10 February 1926, p. 11.
65 ibid., 6 September 1922, p. 21.
66 ibid.
67 ibid., 9 March 1928, p. 10.
68 *Limbless Soldier*, vol. 1, no. 2, 12 December 1923, p. 6.
69 *Argus*, 23 September 1926, p. 20.
70 ibid., 10 July 1928, p. 12.
71 *Limbless Soldier*, vol. 4, no. 2, December 1930, p. 3.
72 ibid., vol. 5, no. 2, September 1931, p. 23.
73 ibid., vol. 1, no. 17, September 1927, p. 22.
74 ibid., vol. 1, no. 18, December 1927, p. 28.
75 ibid., vol. 10. no. 4, June 1937, p. 2.
76 Anson Rabinach, *The Human Motor: Energy, Fatigue and the Origins of Modernity*, New York, Basic Books, 1990, p. 2; Karen Lucic, *Charles Sheeler and the Cult of the Machine*, London, Reaktion Books, 1991, pp. 75–117. See also Roxanne Panchasi, 'Reconstructions: Prosthetics and the Rehabilitation of the Male Body in World War I France', *Differences*, vol. 7, no. 3, 1995, pp. 109–40.
77 See Rabinach, *The Human Motor*, pp. 271–88.
78 *Limbless Soldier*, vol. 1, no. 2, 12 December 1923, p. 1.
79 ibid., vol. 1, no. 2, December 1924, p. 3.
80 ibid., vol. 1, no. 8, June 1925, p. 13.
81 *Argus*, 15 July 1922, p. 8. See extended article on this.
82 *Repatriation Commission for the Commonwealth of Australia, Handbook of Repatriation Artificial Limb Factories and Their Products*, Melbourne, Government Printer, 1945, p. 4.
83 *Limbless Soldier*, vol. 1, no. 3, 17 March 1924, p. 1.
84 *Argus*, 20 August 1929, p. 8.
85 ibid., 15 December 1922, p. 10.
86 ibid., 20 September 1928, p. 6.
87 ibid., 19 September 1928, p. 11.

88 *Limbless Soldier*, vol. 2, no. 2, December 1939, p. 1.
89 For this connection between mourning and militancy, see Crisp, 'Mourning and Militancy', pp. 3–18.

6 ABSENCE AS LOSS ON THE HOMEFRONT AND THE BATTLEFRONT

1 George Vasey to Jessie Vasey, n.d., Box 2, Folder 11, Vasey Papers, MS 3782, NLA. All references to the Vasey correspondence are to this collection, and from George Vasey to Jessie Vasey, unless otherwise stated.
2 *Sydney Morning Herald*, 25 April 1940, p. 6.
3 Eric Hobsbawm, *Age of Extremes: The Short Twentieth Century, 1914–1991*, London, Abacus, 1995, p. 37.
4 Libby Connors, Lynette Finch, Kay Saunders and Helen Taylor, *Australia's Frontline: Remembering the 1939–45 War*, St Lucia, University of Queensland Press, 1992, p. 5.
5 ibid., p. 11.
6 Geoffrey Bolton, *The Oxford History of Australia, Volume 5: 1942–1988*, Melbourne, Oxford University Press, 1990, p. 19; Joan Beaumont, *Australia's War, 1939–1945*, Sydney, Allen & Unwin, 1996, p. xxii.
7 Connors, Finch, Saunders and Taylor, *Australia's Frontline*, p. 5.
8 *Sydney Morning Herald*, 25 April 1940, p. 6.
9 ibid., 26 April 1941, p. 13.
10 ibid., 27 April 1942, p. 4; p. 5.
11 Bolton, *The Oxford History of Australia*, Volume 5, p. 14.
12 Robert Hall, 'Aborigines and Torres Strait Islanders in the Second World War', in Desmond Ball (ed.), *Aborigines in the Defence of Australia*, Canberra, Australian National University Press, 1991, p. 46, p. 52.
13 ibid., p. 32; Alick Jackomos and Derek Fowell (eds), *Forgotten Heroes: Aborigines at War: Somme to Vietnam*, Victoria, Victoria Press, 1993, pp. 1–3.
14 Chesterman and Galligan, *Citizens Without Rights*, p. 157.
15 Raphael, *The Anatomy of Bereavement*, p. 50.
16 9 April 1940, Box 2, Folder 11, Vasey Papers.
17 30 November 1942, Folder 15, ibid.
18 18 December 1942, ibid.
19 19 October 1941, Folder 12, ibid.
20 Christopher Lane, 'In Defence of the Realm: Sassoon's Memoirs and "Other Opaque Arenas of War"', in Christopher Lane, *The Ruling Passion: British Colonial Allegory and the Paradox of Homosexual Desire*, Durham, Duke University Press, 1995, p. 196.
21 Catherine Lutz, 'Depression and the Translation of Emotional Worlds', in Arthur Kleinman and Byron Good (eds), *Culture and Depression: Studies in the Anthropology and Cross-Cultural Psychiatry of Affect and Disorder*, Berkeley, University of California Press, 1985, pp. 80–92.
22 See Fussell, *The Great War and Modern Memory*; Sandra M. Gilbert, 'Soldier's Heart: Literary Men, Literary Women and the Great War', in Higonnet et al. (eds), *Behind the Lines*, pp. 197–226.
23 See Theweleit, *Male Fantasies*; Leed, *No Man's Land*; Winter, *Sites of Memory, Sites of Mourning*.

24 Alison M. Jagger, 'Love and Knowledge: Emotions in Feminist Epistemology', in Elizabeth Harvey and Kathleen Okruhlik (eds), *Women and Reason*, Ann Arbor, University of Michigan Press, 1992, pp. 119–20.
25 ibid., p. 123.
26 See, for instance, David Nott, *Somewhere in France: The Collected Letters of Lewis Windermere Nott, January–December 1916*, Sydney, HarperCollins, 1996; David Horner, *General Vasey's War*, Melbourne, Melbourne University Press, 1992; Judy Barrett Litoff, David C. Smith, Barbara Woodall Taylor, and Charles E. Taylor (eds), *Miss You: The World War Two Letters of Barbara Woodall Taylor and Charles E. Taylor*, Georgia, University of Georgia Press, 1990; Judy Barrett Litoff and David C. Smith (eds), *Since You Went Away: World War Two Letters from American Women on the Homefront*, New York, Oxford University Press, 1991; Tamasin Day-Lewis (ed.), *Last Letters Home*; Jim Mitchell (ed.), *The Moon Seems Upside Down: Letters of Love and War*, Sydney, Allen & Unwin, 1995; Decie Denholm (ed.), *Behind the Lines: One Woman's War, 1914–18, The Letters of Caroline Ethel Cooper*, Sydney, Collins, 1982; Gammage, *The Broken Years*; Lurline Stuart and Josie Arnold (eds), *Letters Home, 1939–1945*, Sydney, Collins, 1987; Ronald Blythe, *Private Words: Letters and Diaries from the Second World War*, New York, Viking, 1991.
27 Horner, *The Commanders*, p. 2.
28 Peter Dennis et al., 'Censorship', *The Oxford Companion to Australian Military History*, p. 139.
29 14 January 1940, Box 2, Folder 11, Vasey Papers.
30 26 October 1941, Folder 12, ibid.
31 8 January 1943, Box 3, Folder 18, ibid.
32 Clark, *No Mean Destiny*, pp. 7–8.
33 ibid., pp. 12–13.
34 ibid., p. 15.
35 ibid., p. 14.
36 Horner, *General Vasey's War*, p. 36.
37 ibid., p. 52.
38 ibid., p. 68.
39 ibid., p. 79.
40 ibid., pp. 90–109.
41 ibid., p. 105.
42 ibid., p. 131.
43 ibid., p. 131.
44 Quoted in Gavin Long, *Greece, Crete and Syria*, Canberra, Australian War Memorial, 1953, p. 74.
45 Bolton, *The Oxford History of Australia, Volume 5*, pp. 6–7.
46 David Horner, 'Major General George Alan Vasey: Commander, 7th Australian Division', in David Horner (ed.), *The Commanders: Australian Military Leadership in the Twentieth Century*, Sydney, Allen & Unwin, 1984, p. 264.
47 ibid., p. 276.
48 ibid., pp. 98, 106.
49 Vasey Papers, Box 2: 29 August 1941, Folder 12; 29 December 1939, 6 September 1940, 23 August 1940, 6 September 1940, 16 March 1940, Folder 11; 10 December 1942, Folder 15; 8 February 1940, 3 April 1940, 8 February 1940, 26 December 1939, Folder 11; 6 October 1941, Folder 12;

Notes to pages 114–122   187

25 March 1940, 30 June 1940, 28 September 1940, 7 August 1940, 11 March 1940, Folder 11; 13 January 1941, 19 October 1941, Folder 12; 8 February 1940, Folder 11.
50 Jean Duruz, 'Suburban House Revisited', in Kate Darian-Smith and Paula Hamilton (eds), *Memory and History in Twentieth-Century Australia*, pp. 177–80; Jean Duruz, 'Suburban Gardens: Cultural Notes', in Sarah Ferber, Chris Healy and Chris McAuliffe (eds), *Beasts of Suburbia: Reinterpreting Cultures in Australian Suburbs*, Melbourne, Melbourne University Press, 1994, pp. 198–213; Ann Game and Rosemary Pringle, 'Sexuality and the Suburban Dream', *Australian and New Zealand Journal of Sociology*, vol. 15, no. 2, 1972, pp. 4–15.
51 Vasey Papers, Box 2: n.d., Folder 11; 25 October 1942, Folder 15; 3, 16 March 1940, 19 October 1940, 24 November 1940, Folder 11; 20 January 1941, Folder 12; 21 April 1940, 30 June 1940, 19 October 1940, Folder 11; 6, 19, 26 October 1941, Folder 12; 22 January 1940, Folder 11; 6 November 1942, Folder 15; 9 November 1941, 26 March 1941, 17 November 1941, Folder 12; 30 June 1940, 5 February 1941, 14 January 1940, 9 December 1940, 1, 19 October 1940, 9 December 1940, Folder 11.
52 25 March, 21 April, 3 June 1940, Folder 11, ibid.
53 Clark, *No Mean Destiny*, p. 3.
54 Vasey Papers, Box 2: 28 June 1940, 7, 15 August 1940, 21 September 1940, Folder 11; 19 February 1941, Folder 12; 6 November 1942, Folder 15; 6 March 1941, Folder 12; 24 November 1940, Folder 11; 2 November 1941, 21 September 1941, Folder 12.
55 *Age*, 7 March 1945, p. 1.
56 *Argus*, 6 March 1945, p. 1.
57 Cannadine, 'War and Death, Grief and Mourning in Modern Britain', p. 206.
58 K. S. Inglis, 'Passing Away', in Gammage and Spearritt (eds), *Australians 1938*, pp. 239, 249–50.
59 Philipe Aries, *Western Attitudes Towards Death: From the Middle Ages to the Present*, trans. Patricia M. Ranum, London, M. Boyards, 1976, p. 85.
60 Hagman, 'Mourning: A Review and Reconsideration', p. 917.
61 Liveris, *The Dismal Trade*, p. 198.
62 Gaines, 'Detachment and Continuity: The Two Tasks of Mourning', p. 559.
63 Roberta Miller to Mrs Burrows, 20 April 1943, PR85/078, AWM.
64 From Ann Quinn 27 December 1943, PR00218, ibid.
65 Emily Hooper to Chaplain Trathen, 20 November (no year), ibid.
66 Mum to My Dear Boy Len, 16 August (no year), PR90/148, ibid.
67 Crissie Prettejohn to Webber, 28 January (no year), Letters to Chaplain Eric Webber, MS 9646, MSB67, La Trobe Library, SLV.
68 From Maude Tanne, 9 April 1945, PR00172, ibid.
69 Mother to Private Allan Tucker, n.d., ibid.
70 To Chaplain Trathen, 6 May 1944, PR00218, ibid.
71 Marjorie Bailey to Father Trathen, 16 November 1943, ibid.
72 Jessie Tonkin to Mr Trathen, 23 November 1943, ibid.
73 Alice Sprone to Chaplain Trathen, 5 November 1943, ibid.
74 Ben Drakes to Chaplain Trathen, 9 December 1943, ibid.
75 See Joan Beaumont, *Gull Force: Survival and Leadership in Captivity, 1941–1945*, Sydney, Allen & Unwin, 1988; Patsy Adam-Smith, *Prisoners of War:*

From Gallipoli to Korea, Ringwood, Vic., Viking, 1992; Hemming, *Doomed Battalion*; Hank Nelson, *Prisoners of War: Australians Under Nippon*, Sydney, ABC Radio Series, 1990.
76 Nelson, *Prisoners of War*, p. 13.
77 ibid.
78 Hugh V. Clarke and Colin Burgess, *Barbed Wire and Bamboo: Australian POWs in Europe, North Africa, Singapore, Thailand and Japan*, Sydney, Allen & Unwin, 1992, p. xiv.
79 Raphael, *The Anatomy of Bereavement*, pp. 50, 53.
80 *Argus*, 24 July 1942, p. 6.
81 ibid., 26 September 1942, p. 2.
82 ibid., 26 June 1942, p. 3.
83 Jeffrey Smart, 'Four Crashing Heart-Twisting Years: The Relatives of Australian Prisoners of War in Japanese Hands, 1941–1945', BA Honours Thesis, University of Melbourne, 1989, pp. 17–18.
84 *Argus*, 12 February 1944, p. 8.
85 Smart, 'Four Crashing Heart-Twisting Years', p. 27.
86 See for instance, Sarah Fishman, *We Will Wait: Wives of French Prisoners of War, 1940–1945*, New Haven, Yale University Press, 1991.
87 *Argus*, 29 August 1944, p. 7.
88 Sydney Smith, Hon. Sec. APWRA (NSW), to John Curtin, PM, 8 February 1945, A1066/4 IC1945/61/15/1 Miscellaneous, Australian Prisoners of War Relatives Association, Rail Priorities, AA, Canberra.
89 Chaplain W. I. Fleming to Mrs Smith, 29 October 1945, PR00460, AWM.
90 Noel Kettlewell to Mrs Smith, 27 October 1945, PR85/141, ibid.
91 Capt. Dodan to Mr Copelin, 2 November 1945, PR91/036, ibid.
92 Clarke and Burgess, *Barbed Wire and Bamboo*, p. xv.
93 Capt. Mills to Mrs Wynn, 3 January 1946, PR86/080, AWM.
94 From W. R. Perkins to Mr and Mrs Wynn, 14 January 1946, ibid.
95 From Lieut.-Col. W. J. Scott, 15 October 1946, PR00145, ibid.
96 Raphael, *The Anatomy of Bereavement*, p. 29.

7 GRIEVING MOTHERS

1 Jack's Mother to My dear Mr Trathen, 7 July 1944, PR00218, AWM.
2 Mother to My Dear Marjorie, 8 August 1942, 3DRL/7945, ibid.
3 ibid.
4 Mother to My Darling, August 1943, ibid.
5 Mother to My dear Darling, August 1943, ibid.
6 Marilyn Lake, 'Female Desires: The Meaning of World War II', in Damousi and Lake (eds), *Gender and War*, pp. 60–80; 'The Desire for a Yank: Sexual Relations between Australian Women and American Servicemen During World War II', *Journal of the History of Sexuality*, vol. 2 no. 4, 1992.
7 See Kate Darian-Smith, 'Remembering Romance: Memory, Gender and World War II', pp. 117–29; Ruth Ford, 'Lesbians and Loose Women: Female Sexuality and the Women's Services during World War II', pp. 81–116; and Lyn Finch, 'Consuming Passions: Romance and Consumerism during World War II', pp. 105–16, in Damousi and Lake (eds), *Gender and War*; Kay Saunders and Geoffrey Bolton, 'Girdled for War: Women's Mobilisations in

Notes to pages 128–133

World War Two', in Saunders and Evans (eds), *Gender Relations in Australia*, pp. 376–95; Rosemary Campbell, *Heroes and Lovers: A Question of National Identity*, Sydney, Allen & Unwin, 1989; Kate Darian-Smith, *On the Homefront: Melbourne in Wartime, 1939–1945*, Melbourne, Oxford University Press, 1990.
8 Betty Goldsmith and Beryl Sandford (eds), *The Girls They Left Behind*, Ringwood, Vic., Penguin, 1990, pp. 203–14.
9 Hobsbawm, *Age of Extremes*, p. 43.
10 ibid.
11 Dennis et al. (eds), *The Oxford Companion to Australian Military History*, p. 176.
12 Raphael, *The Anatomy of Bereavement*, p. 13.
13 See Maurice Halbwach, *On Collective Memory*, trans. Lewis A. Coser, Chicago, University of Chicago Press, 1992, p. 62.
14 Katie Holmes, *Spaces in Her Day: Australian Women's Diaries, 1920s–1930s*, Sydney, Allen & Unwin, 1995, p. xxvi.
15 John Atchinson, 'Franc Brereton Sadleir and Otway Rothwell Falkiner', *Australian Dictionary of Biography, Volume 8*, pp. 465–6.
16 Holmes, *Spaces in Her Day*, pp. 78–9.
17 Frank Doak, *Royal Australian Air Force: A Brief History*, Canberra, Australian Government Publishing Service, 1981, p. 18.
18 Una Falkiner, Diary, 24 September 1942, MSS 4342, Mitchell Library.
19 ibid., 23 September 1942.
20 ibid., 26 December 1942.
21 ibid., 22 September 1943.
22 Horowitz, 'A Model of Mourning', p. 318.
23 Falkiner, Diary, 25 November 1942; 14 May 1944; 22 September 1946; 30 September 1942; 26, 29 October 1942; 13, 24 February 1943; 3 July 1943; 1 January 1943; 24 March 1943; 14, 10, 8 October 1942; 13 November 1942; 18 March 1944; 7 June 1944; 27 September 1942; 12 August 1948.
24 Winter, *Sites of Memory, Sites of Mourning*, pp. 178–203.
25 Most of these studies focus on the nineteenth century. See, for instance, John Rickard, *A Family Romance*, Melbourne, Melbourne University Press, 1996; Jill Roe, *Beyond Belief: Theosophy in Australia, 1879–1939*, Kensington, University of New South Wales Press, 1986; Michael Roe, *Nine Progressives*.
26 Roy Stenman, *One Hundred Years of Spiritualism*, London, Spiritualist Association of Great Britain, 1972, p. 37.
27 ibid., p. 40.
28 See Estelle Roberts, *Forty Years a Medium*, London, Herbert Jenkins, 1959; Ernest Thompson, *The Teachings and Phenomena of Spiritualism*, Manchester, Two Worlds Publishing Company, 1947.
29 Thompson, *The Teachings and Phenomena of Spiritualism*, p. 1.
30 From L. Harrison, 11 July 1944, PR00218, AWM.
31 Hedwige Williams to My Dear Bobbie, 15 April 1943, Charles Rowland Williams Papers, OM95-10/3/1, John Oxley Library, State Library of Queensland (hereafter SLQ).
32 Halbwach, *On Collective Memory*, p. 60.
33 Hedwige Williams to My Dear Bobbie, 15 April 1943, Williams Papers.
34 ibid.
35 ibid.

36 ibid.
37 Sheila to My dear Bobbie, 18 October 1943, ibid.
38 ibid.
39 Hedwige Williams to Dear Bobbie, 8 November 1943, ibid.
40 Peter Dennis et al. (eds), *The Oxford Companion to Military History*, p. 512.
41 Padre Arthur Bottrell, *Cameos of Commandos: Memories of Eight Australian Commando Squadrons in New Guinea and Queensland*, Adelaide, Specialty Printers, 1971, p. 305.
42 Chaplain J. C. Salter, *A Padre with the Rats of Tobruk*, Hobart, J. Walch & Sons, 1946, p. 36.
43 'Royal Australian Army Chaplains Department', in Dennis et al. (eds), *The Oxford Companion to Australian Military History*, p. 512.
44 Agnes Booth to Chaplain Webber, 19 February 1944, Letters to Chaplain Webber, MS 9646, MSB67, La Trobe Library, SLV.
45 Mrs Doggeth to Chaplain Webber, 17 February 1945, ibid.
46 From Ruby Goodisson, 14 September 1943, PR00218, AWM.
47 From Chaplain Fred McKay, 14 August 1943, PR00242, ibid.
48 From the Speaker, Parliament House, 30 November 1945, PR83/021, ibid.
49 From Jean Bonner, 2 April 1944, PR00218, ibid.
50 From Stuart Graham, 24 May 1945, PR00392, ibid.
51 Florence to Heck, 4 November 1945, PR00686, ibid.
52 Michael McKernan, 'Religion and War', in Dennis et al. (eds), *The Oxford Companion to Australian Military History*, p. 497.
53 From A. Taylor to Lois Atock, 3DRL/6372, AWM.
54 From Kathleen, 29 December 1941, ibid.
55 Rosa Taylor, 29 December 1941, ibid.
56 Kathleen to Lois Atock, 3 January 1942, ibid.
57 Anne to Lois Atock, 28 December 1941, ibid.
58 Mrs G. Shipton to Sir/Madam, 26 June 1946, Hough Papers, PRG1055, Mortlock Library, SLSA.
59 ibid.
60 J. Shipton to Mrs Hough, 13 October 1946, ibid.
61 ibid.
62 ibid.
63 From Capt. Keith Bishop, 27 October (1942), 3DRL/7945, AWM.
64 Doak, *Royal Australian Air Force*, p. 17.
65 Sgt J. R. Dixon to Mrs Stark, 3 September 1945, Papers Relating to Russell Stark, 1944–1945, D7214/1(L), Mortlock Library, SLSA.
66 Cutting, *Glenelg Guardian*, 22 November 1945, ibid.
67 Jack Slee to Mrs Manttan, 18 August 1943, PR84/046, AWM.
68 Tom Selby to Mrs Williams, 30 June 1945, PR00057, ibid.
69 Norm Mellett to Mrs Gill, 17 August 1942, 3DRL/7945, ibid.
70 Florence to Heck, 3 June 1943, PR00686, ibid.
71 K. A. Blacker, Hut 103, to Miss Allan, 10 June 1945, PR00666, ibid.
72 W. M. Edwards, Hut 103, 10 June 1945, ibid.
73 J. Moran, Hospital 35, 12 June 1945, ibid.
74 Beryl Audrey Hicks to Mrs Hawes, 6 July 1945, PR85/043, ibid.
75 Ada MacDonald to Mr Muller, 24 June 1946, 3DRL/7892, ibid.
76 Horowitz, 'A Model of Mourning', p. 313.

77 Joy Bowral 20 September, 1945, PR00392, AWM.
78 From Joyce Browning 5 January 1942, 3DRL/6372, ibid.

8 A WAR WIDOW'S MOURNING

1 Mrs M. S. Riordan to Chaplain Eric Webber, 6 March 1944, Letters to Chaplain Webber.
2 Josephine Johnson to Pte Fraser, 1 January 1942, in Len Johnson, *An Australian Family, Volume III: War Letters, 1940–1941*, Brisbane, Rock View Press, 1995, p. 139.
3 ibid., p. 128.
4 ibid.
5 ibid., p. 129.
6 ibid., p. 146.
7 ibid.
8 ibid., p. 145.
9 ibid., p. 146.
10 Josie Arnold, *Mother Superior Woman Inferior*, Melbourne, Dove Communications, 1985, p. 12.
11 N. J. Mackenzie to Mrs Johnson, 4 July 1941, in Johnson, *An Australian Family, Volume III*, p. 133.
12 Dulcie Mackenzie to Josephine Johnson, 15 June 1941, ibid., p. 132.
13 Mary Eileen Wall to Dear Josie, 19 August 1941, ibid., p. 136.
14 Hilda to Josie & Family, 16 June 1941, ibid., p. 130.
15 L. McVean to Mrs Johnson, ibid.
16 ibid., p. 146.
17 Lloyd and Rees, *The Last Shilling*.
18 Clark, *No Mean Destiny*.
19 Santner, *Stranded Objects*, p. 4.
20 Robert G. Moeller, *Protecting Motherhood: Women and the Family in the Politics of Post-War West Germany*, Berkeley, University of California Press, 1993, pp. 112–13, 132–3; Karin Hausen, 'The German Nation's Obligations to the Heroes: Widows of World War I', in Higonnet et al., *Behind the Lines*, pp. 126–40; Janis Lomas, ' "So I Married Again": Letters from British Widows of the First and Second World Wars', *History Workshop Journal*, no. 38, 1994, pp. 218–27; Whalen, *Bitter Wounds*.
21 Clark, *No Mean Destiny*, p. 2.
22 ibid., pp. 30–1.
23 ibid., p. 4.
24 *Argus*, 7 March 1945, p. 1.
25 ibid., p. 3.
26 Circular no. 1, c.1946, Melbourne Branch, War Widows Guild.
27 'War Widows Guild: New Venture Needs Help', *Argus*, 1949, Scrapbook, ibid.
28 *Argus*, 3 July 1947, p. 4.
29 ibid., 18 June 1946, p. 7.
30 ibid., 1 August 1947, p. 2.
31 ibid., 8 August 1947, p. 2.
32 ibid., 4 August 1947, p. 2.
33 ibid., 10 August 1948, p. 5.

34 ibid., 11 October 1947, p. 7.
35 ibid., 7 August 1947, p. 2.
36 Chesterman and Galligan, *Citizens Without Rights*, p. 165.
37 ibid., p. 163.
38 Garton, *The Cost of War*, p. 203.
39 *Argus*, 14 July 1947, p. 24.
40 ibid., 19 July 1947, p. 6; 13 June 1947, p. 3.
41 ibid., 11 June 1947, p. 3.
42 ibid., 9 July 1946, p. 10.
43 ibid., 5 April 1946, p. 2; 8 April 1946, p. 2; 25 February 1946, p. 6; 19 January 1946, p. 13; 9 January 1946, p. 7; 16 July 1946, p. 10.
44 ibid., 4 May 1948, p. 7.
45 Lyons, *Legacy*, pp. 154–5.
46 *Argus*, 12 June 1947, p. 3
47 ibid., 6 June 1949, p. 3.
48 *Sydney Morning Herald*, 3 March 1950, p. 3.
49 ibid., 4 March 1950, p. 4.
50 Minutes of the Ninth Annual Meeting of War Widows, 13 June 1956, NSW Branch, War Widows Guild.
51 Minutes of Executive Committee, 16 May 1951, ibid.
52 Nicholas Brown, *Governing Prosperity: Social Change and Social Analysis in Australia in the 1950s*, Melbourne, Cambridge University Press, 1995, p. 195.
53 *Guild Digest*, November 1957, p. 5.
54 Mrs Thelma Courtman to Rev. Trathen, 27 July 1943, PR00218, AWM.
55 Johnson, *An Australian Family*, Volume III, p. 139.
56 ibid., p. 141.
57 Arnold, *Mother Superior Woman Inferior*, p. 13.
58 Clark, *No Mean Destiny*, p. 64.
59 Jessie Vasey to Mrs Graham, October 1945, Scrapbook, Melbourne Branch, War Widows Guild.
60 Circular no. 22, 2 July 1952, ibid.
61 Nancy Scott to Bruce Ruxton, 13 December 1988, MS 12501, Box 3292/1, La Trobe Library, SLV.
62 Circular no. 29, n.d., Melbourne Branch, War Widows Guild.
63 Minutes of the Executive Meeting 1 June 1950; Minutes of the Council Meeting 16 August 1950; NSW Branch, War Widows Guild.
64 Council of War Widows Guild, 19 August 1954; Minutes of the Meeting of the Executive Committee of the NSW Branch, 21 September 1954, ibid.
65 Jessie Vasey to Mrs Graham, October 1945, Scrapbook, Melbourne Branch, War Widows Guild.
66 Melanie Klein, 'Mourning and Its Relation to Manic Depressive States' (1940), in Melanie Klein, *Love, Guilt and Reparation and Other Works, 1921–1945*, London, Virago, 1988, p. 360.
67 Circular no. 2, April 1946, Melbourne Branch, War Widows Guild.
68 ibid.
69 *Herald*, 27 June 1947.
70 Circular no. 29, August 1948, Melbourne Branch, War Widows Guild.

Notes to pages 154–159

71 'War Widows', *Pix*, 24 January 1948.
72 Circular no. 21, 21 February 1952, Melbourne Branch, War Widows Guild.
73 ibid.
74 ibid.
75 Jean Bethke Elshtain, *Women and War*, Sussex, Harvester Press, 1987, pp. 3–4, 144.
76 See Pick, 'Freud's Group Psychology and the History of the Crowd', pp. 39–61, for a discussion of identity formation within a group.
77 Klein, 'Mourning and Its Relation to Manic Depressive States', p. 354.
78 ibid., p. 354.
79 Annual Report, 1953–1954, Melbourne Branch, War Widows Guild.
80 Circular no. 28, n.d., 1954–1955, ibid.
81 Circular no. 30, 1955, ibid.
82 'War Widows Annoyed with Treatment At Shrine', n.d., Scrapbook, NSW Branch, War Widows Guild.
83 ibid.
84 '200 Widows Angry Over Shrine Seats', ibid.
85 Circular no. 28, n.d., Melbourne Branch, War Widows Guild.
86 Raymond Evans, '"All the Passion of Our Womanhood": Margaret Thorp and the Battle of the Brisbane School of Arts', in Damousi and Lake (eds), *Gender and War*, p. 248.
87 Santner, *Stranded Objects*, p. 3.
88 Wheeler, 'After Grief? What Kind of Selves?', pp. 81–2.
89 Santner, *Stranded Objects*, p. 4
90 Kristeva, *Black Sun*, p. 60.
91 Wheeler, 'After Grief? What Kind of Selves?', p. 82.
92 ibid, p. 82.
93 Flax, *Disputed Subjects*, pp. 94–6.
94 *Sun*, 2 October 1947, Scrapbook, NSW Branch, War Widows Guild.
95 Kristeva, *Black Sun*, p. 60.
96 Wheeler, 'After Grief? What Kind of Selves?', p. 94.
97 Doris McCutcheon to Jessie Vasey, 9 March 1945, Box 1, Folder 1, Vasey Papers.
98 Annette Sage, 7 March 1945, ibid.
99 G. H. Knox, 7 July 1945, ibid.
100 Doris Disher to Vasey, March 1945, ibid.
101 Frank Berryman, 9 March 1945, ibid.
102 Rene Graham, 15 March 1945, ibid.
103 *Sun*, 2 October 1947, Scrapbook, NSW Branch, War Widows Guild.
104 Minutes of the First Annual Meeting of the War Widows Craft Guild in New South Wales, 30 September 1947, Minute Book, 12 July 1946 – 12 December 1947, ibid.
105 Jessie Vasey, Addressing Executive Committee, 21 May 1952, Minutes of Executive Committee 1947–1954, ibid.
106 Jessie Vasey to Mrs Graham, October 1945, Melbourne Branch, War Widows Guild.
107 'War Widows Get Poor Pensions' Deal', *Herald*, 2 October 1945, Scrapbook, NSW Branch, War Widows Guild.

108 Vasey Papers: From Regimental Sgt-Major, School of Infantry, Royal Australian Infantry Corps, 15 July 1957, Folder 27, Box 4; Mrs Vasey to Brigadier John Field, 8 August 1946, Box 4, Folder 28; To Vasey, 9 August 1956, Box 5, Folder 36; Manning to Mrs Vasey, 10 June 1960, Box 4, Folder 28; Clive Morton to Mrs Vasey, 6 October 1955, Mrs G. A. Vasey to Clive Morton, 24 October 1955, and Cleve H. Carney to Mrs Vasey, 11 January 1965, Box 4, Folder 29; 'War Widows Craft Guild', n.d., Box 4, Folder 34; Sir Stanton Hicks to Mrs Vasey, 30 April 1949, Box 4, Folder 29.
109 *Sun*, 2 October 1947, Scrapbook, NSW Branch, War Widows Guild.
110 *Daily Telegraph*, 4 October 1947, ibid.
111 Edith R. McLeod to Vasey, 25 November 1945, Box 4, Folder 28, Vasey Papers.
112 Jessie Vasey, notes on 'Women and Politics', n.d., Box 9, Folder 72, ibid.

CONCLUSION

1 Butler, *The Psychic Life of Power*, p. 148.

Bibliography

PRIMARY SOURCES

MANUSCRIPTS

Anzac Fellowship of Women Papers, MS 2864, NLA.
Australian War Memorial: Accession Numbers 1DRL/0023; 1DRL/0056; 1DRL/0081; 1DRL/0198; 1DRL/0431; 1DRL/0485; 1DRL/0640; 2DRL/0165; 2DRL/0726; 3DRL/6372; 3DRL/7892; 3DRL/7945; PR83/021; PR84/046; PR85/043; PR85/078; PR85/141; PR86/080; PR86/197; PR86/389; PR90/148; PR91/036; PR00145; PR00172; PR00218; PR00242; PR00392; PR00460; PR00686; PR00666; PRG938/2.
Australian Archives: Series A2, Item no. 1919/2673; Series A432/86, Item no. 1932/1616; Series A458, Item no. M382/2; Series A1066/4, Item no. IC1945/61/15/1; Series A2023, Item nos. 110/1/70, 272/8/51(M); Series A2479, Item nos. 17/67, 17/803; Series A2481, Item no. A18/5872; Series A2487, Item nos. 19/2483, 1919/7806, 1919/9472, 1919/11, 1920/5297, 1919/4134, 1920/4304, 1921/9855, 1921/1801, 1919/7500; Series B741/B, Item no. V2741; Series B741/3, Item nos. V/2588(M), V/2721(M), V/2792, V/1940, V/1178, V/1178(M); Series 13741, Item no. V/2779(M).
Bechevaise, Edward, MS 10153 MSB177, La Trobe Library, SLV.
Bettless, Jane, Letters, 1919–1922, D7094(L), Mortlock Library, SLSA.
Falkiner, Una, Diary, MSS 4342, ML.
Higgins, H. B., Papers, MS 2525, NLA.
Hislop, Allan, Papers, MS 10989, MSB349, La Trobe Library, SLV.
Hough Papers, PRG1055, Mortlock Library, SLSA.
Leahy, Claude, Papers, PRG938/2, Mortlock Library, SLSA.
McDonald, Gilbert, Papers, PRG795/2, Mortlock Library, SLSA.
Murrell, Charles, MS 11202, MSB638, La Trobe Library, SLV.
Naylor, George, MS 10024, La Trobe Library, SLV.
Roberts, John, Diary, MS 8183, Box 265/4, La Trobe Library, SLV.
Scott, Nancy, Papers, MS 12501 Box 3292/1, La Trobe Library, SLV.
Stark, Russell, Papers, D 7214/1–2(L), Mortlock Library, SLSA.
Stirling, Malcolm, MS 10739, Box 957/1, La Trobe Library, SLV.
Vasey Papers, MS 3782, NLA.
War Widows Guild, NSW Branch, Annual Reports; Executive Committee Minutes; Council Meeting Reports; Scrapbook, 1945–1956.
War Widows Guild, Melbourne Branch, Scrapbook; Circulars 1945–1955; Annual Reports.
Webber, Chaplain Eric, MS 9646, MSB67, La Trobe Library, SLV.

Williams, Charles Rowland, Papers, OM 95–10/3; 10/5, John Oxley Library, SLQ.

COLLECTED LETTERS

Blythe, Ronald, *Private Words: Letters and Diaries from the Second World War*, New York, Viking, 1991.
Day-Lewis, Tamasin (ed.), *Last Letters Home*, London, Macmillan, 1995.
Denholm, Decie (ed.), *Behind the Lines: One Woman's War 1914–18, The Letters of Caroline Ethel Cooper*, Sydney, Collins, 1982.
Horner, David, *General Vasey's War*, Melbourne, Melbourne University Press, 1992.
Johnson, Len, *An Australian Family, Volume III: War Letters: 1940–1941*, Brisbane, RockView Press, 1995.
Litoff, Judy Barrett, Smith, David C., Taylor, Barbara Woodall, and Taylor, Charles E. (eds), *Miss You: The World War Two Letters of Barbara Woodall Taylor and Charles E. Taylor*, Georgia, University of Georgia Press, 1990.
Litoff, Judy Barrett, and Smith, David C., *Since You Went Away: World War Two Letters from American Women on the Homefront*, New York, Oxford University Press, 1991.
Mitchell, Jim (ed.), *The Moon Seems Upside Down: Letters of Love and War*, Sydney, Allen & Unwin, 1995.
Nott, David (ed.), *Somewhere in France: The Collection of Letters of Lewis Windermere Nott: January–December 1916*, Sydney, HarperCollins, 1996.
Stuart, Lurline, and Arnold, Josie (eds), *Letters Home, 1939–1945*, Sydney, Collins, 1987.

NEWSPAPERS AND JOURNALS

Age
Argus
Australian Worker
Daily Telegraph
Guild Digest
Herald, Melbourne
Limbless Soldier
Medical Journal of Australia
Our Empire: The Official Organ of the Sailors' and Soldiers' Fathers Association of Victoria
Pix
Sydney Morning Herald
Sun (Sydney)

AUTOBIOGRAPHY AND LITERATURE

Arnold, Josie, *Mother Superior Woman Inferior*, Melbourne, Dove Communications, 1985.
Bottrell, Padre Arthur, *Cameos of Commandos: Memories of Eight Australian Commando Squadrons in New Guinea and Queensland*, Adelaide, Specialty Printers, 1971.

Roberts, Estelle, *Forty Years a Medium*, London, Herbert Jenkins, 1959.
Slater, Chaplain J. C., *A Padre with the Rats of Tobruk*, Hobart, J. Walch and Sons, 1946.
Stein, Gertrude, *Wars I Have Seen*, London, Batsford, 1945.
Wiggins, Marianne, *John Dollar*, London, Penguin, 1989.

PARLIAMENTARY PAPERS, GOVERNMENT PUBLICATIONS, TRACTS

Commonwealth Bureau of Census and Statistics, Official Year Books of the Commonwealth of Australia, nos. 8–13, 1915–20, Melbourne, Government Printer, 1916–21.
Fitzpatrick, W., *The Repatriation of the Soldier*, Melbourne, Victorian State War Council, 1916.
MacEwen, Sir William, 'On the Limbless', *The Inter-Allied Conference on the After Care of Disabled Men, Second Annual Meeting, 20–25 May 1918*, London, 1918.
'Progress Report of the Select Committee on Widows' Pensions and Child Endowment', Votes and Proceedings of the Legislative Assembly, *Victorian Parliamentary Papers*, 1936.
Repatriation Commission for the Commonwealth of Australia, Handbook of Repatriation Artificial Limb Factories and their Products, Melbourne, Government Printer, 1945.
United Kingdom, Ministry of Pensions, *Instructions on the Training of Widows*, British Government, 1918.
Widows' Pensions Bill, *NSW Parliamentary Debates*, Sessions 1925–6, Legislative Assembly, Government Printer, Sydney, 1926.

SECONDARY SOURCES

BOOKS

Adam-Smith, Patsy, *Prisoners of War: From Gallipoli to Korea*, Melbourne, Viking, 1992.
Aitken-Swan, Jean, *Widows in Australia: A Survey*, Sydney, Council of Social Service of New South Wales, 1962.
Alexander, Sally, *Becoming A Woman, and Other Essays in 19th and 20th Century Feminist History*, London, Virago, 1984.
Allen, Judith, *Sex and Secrets: Crimes Involving Australian Women Since 1880*, Melbourne, Oxford University Press, 1990.
Antze, Paul, and Lambeck, Michael (eds), *Tense Past: Cultural Essays in Trauma and Memory*, London, Routledge, 1996.
Aries, Philipe, *Western Attitudes Towards Death: From the Middle Ages to the Present*, trans. Patricia M. Ranum, London, M. Boyards, 1976.
Australian Dictionary of Biography, Volumes 7, 8, 11, Melbourne, Melbourne University Press, 1979.
Baldock, Cora, and Cass, Bettina (eds), *Women, Social Welfare and the State*, Sydney, Allen & Unwin, 1983.
Ball, Desmond (ed.), *Aborigines in the Defence of Australia*, Canberra, Australian National University Press, 1991.

Beaumont, Joan, *Gull Force: Survival and Leadership in Captivity, 1941–1945*, Sydney, Allen & Unwin, 1988.
Australia's War, 1939–1945, Sydney, Allen & Unwin, 1996.
Bessel, Richard, *Germany after the First World War*, Oxford, Clarendon Press, 1993.
Bolton, Geoffrey, *The Oxford History of Australia, Volume 5: 1942–1988*, Melbourne, Oxford University Press, 1990.
Bourke, Joanna, *Dismembering the Male: Men's Bodies, Britain and the Great War*, London, Reaktion Books, 1996.
Bremmer, Jan, and van der Bosch, Lourens (eds), *Between Poverty and the Pyre: Moments in the History of Widowhood*, London, Routledge, 1995.
Broughton, Trev Lynne, and Anderson, Lynda (eds), *Women's Lives/Women's Times: New Essays on Auto/Biography*, New York, State University of New York Press, 1997.
Brown, Nicholas, *Governing Prosperity: Social Change and Social Analysis in Australia in the 1950s*, Melbourne, Cambridge University Press, 1995.
Burgmann, Verity, and Lee, Jenny (eds), *Constructing a Culture: A People's History of Australia Since 1788*, Melbourne, McPhee Gribble/Penguin, 1988.
Butler, Judith, *The Psychic Life of Power: Theories in Subjection*, Stanford, Stanford University Press, 1997.
Cain, Frank, *The Origins of Political Surveillance in Australia*, Sydney, Angus & Robertson, 1983.
Campbell, Rosemary, *Heroes and Lovers: A Question of National Identity*, Sydney, Allen & Unwin, 1989.
Charmaz, Kathy, Howarth, Glennys, and Kellehear, Allan (eds), *The Unknown Country: Death in Australia, Britain and the USA*, London, Macmillan, 1997.
Chesterman, John, and Galligan, Brian, *Citizens Without Rights: Aborigines and Australian Citizenship*, Melbourne, Cambridge University Press, 1997.
Clark, Mavis Thorpe, *No Mean Destiny: The Story of the War Widows' Guild of Australia, 1945–85*, Melbourne, Hyland House, 1986.
Clarke, Hugh V., and Burgess, Colin, *Barbed Wire and Bamboo: Australian POWs in Europe, North Africa, Singapore, Thailand and Japan*, Sydney, Allen & Unwin, 1992.
Clemens, Jere (ed.), *The First World War*, London, Macmillan, 1972.
Coetzee, Frans, and Shevin-Coetzee, Marilyn (eds), *Authority, Identity and the Social History of the Great War*, Oxford, Berghan Books, 1995.
Collini, Stefan, *Public Moralists: Political Thought and Intellectual Life in Britain, 1850–1930*, Oxford, Clarendon Press, 1991.
Connors, Libby, et al., *Australia's Frontline: Remembering the 1939–1945 War*, St Lucia, University of Queensland Press, 1992.
Conway, Jill K., Bourque, Susan C., and Scott, Joan W. (eds), *Learning about Women: Gender, Politics and Power*, Ann Arbor, University of Michigan Press, 1989.
Crowley, Frank, *A New History of Australia*, Melbourne, Heinemann, 1974.
Damousi, Joy, and Lake, Marilyn (eds), *Gender and War: Australians at War in the Twentieth Century*, Melbourne, Cambridge University Press, 1995.
Darian-Smith, Kate, *On the Homefront: Melbourne in Wartime, 1939–45*, Melbourne, Oxford University Press, 1990.

and Hamilton, Paula (eds), *Memory and History in Twentieth-Century Australia*, Melbourne, Oxford University Press, 1994.

Davidson, Alastair, *From Subject to Citizen: Australian Citizenship in the Twentieth Century*, Cambridge, Cambridge University Press, 1997.

Davison, Graeme, McCarty, J. W., and McLeary, Ailsa (eds), *Australians 1888*, Sydney, Fairfax, Syme and Weldon, 1987.

Dawes, J. N. I., and Robson, L. L., *Citizen to Soldier: Australia before the Great War: Recollections of Members of the First A.I.F.*, Melbourne, Melbourne University Press, 1977.

Dawson, Graham, *Soldier Heroes: British Adventure, Empire and the Imagining of Masculinities*, London, Routledge, 1994.

de Certeau, Michel, *Heterologies: Discourse on the Others*, trans. Brian Massumi, Minneapolis, University of Minnesota Press, 1986.

Dennis, Peter, et al. (eds), *The Oxford Companion to Australian Military History*, Melbourne, Oxford University Press, 1995.

Doak, Frank, *Royal Australian Air Force: A Brief History*, Canberra, Australian Government Publishing Service, 1981.

Doane, Mary Ann, *'Femmes Fatales': Feminism, Film Theory, Psychoanalysis*, New York, Routledge, 1991.

Duby, Georges, and Perrot, Michelle (eds), *A History of Women in the West, Volume V: Towards a Cultural Identity in the Twentieth Century*, London, Belknap Press, 1994.

Dyer, Colin, *Population and Society in Twentieth-Century France*, London, Hodder and Stoughton, 1978.

Eksteins, Modris, *Rites of Spring: The Great War and the Birth of the Modern Age*, Boston, Houghton, 1989.

Elshtain, Jean Bethke, *Women and War*, Sussex, Harvester Press, 1987.

Evans, Raymond, *Loyalty and Disloyalty: Social Conflict on the Queensland Homefront, 1914–18*, Sydney, Allen & Unwin, 1987.

Felski, Rita, *The Gender of Modernity*, Cambridge, Harvard University Press, 1995.

Ferber, Sarah, et al. (eds), *Beasts of Suburbia: Reinterpreting Cultures in Australian Suburbs*, Melbourne, Melbourne University Press, 1994.

Field, H. John, *Toward a Programme of Imperial Life: The British Empire at the Turn of the Century*, New Haven, Greenwood Press, 1982.

Fishman, Sarah, *We Will Wait: Wives of French Prisoners of War, 1940–1945*, New Haven, Yale University Press, 1991.

Fitzpatrick, David, *Oceans of Consolation: Personal Accounts of Irish Migration to Australia*, Melbourne, Melbourne University Press, 1995.

Flax, Jane, *Disputed Subjects: Essays on Psychoanalysis, Politics and Philosophy*, New York, Routledge, 1993.

Frances, Raelene, and Scates, Bruce, *Women and the Great War*, Melbourne, Cambridge University Press, 1992.

Freud, Sigmund, *Civilisation, Society and Religion: Group Psychology, Civilisation and Its Discontents and Other Works*, London, Penguin, 1985.

—— *On Metapsychology: The Theory of Psychoanalysis, Volume 11: The Penguin Freud Library*, London, Penguin, 1991.

Friedlander, Saul (ed.), *Probing the Limits of Representation: Nazism and the 'Final Solution'*, Cambridge, Harvard University Press, 1992.

Fussell, Paul, *The Great War and Modern Memory*, Oxford, Oxford University Press, 1975.
Gabay, Al, *The Mystic Life of Alfred Deakin*, Melbourne, Cambridge University Press, 1992.
Gammage, Bill, *The Broken Years: Australian Soldiers in the Great War*, Ringwood, Vic., Penguin, 1975.
 and Spearritt, Peter (eds), *Australians 1938*, Sydney, Fairfax, Syme and Weldon, 1987.
Garton, Stephen, *The Cost of War: Australians Return*, Melbourne, Oxford University Press, 1996.
 Out of Luck: Poor Australians and Social Welfare, 1788–1988, Sydney, Allen & Unwin, 1990.
Giddens, Anthony, *The Consequences of Modernity*, Stanford, Stanford University Press, 1990.
Gilding, Michael, *The Making and Breaking of the Australian Family*, Sydney, Allen & Unwin, 1991.
Gillis, John (ed.), *Commemorations: The Politics of National Identity*, Princeton, Princeton University Press, 1994.
Goldsmith, Betty, and Sandford, Beryl (eds), *The Girls They Left Behind*, Melbourne, Penguin, 1990.
Goodall, Heather, *Invasion to Embassy: Land in Aboriginal Politics in New South Wales, 1770–1972*, Sydney, Allen & Unwin/Black Books, 1996.
Gregory, Adrian, *The Silence of Memory: Armistice Day, 1919–1946*, Oxford, Berg Publishers, 1994.
Griffin, Graeme M., and Tobin, Des, *In the Midst of Life: The Australian Response to Death*, Melbourne, Melbourne University Press, 1997.
Griffiths, Tom, *Hunters and Collectors: The Antiquarian Imagination in Australia*, Melbourne, Cambridge University Press, 1996.
Grimshaw, Patricia, et al. (eds), *Families in Colonial Australia*, Sydney, Allen & Unwin, 1985.
 et al., *Creating a Nation: 1788–1990*, Melbourne, Penguin, 1994.
Gunew, Sneja (ed.), *A Reader in Feminist Knowledge*, London, Routledge, 1990.
Halbwach, Maurice, *On Collective Memory*, trans. Lewis A. Coser, Chicago, University of Chicago Press, 1992.
Hamilton, Paula, and Darian-Smith, Kate (eds), *Memory and History in Twentieth-Century Australia*, Melbourne, Oxford University Press, 1994.
Harpham, Geoffrey Galt, *On the Grotesque: Strategies of Contradiction in Art and Literature*, Princeton, Princeton University Press, 1982.
Hartman, Geoffrey (ed.), *Holocaust Remembrance: The Shapes of Memory*, Oxford, Basil Blackwell, 1994.
Harvey, Elizabeth, and Okruhlik, Kathleen (eds), *Women and Reason*, Ann Arbor, University of Michigan Press, 1992.
Healy, Chris, *From the Ruins of Colonialism: History as Social Memory*, Melbourne, Cambridge University Press, 1997.
Hemming, Peter, *Doomed Battalion: Mateship and Leadership in War and Captivity: The Australian 2/40 Battalion, 1940–45*, Sydney, Allen & Unwin, 1995.
Higgonet, Margaret, et al. (eds), *Behind the Lines: Gender and the Two World Wars*, New Haven, Yale University Press, 1987.

Hobsbawm, Eric, *The Age of Extremes: The Short Twentieth Century, 1914–1991*, London, Abacus, 1995.
Holmes, Katie, *Spaces in Her Day: Australian Women's Diaries, 1920s–1930s*, Sydney, Allen and Unwin, 1995.
Horner, David (ed.), *The Commanders: Australian Military Leadership in the Twentieth Century*, Sydney, Allen & Unwin, 1984.
Hynes, Samuel, *The Soldier's Tale: Bearing Witness to Modern War*, New York, Allen Lane/The Penguin Press, 1977.
Jackomos, Alick, and Fowell, Derek (eds), *Forgotten Heroes: Aborigines at War: Somme to Vietnam*, Melbourne, Victoria Press, 1993.
Jalland, Pat, *Death in the Victorian Family*, Oxford, Oxford University Press, 1997.
Kennedy, Richard (ed.), *Australian Welfare: Historical Sociology*, Melbourne, Macmillan, 1989.
Kent, Susan Kingsley, *Making Peace: The Reconstruction of Gender in Inter-War Britain*, Princeton, Princeton University Press, 1993.
Kewley, T. W., *Social Security in Australia: Social Security and Health Benefits from 1900 to the Present*, Sydney, Sydney University Press, 1965.
King, Clemens Jere (ed.), *The First World War*, London, Macmillan, 1972.
Klein, Melanie, *Love, Guilt and Reparation and Other Works, 1921–1945*, London, Virago, 1988.
Kleinman, Arthur, and Good, Byron (eds), *Culture and Depression: Studies in the Anthropology of Cross-Cultural Psychiatry of Affect and Disorder*, Berkeley, University of California Press, 1985.
Kociumbas, Jan, *Australian Childhood: A History*, Sydney, Allen & Unwin, 1997.
Kristeva, Julia, *Black Sun: Depression and Melancholia*, trans. Leon S. Roudiez, New York, Columbia University Press, 1985.
Kristianson, G. L., *The Politics of Patriotism: The Pressure Group Activities of the Returned Servicemen's League*, Canberra, Australian National University Press, 1966.
Lake, Marilyn, *A Divided Society: Tasmania During World War One*, Melbourne, Melbourne University Press, 1975.
The Limits of Hope: Soldier Settlement in Victoria, 1915–38, Melbourne, Oxford University Press, 1987.
and Kelly, Farley (eds), *Double Time: Women in Victoria – 150 Years*, Melbourne, Penguin, 1985.
Lane, Christopher, *The Ruling Passion: British Colonial Allegory and the Paradox of Homosexual Desire*, Durham, Duke University Press, 1995.
La Rossa, Ralph, *The Modernisation of Fatherhood: A Social and Political History*, Chicago, University of Chicago Press, 1997.
Leed, Eric, *No Man's Land: Combat and Identity in World War I*, Cambridge, Cambridge University Press, 1979.
Liveris, Leonie B., *The Dismal Trader: The Undertaker Business in Perth, 1860–1939*, Perth, Park Printing, 1991.
Lloyd, Clem, and Rees, Jacqui, *The Last Shilling: A History of Repatriation in Australia*, Melbourne, Melbourne University Press, 1994.
Long, Gavin, *Greece, Crete and Syria*, Canberra, Australian War Memorial, 1953.
Lucic, Karen, *Charles Sheeler and the Cult of the Machine*, Reaktion Books, London, 1991.
Lyons, Mark, *Legacy: The First Fifty Years*, Melbourne, Lothian, 1978.

Lyons, Martyn, and Taksa, Lucy, *Australian Readers Remember: An Oral History of Reading, 1890–1930*, Melbourne, Oxford University Press, 1992.

Macintyre, Stuart, *The Oxford History of Australia, Volume 4: 1901–1942*, Melbourne, Oxford University Press, 1986.

Mangan, J. A., and Walvin, James (eds), *Manliness and Morality: Middle Class Masculinity in Britain and America, 1800–1940*, Manchester, Manchester University Press, 1987.

Markus, Andrew, *Governing Savages*, Sydney, Allen & Unwin, 1990.

McGregor, Russell, *Imagined Destinies: Aboriginal Australians and Doomed Race Theory, 1880–1939*, Melbourne, Melbourne University Press, 1997.

McKernan, Michael, *Australian Churches at War: Attitudes of the Major Churches, 1914–1918*, Canberra, Australian War Memorial, 1980.

The Australian People and the Great War, Melbourne, Nelson, 1980.

Padre: Australian Chaplains in Gallipoli and France, Sydney, Allen & Unwin, 1986.

and Browne, M. (eds), *Australia: Two Centuries of War and Peace*, Sydney, Allen & Unwin/Australian War Memorial, 1988.

Minsky, Rosalind, *Psychoanalysis and Gender: An Introductory Reader*, London, Routledge, 1996.

Moeller, Robert G., *Protecting Motherhood: Women and the Family in the Politics of Post-War Germany*, Berkeley, University of California Press, 1993.

Mosse, George, *Fallen Soldiers: Reshaping the Memory of the World Wars*, New York, Oxford University Press, 1990.

Nelson, Hank, *Prisoners of War: Australians under Nippon*, Sydney, ABC Radio Series, 1990.

Nora, Pierre, *Realms of Memory and Rethinking the French Past*, New York, Columbia University Press, 1996.

Pankhurst, E. Sylvia, *The Home Front: A Mirror to Life in England During the First World War*, London, Cressett Library, 1987.

Pedersen, Susan, *Family, Dependence and the Origins of the Welfare State: Britain and France, 1914–1945*, Cambridge, Cambridge University Press, 1993.

Phillips, Adam, *On Flirtation*, London, Faber & Faber, 1994.

Pound, Reginald, *The Lost Generation*, London, Constable, 1964.

Rabinach, Anson, *The Human Motor: Energy, Fatigue and the Origins of Modernity*, New York, Basic Books, 1990.

Raphael, Beverley, *The Anatomy of Bereavement*, New York, Basic Books, 1983.

Read, Peter, *Returning to Nothing: The Meaning of Lost Places*, Melbourne, Cambridge University Press, 1996.

Reiger, Kerreen, *The Disenchantment of the Home: Modernising the Australian Family, 1880–1940*, Melbourne, Oxford University Press, 1985.

Rickard, John, *H. B Higgins: The Rebel as Judge*, Sydney, Allen & Unwin, 1984.

A Family Romance, Melbourne, Melbourne University Press, 1996.

and Spearritt, Peter (eds), *Packaging the Past: Public Histories (Special Issue of Australian Historical Studies)*, vol. 24, no. 6, Melbourne, Melbourne University Press, 1991.

Roberts, Mary Louise, *Civilisation Without Sexes: Reconstructing Gender in Post-War France, 1917–1927*, Chicago, University of Chicago Press, 1994.

Roe, Jill, *Beyond Belief: Theosophy in Australia, 1879–1939*, Kensington, New South Wales University Press, 1986.

Roe, Michael, *Nine Australian Progressives: Vitalism in Bourgeois Social Thought, 1890–1960*, St Lucia, University of Queensland Press, 1984.
Roper, Lyndal, *Oedipus and the Devil: Witchcraft, Sexuality and Religion in Early Modern Europe*, London, Routledge, 1994.
Samuel, Raphael, and Thompson, Paul (eds), *The Myths We Live By*, London, Routledge, 1990.
Theatres of Memory, Volume 1: Past and Present in Contemporary Culture, London, Verso, 1994.
Santner, Eric, *Stranded Objects: Mourning, Memory and Film in Postwar Germany*, Ithaca, Cornell University Press, 1990.
Saunders, Kay, and Evans, Raymond (eds), *Gender Relations in Australia: Domination and Negotiation*, Sydney, Harcourt, Brace and Jovanovich, 1992.
Sayers, Janet, *The Man Who Never Was: Freudian Tales*, London, Chatto and Windus, 1995.
Scarry, Elaine, *The Body in Pain: The Making and Unmaking of the World*, New York, Oxford University Press, 1985.
Schatzki, Theodore, and Natter, Wolfgang (eds), *The Social and Political Body*, New York, Guilford Press, 1996.
Spillman, Lyn, *Nation and Commemoration: Creating National Identities in the United States and Australia*, New York, Cambridge University Press, 1997.
Stenman, Roy, *One Hundred Years of Spiritualism*, London, Spiritualist Association of Great Britain, 1972.
Stevens, Charles H., *Limbless Soldiers' Association of Victoria, 1921–1971*, Melbourne, Limbless Soldiers' Association of Victoria, 1971.
Stokes, Geoffrey (ed.), *The Politics of Identity in Australia*, Melbourne, Cambridge University Press, 1997.
Swain, Shurlee, with Howe, Renate, *Single Mothers and Their Children: Disposal, Punishment and Survival in Australia*, Melbourne, Cambridge University Press, 1995.
Theweleit, Klaus, *Male Fantasies, Volume 1: Women, Floods, Bodies, History*, trans. Stephen Conway, Minneapolis, University of Minnesota Press, 1987.
Thomson, Alistair, *Anzac Memories: Living with the Legend*, Melbourne, Oxford University Press, 1994.
Thompson, Ernest, *The Teachings and Phenomena of Spiritualism*, Manchester, Two Worlds Publishing Company, 1947.
Walker, R. B., *The Newspaper Press in New South Wales, 1803–1920*, Sydney, University of Sydney Press, 1976.
Watson, Sophie (ed.), *Playing the State: Australian Feminist Interventions*, London, Verso, 1990.
Whalen, Robert Weldon, *Bitter Wounds: German Victims of the Great War, 1914–1939*, Ithaca, Cornell University Press, 1984.
Whaley, Joachim (ed.), *Mirrors of Mortality: Studies in the Social History of Death*, London, Europa Publications, 1981.
Wilkinson, Alan, *The Church of England and the First World War*, London, SPCK, 1978.
Williams, John, *The Home Front: Britain, France and Germany 1914–1918*, London, Constable, 1972.
Winter, Jay, *The Great War and the British People*, London, Macmillan, 1987.

Sites of Memory, Sites of Mourning: The Great War in European Cultural History, Cambridge, Cambridge University Press, 1995.

Young, James (ed.), *The Art of Memory: Holocaust Memorials in History*, New York, Prestel Verlag, 1994.

ARTICLES

Bergmann, Linda S., 'The Contemporary Letter as Literature: Issues of Self-Reflexivity, Audience and Closure', *Women's Studies Quarterly*, nos. 3 & 4, 1989.

Bourke, Joanna, 'The Battle of the Limbs: Amputation, Artificial Limbs and the Great War in Australia', *Australian Historical Studies*, vol. 29, no. 110, 1998.

Brandt, Susanne, 'The Memory Makers: Museums and Exhibitions of the First World War', *History and Memory*, vol. 6, no. 1, 1994.

Chodorow, Nancy, 'Gender as a Personal and Cultural Construction', *Signs*, vol. 20, no. 1, 1995.

Confino, Alon, 'Collective Memory and Cultural History: Problems of Method', *American Historical Review*, vol. 102, no. 5, 1997.

Crane, Susan A., 'Writing the Individual Back into Collective Memory', *American Historical Review*, vol. 102, no. 5, 1997.

Crisp, Douglas, 'Mourning and Militancy', *October*, no. 51, 1989.

Curthoys, Ann, 'Eugenics, Feminism and Birth Control: The Case of Marion Piddington', *Hecate*, vol. 15, no. 1, 1989.

Elliot, Patricia, 'Politics, Identity and Social Change: Contested Grounds in Psychoanalytic Feminism', *Hypatia; A Journal of Feminist Philosophy*, vol. 10, no. 2, 1995.

Faye, Esther, 'Psychoanalysis and the Barred Subject of Feminist History', *Australian Feminist Studies*, no. 22, 1995.

Figlio, Karl, 'Historical Imagination/Psychoanalytic Imagination', *History Workshop Journal*, no. 45, 1998.

Gaines, Robert, 'Detachment and Continuity: The Two Tasks of Mourning', *Contemporary Psychoanalysis*, vol. 33, no. 4, 1997.

Game, Ann, and Pringle, Rosemary, 'Sexuality and the Suburban Dream', *Australian and New Zealand Journal of Sociology*, vol. 15, no. 2, 1972.

Hagman, George, 'Mourning: A Review and Reconsideration', *International Journal of Psychoanalysis*, no. 76, 1995.

'The Role of the "Other" in Mourning', *Psychoanalytic Quarterly*, no. LXV, 1996.

Hunt, Lynne, 'Psychoanalysis, the Self, and Historical Interpretation', *Common Knowledge*, vol. 6, no. 2, 1997.

Horowitz, Mardi J., 'A Model of Mourning: Change in Schemes of Self and Other', *Journal of the American Psychoanalytic Association*, vol. 38, no. 2, 1990.

Inglis, Ken S., 'Entombing Unknown Soldiers: From London to Paris to Bagdad', *History and Memory*, vol. 5, no. 2, 1993.

Karskens, Grace, 'Death Was in His Face: Dying, Burial and Remembrance in Early Sydney', *Labour History*, no. 74, 1998.

Koven, Seth, 'Remembering and Dismemberment: Crippled Children, Wounded Soldiers, and the Great War in Great Britain', *American Historical Review*, vol. 99, no. 4, 1994.

Lake, Marilyn, 'The Desire for A Yank: Sexual Relations between Australian Women and American Servicemen During World War II', *Journal of the History of Sexuality*, vol. 2, no. 4, 1992.
'The Independence of Women and the Brotherhood of Man: Debates in the Labor Movement over Equal Pay and Motherhood Endowment in the 1920s', *Labour History*, no. 63, 1992.
'Mission Impossible: How Men Gave Birth to the Australian Nation: Nationalism, Gender and Other Seminal Acts', *Gender and History*, vol. 4, no. 3, 1992.
'Feminism and the Gendered Politics of Antiracism, Australia, 1927–1957: From Maternal Protectionism to Leftist Assimilationism', *Australian Historical Studies*, vol. 29, no. 10, 1998.
Lomas, Janice, ' "So I Married Again": Letters from British Widows of the First and Second World Wars', *History Workshop Journal*, no. 38, 1994.
Manuel, Jacqueline, ' "We are the women who mourn our dead": Australian Civilian Women's Poetic Responses to the First World War', *Journal of the Australian War Memorial*, no. 29, 1996.
'Men/Women of Letters', *Yale French Studies (Special Issue)*, no. 71, 1986.
Morris, Humphrey, 'Narrative Representation, Narrative Enactment, and the Psychoanalytic Construction of History', *International Journal of Psychoanalysis*, no. 74, 1993.
Panchasi, Roxanne, 'Reconstructions: Prosthetics and the Rehabilitation of the Male Body in World War I France', *Differences*, vol. 7, no. 3, 1995.
Pick, Daniel, 'Freud's Group Psychology and the History of the Crowd', *History Workshop Journal*, no. 40, 1995.
Roe, Jill, 'Chivalry and Social Policy in the Antipodes', *Historical Studies*, vol. 22, no. 88, 1987.
Sherman, Daniel, 'Mourning and Masculinity in France after World War One', *Gender and History*, vol. 8, no. 1, 1996.
'Bodies and Names: The Emergence of Commemoration in Interwar France', *American Historical Review*, vol. 103, no. 2, 1998.
Speck, Catherine, 'Women's War Memorials and Citizenship', *Australian Feminist Studies*, vol. 11, no. 23, 1996.
Tosh, John, 'What Should Historians Do with Masculinity? Reflections on Nineteenth-Century Britain', *History Workshop Journal*, no. 38, 1994.
Tsokhas, Kosmas, 'Modernity, Sexuality and National Identity: Norman Lindsay's Aesthetics', *Australian Historical Studies*, vol. 27, no. 107, 1996.
Wheeler, Wendy, 'After Grief? What Kind of Selves?', *New Formations*, no. 25, 1995.
Woodward, Kathleen, 'Freud and Barthes: Theorizing Mourning, Sustaining Grief', *Discourse*, vol. 13, no. 1, 1990–91.

UNPUBLISHED THESES

Smart, Jeffrey, 'Four Crashing Heart-Twisting Years: The Relatives of Australian Prisoners of War in Japanese Hands, 1941–1945', BA (Hons) thesis, University of Melbourne, 1989.

Index

Aboriginal people, 4, 37–9, 56, 68, 95, 106, 150, 163
Adams family, 81–2
Adamson, C. S. D., 13
AIF *see* volunteers
Albert family, 15, 17
Allan, Sheila, 142
Allen, Morton, 11, 14
Alston, Edith (Miss), 62
Anderson family, 13
Anderson, Frances, 19–20, 24, 65–6
Anderson, R. M. (Captain), 15
anger, 3, 106, 161; disabled, 102; fathers, 52, 54, 57–9; mothers, 2, 27, 30, 39, 44–5, 135, 162; widows, 6, 39, 44, 77–8, 84, 147, 155–6
anniversaries, 63, 107, 116–17, 130
anticipation of bereavement, 5–6, 19, 23, 25, 107, 120, 125, 161
Anzac Day commemorations, 35–8, 57, 81, 96, 105–6, 111, 152, 155–6
Anzac spirit, 35, 89, 96, 106, 162
Appleton, Bob, 131
Archibald, John (Lieutenant), 16
Armistice Day commemorations, 34, 44, 54
Armstrong family, 17–18
Arnold, Josie, 145, 152
artificial limbs, 86–7, 89, 93, 100
Atcock family, 138
Australian Army Nursing Service, 158
Australian government *see* federal government
Australian Imperial Force (AIF) *see* volunteers
Australian spirit *see* national character

'baby bonus', 38–9
badges: disabled soldiers, 88, 91, 94; Fathers Association, 54–5; mothers of dead sons, 26; returned service groups, 54; widows, 153
Bagenal, B. W. (Mr), 88, 93
Bailey family, 50, 121–2
Bairnsfather family, 140
Baker, Arnold, 22
Baker, Les, 61
Barker family, 22
Barrett family, 21–2
Basham, W. J., 53
Bavin, Thomas, 44
Bayliss family, 137, 141–2
Bechevaise, Edward, 49
begging and canvassing, 88, 97, 101
Berryman, Frank, 158
Billing, Fannie, 22
Birdwood, William (General), 41–2
Black, Amelia (Mrs), 74
Blackburn, Archer, 68
Blacker, K. A., 142
Blackmore family, 62
blind and partially sighted returned soldiers, 86, 89–91, 94, 96–7, 100
Bond family, 120
Bonner, Jean, 136–7
Booth, Mary, 67, 81
Booth family, 135–6
Bowral family, 142–3
breadwinners and dependents, 39–43, 47, 69–71, 78–80, 82–3, 90, 99–100, 145, 148–52, 154
Bridges, Tom (Sir), 95
Briggen family, 13
Brisbane (Qld), 16, 40
Brock, G. H. (Mrs), 150
Brooks family, 13, 21
Browning, Joyce, 143
Bruce, S. M., 44, 80
Brydie, Will, 13
Bullock, C. (Chaplain), 17–18
Burrows family, 120
Butler, Judith, 3, 161

Cannadine, David, 2, 49, 119
Carney, Cleve H., 159
Caroline, L. (Mrs), 74
casualty lists, 18, 21–2, 25, 42, 46, 66
casualty statistics, 26, 65, 68, 106, 119–20, 122–3, 128–30, 135, 140

Index

Cazale, J., 139
censorship, 21, 109
Centre for Soldiers' Wives and Mothers, 34–5, 81–2
Chalmers family, 33
Champion, Kazan, 75
Chandler family, 40
chaplains: First World War, 14, **16–18**, 34; Second World War, 121–2, 124, 133, **135–7**
Chapman family, 11–12, 14, 18
charities, 39, 68–9, 78, 81–3, 89–90, 154, 158; *see also* fund-raising
Charlwood family, 120
childrearing, 38, 47, 152
children: Aboriginal, 38; loss of, 128–9; public commemorations, 36–7; welfare, 44, 47, 68–9, 72–80, 82–4, 144–5, 148–52
chivalry, 15, 37, 47, 52, 83, 89; *see also* heroic ideals
Christian beliefs, 10, 16–18, 21, 28, 48–9, 71, 109, 120, 129, 137, 143; *see also* chaplains; clergy
CIB *see* Commonwealth Investigation Branch
citizenship: Aboriginal people, 4, 68, 106, 150; disabled soldiers, 85, 87, **95–7**; fathers, 52, 54–5; women, 4, 31, 38, 68, 70
Clark, Mavis Thorpe, 109, 147
Clarke family, 22, 24, 40
Clayton, John, 68, 90
clergy, 16–19, 25; *see also* chaplains
Cole family, 126
collecting, 24, 59–62, 114, 159
collective memory: Aborigines, 56, 95; fathers' place, 53, 55–8; shifts, 2–3, 25, 30, 96, 101–2; women's place, 37, 42, 51, 81, 147–9, 152, 162–3
collective support, 1, 4–5, 161; fathers, 51, 61–2; Second World War, 119–25, 128, 135–7; soldiers, 11; women, 5, **21–5**, 42, 51, 146–7, 153–7, 160
commanders and leaders, 11, 41–2, 50, 57, 62, 95, 158–60; *see also* Vasey, George
Commonwealth government *see* federal government
Commonwealth Investigation Branch (CIB), 70, 74–6, 82
Commonwealth Repatriation Commission *see* repatriation programmes
community *see* collective support
Conlon, Mildred May Teresa, 72
Connell, H., (Mrs), 42
conscription, 30–1, 81, 128
Copelin family, 124–5

Coppin family, 33
Corkett family, 83
Courtman family, 152
Cullen family, 22
Curtin, John, 124, 128, 148, 162

David, A. M. (Mr), 87
Day, A. J., 94–5
de facto relationships, 72, 149
Dean, A., 67
death: acceptance, 1, 20, 62, 135, 142–3; accidental, 118–19, 121, 129, 148; details, 5, 10–12, 14, 136, 141; experience, 9–12, 16–18, 50, 61; messages after, 20, 59–60; notices, 18, 21, **32–3**; notification, 5, 19, 24–5, 50, 58, 63, 126, 144–5; premature, 131; prisoners of war, 123–5; understanding, 48–51, 162; *see also* anticipation of bereavement; casualty lists; casualty statistics; families: grief; rituals of death and mourning
Department of Repatriation *see* repatriation programmes
dependents *see* breadwinners and dependents
Depression, 35, 39, 70, 72, 83, 98–9
Derham family, 12, 19–24, 29, 33–4, 45, 52, 65–6
deserters, 71–2
Dickson family, 62
disabled returned soldiers, 6, 40–1, 47, 53, 68–9, 80, **85–102**; employment, 87–90, 92, **96–101**; preferential treatment, 85, 87, 91–2, 97–8; travelling concessions, 92–5; *see also* blind and partially sighted soldiers; limbless soldiers; lung diseases
disarmament *see* peace movement
Disher, Doris, 158
Dixon, D. (Mrs), 153
Dixon, J. R., 140
Dobson, G. F., 61
Doggeth family, 136
Doherty (Mrs), 43
Doig family, 28
domesticity, 29, 36, **107–19**, 126–8, 155
Dowell family, 62
Drakes family, 122
drunkenness, 67–8, 73, 76, 86
Duncan family, 16
Dutton family, 139
duty, 15, 32, 42, 48–9, 52, 54–8, 101; *see also* shirkers and slackers

Eadie family, 82

Index

economic hardship: Depression, 35, 39, 70, 72, 83, 98–9; fathers, 51; mothers, **38–41**: returned soldiers, 53, 98–9; widows, 4, 69–72, 80–1, 84, 145, 148; *see also* welfare
Edwards family, 61
Elliot (Senior Constable), 74
Elshtain, Jean, 155
emotions, 1–6; families, 18, 24–5, 33, 105, 120; fathers, 46, 48–9, 58–9; mothers, 27–31, **126–35**; soldiers, 11, 13, 27–8, 107–9, 112, 114; widows, 146–8, 154–7
Empire, 15, 30–2, 46, 48–52, 54, 57, 59, 87, 140, 158
employment, 53, 97–101; *see also under* disabled returned soldiers; returned soldiers; women
engaged couples, 20, 24, 29, 65, 126, 133–4
etiquette, 10, 48, 69; *see also* rituals of death and mourning
eugenics *see* racial attitudes
Evans, Raymond, 42, 156
ex-servicemen *see* returned soldiers

Falkiner family, **128–33**
Falkingham, Ruth, 22
families: broken, 151; disabled soldiers, 89, 98; fathers in, 48, 51, 53; grief, 2, 6, 51, 58–9, 61–3, 106, 128, **133–5**, 144–5; homefront, 107–10, 113–18, 120, 124–5; myths and narratives, 130–1, 133–4, 162; welfare, 26, **38–41**, 69, 72–80, 147, 151; *see also* correspondence
Farrell (Alderman), 42
Farrow, G. Martin, 95
fatherhood, 19, 55
fatherless families, 5, 47, 68–9, 78, 152; *see also* war widows
fathers: during First World War, 19, 29, 46, 49; during Second World War, 121, 135; mourning, 1, 4–5, 27, 41–2, 47–52, 57–64, 161; organisations, **52–7**, 90, 163
federal government: First World War and earlier, 30, 38–9, 68–70, 77–9; between wars, 26–7, 39, 43–4, 56, 68, 70–1, 76, 79–81, 91–2, 98; Second World War, 68, 124, 148; after Second World War, 145, 147–51, 155; *see also* government employees; repatriation programmes; welfare
feminists, 38, 67
Field, John (Brigadier), 159
Fielder family, 139
financial assistance *see* welfare

Fisher, Andrew, 38, 77
Fitzalan family, 33
Fitzpatrick, W., 89–90
Forrester family, 22, 40
Forsyth family, 12, 23
Fox, Alf, 61
Frances, Raelene, 3–4
Fraser, Charlie (Private), 144
Fraus, Kitty, 22
French, R. F. (Captain), 13
Freud, Sigmund, 1–2, 48, 147
friendships between soldiers, 11–12, 131, 139–41, 144; *see also* mateship
Fulcher, Marjorie, 126
funerals, 10, 13, 58, 75, 119, 161
Fussell, Paul, 11, 15
future, loss of, 50–1, 126, 133, 145

Gallipoli (Dardanelles), 20, 22–3, 30–2, 41–2, 49, 55, 61–2, 105, 110
Gapper family, 82
Garton, Stephen, 3, 39, 68
Gell family, 33
gender roles, 2, 4–5, 69–71, 78, 108, 115, 154–5, 160; *see also* women's roles
Germany: First World War, 13–15, 19, 59–60, 71, 111; Second World War, 116, 128, 133–5, 140, 146–7
Gibson, Eric, 22
Gibson, Mary, 21
Gilbert family, 140
Gill family, 126–7, 141
Goodisson family, 136
Goodman, William, 13–14
government employees, 53, 92, 97–9, 145
Graham, Rene, 158
Graham, Stuart (Captain), 137
Griffin family, 40
Groom, Margaret, 37
Groom, W., 99
guilt, 9, 14, 59, 139, 162
Guthrie (Senator), 92, 94, 96, 98
Gwyther family, 32

Haase (Mrs), 153
Halbwach, Maurice, 128, 133
Hall, N. R. (Mrs), 156
Hamilton family, 32
Harrison family, 132–3
Hay family, 33
Hayes family, 73
health, 29, 50, 53, 57, 74, 80, 82–3, 120, 124–5; *see also* disabled returned soldiers; medical services
Heath family, 32
Henderson family, 23
Henry family, 139

Index

heroic ideals: disabled soldiers, 85, 89, **95–7**, 102; fathers, 19, 41, 46, 48–9, 51–2, 55, 57–60, 63, 163; mothers, 30–3, 35, 41, 45; returned soldiers, 67, 162; soldiers, 15–17, 106, 111, 135, 140, 146–7
Hicks, Stanton (Lady), 151
Hicks, Stanton (Sir), 160
Higgins, Henry Bourne, 50–1, 54, 59
Higgins, Mervyn, 29
Hilliard, R. E., 61
Hislop family, 12–14, 16
Hollway family, 74
Holt family, 83
honour, 26–8, 30–1, 35, 42, 56, 58, 64, 131, 156
Horner, David, 108, 110–11
Hough family, 138–9
housing, 83, 152–3
Hughes, Eva, 31
Hughes, William Morris, 30, 79, 81

illegitimate children, 72
imperialism *see* Empire
incapacitated *see* disability
Inglis, K. S., 4
Isaacs, Isaac (Sir), 101

Jalland, Pat, 2, 48
Japanese, 111, 122–5, 142, 162
Johnson family, **144–7**, 152
Joyce, Mr (RSL), 36
Jung, C. G., 67

Keddie (Mrs), 120
Kettlewell, Noel (Captain), 124
Killeen, Francis, 97
Kipling, Rudyard, 49, 66
Kirkwood family, 75
Klein, Melanie, 3, 154–5
Knight, R. J. (Private), 61
Knox, G. H., 158
Kristeva, Julia, 3

Lager family, 40–1
Laing, E. W. D., 9
Lake, Marilyn, 38, 127
Lang, Jack, 69, 73
language: death notices, 32–3; heroic, 15; inadequacy, 11, 13, 143; of grief, 27, 143; self and identity, 85; widows and soldiers, 157, 160; *see also* rhetoric
Lapthorne, A. E. (Chaplain), 16–17
Laqueur, Thomas, 14
Lauder, Harry (Sir), 49
Laurie family, 76
Laver family, 136
Lawerson (Sergeant), 61

Lawson, J., 67
Leahy family, 16–17
Leckie family, 62
Lee family, 33
Leed, Eric, 2
Legacy, 43, 47, 68, 82, 127, 151
letter-writing *see* correspondence
limbless soldiers, 6, **85–104**, 161
Lindsay, W. H. (police officer), 73
Livingstone (Sergeant), 11
Lofts family, 32
Lovett family, 140
lung diseases, 86, 91–2
Lynch family, 76
Lyne, Amelia (Mrs), 74
Lyons, Joseph, 39

McCarthy (Inspector), 74
McCutcheon, Doris, 157–8
MacDonald family, 17, 50–2
McDonald family, 15, 49
McEwen, William (Sir), 86
McGregor (Mr), 57
McInerney family, 14–15
Mackay (Councillor), 101
McKay, Fred (Chaplain), 136
McKenzie, J. (Mr), 83
Mackenzie family, 146–7
McKernan, Michael, 4, 137
McLarty, Mary, 131
McLeod, Edith, 160
Macmillan, Harold, 49
manliness: disabled returned soldiers, 89–91, 97–9; fathers, 5, 47, 51–4, 58, 64; mourning, 2; soldiers, 15, 37, 48, 61, 64, 158; women's assumption, 160
Manning, H. J., 159
Manttan family, 141
marriage, 27, 66, 68–9, 78, 101, 150; examples, 63, 106–19, 128–9, 158; war widows' remarriage, 5, 71–2, 74, 77, 151, 153–4; *see also* engaged couples
Martin, Susan, 23
Martin family, 15
mateship, 27, 163; *see also* friendships between soldiers
Maxwell (Mr), 97
Meagher family, 62
medical services, 86, 148; *see also* artificial limbs
melancholia, 2–3, 157
Melba, Nellie (Dame), 90
Melbourne family, 32
Mellett family, 141
memorials, 2, 5, 18, 35–7, 57–8, 60–2, 139, 162
Mercer, May, 42, 44

Millen, Edward (Senator), 76, 80
Miller family, 120
Mills (Captain), 125
Mitchell, Ede, 126
modernity, 89, 95
Monash, John (Sir), 57, 62
monuments *see* memorials
Moore, William (Chaplain), 18
Moors, Clement, 74
morale, 29–30, 123, 135
morality (war widows), 4–5, **69–78**, 80, 84, 151, 163
Moran, J., 142
Moran family, 83
Morphett family, 61, 120
Morrissey, Michael J., 75
Morton, Clive, 159
Mosse, George, 2
mothers, 1–2, 4–6, 161; collective support, 51, 128, 131, 135–42, 146, 163; First World War, **26–45**, 54–5; other mothers and, **137–9**, 161; sacrifice, 5, **29–45**, 91, 128, 136, 143, 162; Second World War, 106, **126–43**; soldiers and, 48, **139–42**, 161; sons and, **27–9**, 46, 48, 121–2; welfare, 38–41, 43–4, 68–70, 73, 149
Mothers' Day, 130
Murrell family, 29

national character, 18, 89, 106, 137
national mythologies, 4, 37–8, 105
Naylor family, 12
neglect, sense of, 145, 155–6
Nelson, Hank, 122
Nestor family, 41
Newman family, 131
news: battlefront, 12, 14–15; homefront, 19–25; yearning for, 50, 107, **119–25**, 135–6
newspapers: accidental death, 119; Anzac spirit, 105–6; clippings, 60; disabled returned soldiers, 88, 92–3; prisoners of war, 123, 125; recruitment, 30–3; source of news, 6, 18–19, **21–2**, 59, 115, 140; women, 30–2, 34–7, 39, 43–4, 149–50, 158–60
Newton family, 136
Nitchie family, 31
Norman, J. E., 15
nostalgia, 2–3, 162; couples, 66, 118–19; fathers, 62–3; mothers, 129–30, 133–5, 139, 143; widows, 157

obsession for detail, 58–63, 120, 141, 161–2; *see also* collecting
orphans *see* children
Osborne, N., 37

Owen, Evelyn, 159

Pankhurst, Sylvia, 71
parenting *see* childrearing
Parfitt, Gwen, 133–4
paternalism, 47, 51, 70, 98
patriotism: First World War, 15–16, 28, 31–3, 42, 48–9, 51, 59; between wars, 34, 46, 54, 69, 81; after Second World War, 150, 158; *see also* national mythologies
peace movement, 54, 105
Peake, A. H., 16
Pearce, George (Senator), 26, 68, 77–8
pensions: disabled servicemen, 68, 91, 93–4, 99; mothers, 38–40, 43–4, 69; old age, 43; widows, 39, 43–4, 47, 53, 68–9, 71–3, 75–83, **148–55**, 162–3
Phillips, Adam, 45
Piehler, G. Keirt, 31
police, 73–6, 82, 144
political campaigns and environment, 1, 3–6, 161, 163; disabled returned soldiers, 86, 88, 97–8, 102; fathers, 27, 48; mothers, 27, 31, 38–9, 41; prisoners' relatives, 123–4; returned soldiers, 47, 56; soldiers' wives, 117–18; war widows, 27, 69, 71, **78–81**, 84, **147–55**
Poppy Day, 44
possessions of dead soldiers, 130, 142, 159
postal services, 19–20, 24, 123
press *see* newspapers
pressure groups *see* political campaigns
Prettlejohn family, 122
pride: civic, 33; fathers, 49, 54, 58–60; mothers, 28, 31, 34, 127, 129, 135; soldiers' friends, 13; widows, **148–55**, 158
prisoners of war (POWs), 163; First World War, 13; Second World War, **121–5**, 128, 131, 135, 140, 142
protest *see* political campaigns
psychoanalysis, 1–3, 48, 67, 147, 154, 157
psychological processes, 1–5, 10, 47, 54, 58, 108–9, 119–20, 143; *see also* emotions; obsession for detail; violence
public commemorations, 2, 51, 53, 105–6, 163; women's role, 4, 34–8, 84, 106, 127–8, 143, 145; *see also* Anzac Day commemorations
public memory *see* collective memory
public mourning, 34, 51, 58, 61, 147, **155–7**
public service *see* government employees
public transport, 92–5

Queensland, 32, 53, 96, 111, 119, 150
Quinn family, 120

Index

racial attitudes, 31, 37–9, 95, 163; *see also* Aboriginal people
Read (Councillor), 101
Read, Peter, 4
recruitment *see* conscription; volunteers
Red Cross, 14, 90, 117, 123, 150
religion *see* Christian beliefs; spiritualism
remarriage (war widows), 5, 71–2, 74, 77, 151, 153–4
remembrance *see* collective memory; public commemorations
Remembrance Day, 156
remuneration *see* financial welfare
repatriation programmes, 2–3, 68, 147; incapacitated soldiers, 68, 86–7, 89, 91–4, 98; mothers, 39–40, 43–4; returned soldiers, 47, 55–6, 68–9, 83, 151; widows, 5, 39, 43–4, 68, 74–5, 80, 83, 151
repressions, 30, 52, 85, 89, 95, 156, 162
resentment, 3, 106; fathers, 59; limbless soldiers, 6, 85–7, 98–9, 102; mothers, 2, 30, 42, 45, 135, 162; widows, 5–6, 75, 77, 146–7, 155–6, 162–3
respectability *see* morality
returned soldiers: attitudes and behaviour, 3, 66–8, 86, 110, 114, 162–3; fathers' duty, 52–7; organisations and commemorations, 42–4, 47, 51, 87, 106 (*see also* RSL); preference in employment, 53, 56–7, 70, 79–80, 97–8; *see also* disabled returned soldiers; repatriation programmes; soldier settlement
Returned Soldiers' and Sailors' Imperial League of Australia *see* RSL
Reynolds family, 79
rhetoric, 11, 16, 38, 42, 48, 51, 89, 95, 106
Richard, R., 82
Riggall, W. (Mrs), 149
rituals of death and mourning, 4, 161–2; Victorian, 10, 48, First World War, 16, 59–60, 78; sesquicentenary (1938), 37; Second World War, 119–20, 127–8, 130, 132–3, 155; *see also* obsession for detail; public commemorations
Roberts family, **58–64**
Robinson, Annie, 45
Roe, Jill, 38
Rolland, F. W. (Chaplain), 17
romance, 27, 107–8, 114, 127
Rosebery (Lord), 49
Ross family, 31–2
Rousel family, 140
Rowles family, 62
Royal Tour (1954), 154–6
RSL, 36, 42, 44, 47, 54, 83, 87, 101, 150–1

sacrifice, 1–2, 4–5, 161–3; Aborigines, 95; disabled, 95–7, 102; fathers, 49, 51–2; hierarchy, 25–7, 70, 77; mothers, 5, **26–45**, 91, 128, 136, 143, 162; soldiers (First World War), 16, 21, 35–8, 56, 59, (Second World War) 119, 131, 138, 140, 143, 162–3; widows, 69–71, 77–8, 81–2, 84, 128, 143, 147, 154–5, 159
Sage, Annette, 158
Salter, J. C. (Chaplain), 135
Samuel, Annie, 22
Sandy, J. M., 41
Santner, Eric, 2, 157
Scates, Bruce, 4
Scott family, 153
Selby, Tom, 141
sesquicentenary celebrations (1938), 37–8
Seton, C. J. (Trooper), 72
sexual adventure, 127–8
Sheills, W. H. (Trooper), 32
Sheldon, A. B., 95–6
Shipton family, 138–9
shirkers and slackers, 49, 55–7, 60, 78
Singapore, 111, 121, 123, 135
Skinner family, 70
Skow family, 40
slackers *see* shirkers and slackers
Slee, Jack, 141
Smith, David (Warrant Officer), 124
Smith, Sydney, 124
Smith, Vernon (Flying Officer), 124
social functions, 52–3, 87–8, 90
social networks *see* collective support
social welfare *see* welfare
soldier settlement, 56, 86, 106, 163
Soldiers' Club (Sydney), 67–8, 81
sons: relations with fathers, 46, 55; relations with mothers, **27–9**; surrogate, 14, 25, 61, 131, 141–2
spiritualism, **131–3**, 137
Spoule, Miss, 22
Staff family, 62, 75
Stark family, 140–1
state *see* federal government
statistics *see* casualty statistics
Stein, Gertrude, 6
Stirling family, 28
Strutt, Nellie, 79
Sugden, Edward, 28
suicide, 67
Sunder, Norman W. (Captain), 14
surrogate sons, 14, 25, 61, 131, 141–2
surveillance, 4–5, **70–6**, 151
survivors, 9–10, 139–40

Taylor family, 138
Taylorism, 100

telegrams, 18–19, 25, 50, 126, 133
Templeton (Mrs), 132
Tennyson, Alfred (Lord), 15
Thomas, G. L. (Mrs), 156
Thompson, D. R. (Mrs), 77–8
Thompson family, 62
Thomson, Alistair, 3
'totally and permanently incapacitated' (TPI) *see* disability
Trathen (Chaplain), 121–2, 136, 152
Tregent, Dudley A., 96
trench warfare, 11–12, 14–15, 17, 105
Trice (Mr), 89
tuberculosis, 91–2

unemployment *see* employment

VAD (Volunteer Aid Detachments), 90
Vasey, George (General), **107–17**, 118–19, 148, 158–60
Vasey, Jessie (Mrs), 107, 109–10, 113–16; correspondence with George, **117–19**; War Widows Guild, **147–60**
Vaughan, C. A. (Mrs), 149
veterans *see* returned soldiers
Victorian values, 16, 48, 52, 54, 56, 58, 63–4, 89
violence, 4, 66–8, 86, 163
Volunteer Aid Detachments (VAD), 90
volunteers: First World War enlistment, 28, 30–3, 49, 52, 54, 65, 105–6; First World War experience (AIF), 18, 32–3, 39, 50, 58, 60–2, 71; demobilisation (1921), 46; Second World War, 106, 110–11, 128, 160

Wade family, 62
Walker, Isabelle, 21
Walker family, 139
Wall, Mary, 146
Wallace (Private), 12
war graves, 2, 10, 15–18, 53, 61–2, 135–6, 138–9, 161

war pensions *see* pensions
war widows, 1, 3–6, 161, 163; First World War, 27, 36, 43–4, 47, 53–4, 59, **65–84**, 92; Second World War, 127, 142–3, **144–60**; remarriage, 5, 71–2, 74, 77, 151, 153–4
War Widows Guild, **147–58**, 160
Watson family, 40
Webber, Eric (Chaplain), 121, 135–6
welfare, 2, 5; disabled returned soldiers, 85–7, 90, 101; mothers, 27, 38–41, 43–4, 68–70, 73, 149; returned soldiers, 55; widows, 43–4, **68–84**, 145, 148, 150, 158, 163; *see also* charities; pensions
White, Richard, 27
Whittle family, 78–9
widows *see* war widows
Wiggins, Marianne, 20
Wignall (Sergeant), 61
Williams family, 30, 45, 71, 121, 133–5
Wilson, Charles, 67
Wilson (Nurse), 130
Winter, Jay, 2, 4, 57
womanhood, 27, 34–5, 45, 84, 127–8, 157, 162
women: collective support, 5, **21–5**, 61; experience of Second World War, 106, 121, 127–8; *see also* mothers; war widows
women's employment: between wars, 53, 68, 70–1, 73, 78–80, 98–100; during Second World War, 106, 121, 127; after Second World War, 149, 151–2
women's memory, 15, **34–7**, 45, 128, 130, 133, 135, **142–3**
women's roles, 2, 4, 11, 17, 30, 35–8, 47, 90, 155, 160; *see also* womanhood
Wood family, 32
Wynn family, 125

Youdale, Roy, 15
Young family, 76–7